Rewriting Gender

Rewriting Gender
Reading contemporary Chinese women

RAVNI THAKUR

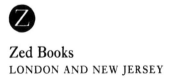

Zed Books
LONDON AND NEW JERSEY

Rewriting Gender: Reading contemporary Chinese women was first published by Zed Books Ltd, 7 Cynthia Street, London N1 9JF, UK, and 165 First Avenue, Atlantic Highlands, New Jersey 07716, USA, in 1997.

Cover designed by Andrew Corbett.
Set in Monotype Ehrhardt by Ewan Smith.
Printed and bound in the United Kingdom by Biddles Ltd, Guildford and King's Lynn.

A catalogue record for this book is available from the British Library.

US CIP data is available from the Library of Congress.

Contents

Acknowledgements

My grateful thanks goes to the Dutch organisation WOTRO, which provided financial support enabling me to carry out this research. Financial help was also provided by Leiden University, for which I would like to thank M. M. Hedeman and the Stichting Mohummed Yakoubi.

I would like to thank my two supervisors, Professor Wilt Idema and Professor Els Postel, for their constant help and encouragement and their painstaking reading of the draft and final copies of my thesis.

I would also like to acknowledge my debt to Professor Carla Risseeuw, who introduced me to the work of Pierre Bourdieu and proved a constant source of help and guidance. A special thanks is due to Rosy Risseeuw who, though no longer in this world, was a special friend.

Professor Gao Xian from China was of great help in arranging interviews with several writers in China and for generally helping me during my stay there. His assistance and the friendship of the whole family is greatly appreciated.

I would also like to thank Professor Tan Chung, who first introduced me to Chinese Studies and stimulated me to pursue research in the field.

A very special thanks goes to Michel Hockx, who helped in the finalisation of all the details – help which I very much appreciate; and to Frank Pieke for reading parts of this thesis and for helping with the public defence.

On a more personal level, I would like to thank Thandham Truong, Amrita Chachhi and Karamat Ali. Their support has been invaluable in countless ways during my stay in Holland. This book could never have been written without their encouragement, constant affection and rich intellectual stimulation.

I would like to thank my friends Mila Avramovic, Gary Debus, Vera Goedhart, Gina Vargas, Danny Waterman, Peter Waterman and Ruth Waterman, for their warm and generous friendship; Hans Verolme for help with managing my computer; Ruta Aidis for her help with the bibliography; and Linda McPhee for help with setting up the thesis for printing.

Finally, I would like to thank Krishan for his encouragement to finish this book.

To my mother Viplove

Introduction

Women writers have been at the forefront of literary innovation in post-Mao China. *Nüxing Wenxue*, as the writings of women collectively came to be called, has led to debate among scholars both within and outside China. This study is a contribution to the ongoing attempt to understand and analyse the role, contribution and significance of women writers in contemporary China. It focuses specifically on an analysis of the social relations of gender in post-Mao China through reading a representative work of each of four prominent women writers: Zhang Jie, Zhang Xinxin, Wang Anyi and Shen Rong. The works were chosen because their female protagonists show how social ideas about male–female relations are experienced by women. The early post-Mao period was chosen because this was the time when an orthodoxy of gender was being questioned for the first time.

Using the work of women writers as my basic research material, I hoped to answer the following questions:

1. What is the dominant way of viewing male–female relations (gender relations) in China and how is this dominant view expressed in different areas or fields of discourse such as literature? This dominant view I shall classify as 'orthodoxy'.
2. What different types of responses do women have to the prevailing dominant view of gender relations? In other words, how do women situate themselves in relation to orthodoxy?

Answers to these questions may help us arrive at an understanding of the lives of women in contemporary China from an alternative perspective.

Several important socio-political and anthropological studies have focused on Chinese women. Most of them have sought to understand the changing position of women by concentrating on the economic and political changes that have occurred in post-Revolutionary China. Most of these studies point to the existence of a widespread belief in the inferiority of women in all spheres of society (*Zhongnan Qingnü*). Scholars have pointed out that it is this belief in women's inferiority which justifies and helps to maintain their secondary position in society. Some have termed this belief a 'patriarchal family ideology' which goes back to China's feudal past (Croll 1978; Andors 1981).

The existence and common acceptance of this 'patriarchal ideology' prompted my own research. It raised two major questions. First, I was interested in learning how this belief in women's inferiority could be identified and what were its elements of continuity and change. Second, I was interested in how women's relationship to this belief could be uncovered: did women in China accept the terms of patriarchal ideology or were they critical of it?

Until a few years ago, the voices of Chinese women were rarely heard. The Communist Party with its official publications exercised a strict control over researchers and contacts between foreigners and Chinese people. Outsiders were forced to rely on statistics about the 'position' of Chinese women in society without learning how Chinese women actually experienced their lives.

While it is easy to speak of 'patriarchal ideology' and even find indicators that show it at work, the effect of this 'ideology' on people is much harder to analyse. Yet it is this area which needs to be brought to the fore if we are to deepen our understanding of how beliefs about social relations work in practice. It is only by focusing on the relationship that those affected by a particular ideology have with that ideology that can we assess the potential for change. In other words, the relationship of 'agents' with ideology becomes crucial for understanding how social beliefs produce and maintain themselves.

In order to answer these questions, I turned to literary sources and literature, for several reasons. Reading the various women writers who have emerged in China in recent years, I was astonished to find a wealth of material that would allow me an understanding of precisely these questions. Within the field of Chinese literary criticism, the question of why women write like women seemed to dominate the discussion. In my readings, I discovered that the criticism was often prescriptive in nature. It expected women's writings to conform with 'social ideas' about their lives. It was an attempt to group women together on the basis of their sex and presumed nature. It allowed me to identify a particular belief about women and showed how traditional ideas about women could surface in different areas.

In reading the work of women writers themselves, I noted a great deal of diversity. Even those women who focused solely on urban intellectual women seemed to do so from different perspectives. The content of their writing did not always correspond with the claims being made by critics about women's literature.

Studying this diversity among women writers can help us to understand the ways in which women relate to dominant beliefs and expectations about their nature, role and position in society. The writings reveal the complex relationship that women have with social ideas and beliefs. Thus, the field of literature and literary representation provided me with resources on which to base an understanding of the nature of dominant beliefs about the position of women, at the same time as helping me arrive at an understanding of women's responses to these beliefs. By focusing on responses by women, I hoped to understand the role of women as active agents, taking action and expressing their interaction with social beliefs, not just as a group which is the passive recipient of ideas. This study, therefore, focuses on women writers who, by writing about women's lives, are participating in the way women are represented in social discourse.

The field of literature represents an excellent example of the increasing multi-disciplinary nature of the social sciences today. It is a subject that can be approached from divergent standpoints and through different methods. Common to many sociological studies of literature is the belief that novels and short stories, among other forms of literature, provide us with information regarding the workings of society. Speaking of the relationship between society and its literature, Raymond Williams says: 'If we compare art with its society, we find a series of real relationships showing its deep and central connexions with the rest of general life' (1965: 86). Writing more recently, Ferguson, Desan and Griswold point out that while literary critics look at works, texts, writers and readers and focus on the creation, reception and interpretation of literature, social scientists, on the other hand, discuss books and literary institutions, and dwell upon the production, distribution and consumption of cultural products (1988: 423) Thus, a social scientist uses literature to reveal, exemplify or interpret social process. The literary critic, on the other hand, sees the literary work as an end in itself.

Since the purpose of this book is to attempt an understanding of the social relations of gender through reading the works of women writers, I was drawn to theories which have attempted this task before me. Feminist theories of literature have all attempted to uncover the specific relationship of women to literature as writers, critics and readers, and through this focus to shed light on the social context of women's lives. Whether concerned with the literary representations of sexual difference, with the ways in which literary genres have been shaped by masculine or feminine values, or with the exclusion of the female voice from the institutions of literary criticism and theory, feminist criticism has consistently sought to challenge the previous notions of literature (Showalter 1985: 3).

However, my concern with women writers in China forced me to conclude that concern with a female tradition of representation and a female style of writing must not exclude the attempt to understand the way women's texts relate to their cultural contexts. In societies where the term 'literature' itself means something totally different from its meaning in the West, an understanding of its specificity becomes crucial. Literature in China is grounded on Marxist literary thought. Here literary representations are meant to reproduce a certain ideological position. Women writers are, likewise, supposed to concern themselves with the propagation of certain images. Thus, any analysis of women writers in China must understand their works and their representations of women on the basis of their relationship as writers and as women to the dominant discourse which expects women to conform to certain criteria.

It was this cultural specificity of the context in which women writers work in China which made me turn to a more sociological methodology for analysing their work. Since I was specifically interested in relating the work of women writers to the socially accepted gender discourse, my first task was to arrive at an understanding of how 'discourse' operates in society before I could talk of 'gender discourse'. Michel Foucault has convincingly argued that 'discourse', or the practice of writing and reading, plays an important role in legitimising and maintaining particular power relations in society.

Feminists have taken Foucault's notion of discourse and used it to study gender relations. They have argued that the operation of discourse on gender can be made visible by examining the way women are spoken of within particular discourses in society and in what is attributed to them as their nature (Martin 1988; Flax 1990). It is this theoretical understanding of discourse that I have used as my point of departure in order to analyse how women and their writing are spoken of within the specific discourse of the literary field in China.

However, while Foucault talks about the function and practice of discourse in society, his framework needs to be complemented by the work of others who have examined the different way people relate to discourses. My concern with understanding women's responses to gender discourse led me to use an approach which would allow me to articulate women's relationship to discourses.

The work being done by Pierre Bourdieu in this tradition of enquiry seemed both contemporary and appropriate for providing a method to understand my research material. I was drawn specifically to the work of Bourdieu because he departs from previous concerns with discourse theory by bringing back the role played by individuals as agents: those who participate in the production of discourses in society and respond differently to dominant social values (1990a). Bourdieu's effort is to delineate the mechanisms of symbolic domination and control by which the existing social order is maintained in society as natural. He attempts to describe a general sociological practice which unmasks this attempt of society to see dominant value systems as natural. According to Bourdieu, discourses in society can be differentiated, according to the degree of legitimacy they enjoy, into orthodoxies and heterodoxies (1977; 1988). While orthodox discourse attempts to maintain the status quo of society as natural and inevitable, heterodox discourses attempt to unmask the 'naturalness' of social actions by questioning them and articulating different social practices (1988).

This book, then, uses an interdisciplinary theoretical framework, based on gender theory, discourse analysis as put forward by Michel Foucault and the sociological model provided by Pierre Bourdieu both for understanding the concept of a culturally specific literary field and the relationship of agents to this literary field. It emphasises that an analysis of women writers, if placed within the framework provided by a sociology of literature approach, deepens our understanding of the relationship women have to forms of cultural representation such as literature.

This study thus attempts to use discourse analysis for a study of how a 'women's literature' (*nüxing wenxue*) is being defined in China and how statements about the texts of women writers relate to other statements on the subject of women. My main argument stresses that a wider discourse on gender relations can be seen to operate in the way the work and the place of women writers are being defined. I shall further argue that, apart from identifying the orthodox institutional discourse on gender, reading women writers can also help us to identify how women relate and respond to this orthodox discourse. Discourse analysis combined with the use of relevant sociological concepts can both help us unmask the workings of orthodoxy on gender, an orthodoxy legitimised through insitutional practices, and can also help us see how this orthodoxy actually comes into conflict with other discourses.

This book is divided into two parts. The first examines the content and construction of an orthodoxy on gender relations in China; it then examines how this orthodoxy can be shown as operating in the literary field. The second part is concerned with analysing women's responses to this orthodoxy through an in-depth analysis of the female characters in four novellas.

PART I

Orthodox Gender Discourse and the Literary Field

Gender relations and literature: an inter-disciplinary approach

The landscape: feminist theories of literature

Annette Kolodyny's (1980) phrase 'dancing through a minefield' has always appealed to me as an appropriate way to define the field of feminist literary theory. In recent years, the enormous upsurge in works attempting a feminist analysis of literary practices has indeed made feminist literary studies a virtual minefield of approaches. The dispute starts with the very word 'feminism' and goes on to problems of what characterises a 'feminist text'.[1]

The differences between feminist approaches to literature can be seen as related to the ways in which they have conceptualised the social relations of gender.[2] This divergence of approaches has also been related to the various aims of feminist politics. Toril Moi (1985), for example, identifies three main trends within feminist literary theory: liberal approaches, French feminism and Marxist-socialist feminism. Nevertheless, what ties these theories together has been their concern with literary representation.[3]

Feminism entered the politics of representation by examining the various ways in which women have been depicted in literature and showing the patriarchal and sexist bias of these images.[4] This type of criticism was spearheaded by Kate Millet (1970). She attempts to show the sexist way in which particular male authors, such as Henry Miller, Jean Genet, Norman Mailer and D. H. Lawrence, depict women characters in their works. Her work was followed by a spate of studies which sought to examine the 'images' of women in literature (for example, Jacobus 1979; Moers 1978; Palmer 1989).

Following this initial feminist engagement came a renewed interest in revalidating and re-reading women writers of the past. The predominant concern among a number of Anglophone critics was to posit a female tradition in literature as opposed to a male tradition. This approach is most noticeable in the works of Showalter with her notion of 'gyno-criticism' which she defines as the attempt to 'construct a female framework for the analysis of women's literature' (1985: 131). Other writers, focusing on a study of nineteenth-century women writers, have been especially effective in showing how male critics have denigrated and dismissed women as authors (Gilbert and Gubar 1979). Within the same tradition of pointing out a female culture, Annette Kolodyny (1976a) has developed a notion of a 'resisting or feminist reader'. According to her, the different types of feminist literary criticism come together in the attention they pay to 'male structures of power' in literary criteria (1980: 20).

Other feminist readings of literature draw upon the insights made in the fields of linguistics and psychoanalysis, an influence which is visible in feminist theory as a whole (Mitchell 1975; 1984). French feminists, such as Kristeva, Cixous, Irigaray and Wittig, are usually credited with this approach (Marks and de Courtivron [eds] 1980). Influenced by the work of Lacan and Derrida,[5] these feminists have focused on methods of textual analysis (Kuhn 1978: 9).

This French approach, especially in the work of Cixous and Wittig, also makes an attempt to identify a specific form of female creativity and sees it as different from the forms taken by male creativity. As Cixous says: 'Woman must write herself: must write about woman and bring woman to writing ... woman must put herself into text – as into the world and into history' (1976: 878).

Wittig takes the point further by characterising our use of language itself as patriarchal. She makes an attempt to construct a female language by creating new words to describe female experience. She does this by using only feminine genders for universal pronouns, such as elles (fem. plural), or by using the word *on* which is gender neutral. She sees this as a way for women to regain their subjectivity, which the gendered nature of language 'seeks to annul as far as women are concerned' (1985: 6).

In literary analysis, the Marxist term 'ideology' has also been used to analyse the role played by gender relations in literature (Williams 1988). Ideologies are, for Marxists, systems of misleading ideas about the nature of human beings and society and serve to legitimise unequal power relations.[6] Thus, gender relations work as an ideology which serves to keep women in a subordinate position (Kuhn and Wolpe 1978).

Marxist feminists have, consequently, attempted to link the cultural representation of women with the existing social subordination of women. They argue that because women are in a materially subordinate position to men, the representations of women will directly or indirectly reflect this fact (Caplan 1986). Thus, literature should be seen as a site where the material subordination of women can be made visible. They advocate a 'materialist feminist criticism', a criticism concerned with incorporating elements of race and class with gender (Newton and Rosenfelt 1985: xxvii).

Feminist theory has, as the above very brief review shows, brought important insights to bear upon the study of literature and has fundamentally changed the way we think of women's engagement with literature. Nevertheless, certain shortcomings persist within the framework of feminist criticism.

Liberal feminist theories, such as the model of gynocriticism put forward by Showalter (1981; 1985), and certain psychological theories such as those represented by Cixous (1976) and Wittig (1985), can be criticised for a notion of essentialism as regards gender differences. Hindess points out that 'essentialism refers to a mode of analysis in which social phenomena are analyzed not in terms of their specific conditions of existence ... but as the expression of an essence' (1977, 95). The above theories are also essentialist in this respect. Within this persepective, male and female identities are considered immanent and pre-given and marked by unified characteristics rather than seeing male and female identity as historically constructed and linked to changing social ideologies (Caplan 1986: 149–50). The dangers of accepting an unquestioned female nature are especially grave in contexts such as China where, as will be shown in Chapter 3, it is precisely notions of an essential female nature which operate within literary discourse to ensure certain definitions of women's literature (*nüxing wenxue*).

This belief in a universal female nature leads to my second criticism: the overlooking, at the level of theoretical formation, of the notion of difference between women. The emphasis in feminist theory has always been on difference from men. This has meant that, until recently, most debates tended to ignore the issue of differences among women writers.

This oversight has also been the focus of criticism by women from different cultural contexts outside the West. Critics have pointed out that even those western women writers who can be seen as the explorers of feminist themes in literature suffered from the limitations imposed by the context of their cultures and the history of colonialism. This context influenced their vision of themselves and the ideas they had of non-white women (Spivak 1986). Others have pointed out that most of these attempts have not examined the influence of imperialism in the way a 'dominant language' like English has been used to create differences between colonised and coloniser (Ashcroft et al., 1990). Further, the way in which western conceptions of what qualifies as literature have marginalised the works of other cultures has also not been seriously examined.

Speaking of a universal female knowledge and language outside male culture also seems to imply that an exclusive female regime will suffer from none of the problems of male-dominated society. Issues of inequality, exploitation and, above all, power will wither away as if by magic. Yet, black and working-class women have documented the fact that women do not escape the influence of prevailing racist or class ideologies (Tate 1985; Truong 1990). Literary critics have also highlighted the difference of perception among writers who belong to a different race (Schipper 1989). We cannot afford to focus our analysis only on texts by women which satisfy some criteria of feminism. Any comprehensive theory has to be able to examine the complex ways in which women themselves participate in the production of gendered practices.

Finally, these approaches tend to focus their analysis on the text as such, rather than explaining clearly which aspect of the text they are dealing with. Is it with the language, the author, the reader or with the character? Very little work has been done on the development of a comprehensive theory of character analysis, for example, to show how character representation provides a clue to examining the social relations of gender.

The psychoanalytic theories of language acquisition and the different way in which this process works for the two sexes have meant that the use of and relationship to language are seen as different for men and women. Thus, in this perspective as well, women's writing is seen to be distinct from male writing. As Anna Rosalind Jones points out: 'psychoanalytic theory and social experience both suggest that the leap from body to language is especially difficult for women, since language use is dependent on social values and norms' (1981: 229). Claims towards a feminine language seem to ignore the context of social interaction. They speak of a Utopia of female language, as put forward by Cixous (1976) and Wittig (1985), which is uncorrupted by patriarchal influence. The other problem with such positions is that, like liberal feminism, they seem to slip into an essentialist and universalist position when speaking of female nature, which is seen as the precursor to a female language.

We find ourselves constantly asking the question, which women and whose language are being privileged here? Is it the language of middle-class women who are part of academic discourse, or is it a state of being attributed to all women irrespective of class and cultural differences? Further, is it the language of the text as a whole, which is seen to be the language of the author, or is it the language of different characters in the work? Thus, for example, will male dialogue in a text written by a woman be female language or male language? Here, Wiegel's criticism holds true when she argues that though one can agree with thinkers like Irigaray and Cixous about the place of the other (in this case woman as the other of man), their 'programmatic remarks about female praxis seem highly problematic' (Weigel 1986: 79). It also seems a cruel trick to play on those writers who are struggling against the insidious claim that women's nature makes them especially suitable for certain types of work and certain types of literary styles, which are always defined in terms of difference from male style.

Further, the work of these writers seems to be doing away with notions of agency. The focus on the unconscious, essential though it is, also makes it problematic to work with if one wants to speak of conscious actions performed by agents making critical choices; in other words, if one wants to deal with surface relations rather than hidden relations. Another problem with these approaches is that most theories are centred round the 'western family'.[7] The different socialisation processes in other cultures make it difficult to apply this approach outside its context.

To a certain extent, socialist feminist stances, with their emphasis on ideology as the mechanism which links the social experience of gender relations, do attempt to break out of the trap of essentialism. They also provide a means of understanding difference among women by speaking of ideologies such as that of race, class and gender. This implies that any analysis of gender relations sees them as ultimately determined by the material basis of society, ignoring the power of traditions which persist despite changes in the material production of society. Though the material position of people is an extremely important factor, these theories provide us with an adequate link between social context and literature; they do not provide an adequate means to analyse women's responses within the same field or class, a point I will take up later.

My main criticism of feminist attempts to deal with literary theory are thus focused on the way they have attempted, first, to understand the way gender relations function in society and, second, the way these social relations of gender have been studied from a literary perspective. In fact, the dominant feminist problem has remained one of attempting to study literature either as a reflection of social ideology or of studying literary texts as the expression of a special female nature and language. An adequate study of cultural factors including gender, and the organisation of literature within this specific set of cultural factors, still need to be undertaken.

My approach, consequently, argues that any attempt at criticism of women writers has to locate itself within a specific cultural and historical context. This requires an understanding of, first, how the field of literature is organised and, second, how this organisation affects all aspects of literature. Further, we need to understand not only whether women write differently from men but also how this difference is deployed within the literary field. In other words, what is said about it by the different agents who participate in the literary field. This requires an idea of the organisation of the field in China and an examination of the limits exercised by this on the participation of different agents who address the issue. This would include a critical examination of the participation of women. In this respect I entirely agree with Chris Weedon when she says:

> The analysis of the patriarchal structures of society and the positions that we occupy within them requires a theory which can address forms of social organisation and the social meanings and values which guarantee or contest them. Yet it must also be able to theorize individual consciousness. We need a theory of the relation between language, subjectivity, social organisation and power. (Weedon 1987: 12)

Following Weedon, it is my contention that only such an integrated approach to literature can allow us to escape the circle of debate within which feminism now finds itself located. It is in this context that I feel the work of Pierre Bourdieu provides a comprehensive approach to a study of women writers within the literary field. The following sections will expand on these ideas and put forward a method for the study of women writers in the specific context of China.

The concept of discourse: a Foucaultian approach

The work of Michel Foucault has been one of the mainstays behind the post-structuralist focus on an analysis of the effects of discourse and its role in the constitution of social power.[8] Foucault's work, at a philosophical level, is directed against the notion of rationality and objective knowledge claims.[9] He has sought to show the linkages between knowledge and power in modern society (Poster 1982). Given the complexity of Foucault's work and the various discussions that have emerged around his theories, I have chosen to deal only with his concept of discourse and its relationship to power.

In his book *The Archeology of Knowledge and the Discourse on Language* (1972), Foucault defines discourse as being linked to the production of statements. For Foucault, it is statements which form the basic unit of discourse.[10] Foucault's task, as Poster points out, is to uncover the 'specificities' of a particular discourse. Poster further clarifies Foucault's object as being 'discourses which are composed of statements, statements that are constituted by rules of formation and that have types of relations with other statements' (Poster 1982: 146).

Foucault goes on to tell us that this system works through the principle of 'exclusion and disclosure' (1972). The manner in which this system of relationships operates becomes the target of analysis. As Foucault explains, discourse analysis is not only the examination of the content of discourse:

> it is more a question of determining the conditions under which it may be employed, of imposing a certain number of rules upon those individuals who employ it, thus denying access to everyone else. This amounts to a rarefaction among speaking subjects: none may enter into discourse on a specific subject unless he [sic] has satisfied certain conditions or if he is not, from the outset, qualified to do so. (Foucault 1972: 224)

In other words, Foucault's method prompts us to look at what governs statements, what allows them to be said in the first place, who says them, who is allowed to say them and how they relate to other statements and ways of speaking about a subject.

Here again, Poster's reading of Foucault is appropriate when he says: 'Foucault wants to determine how discourse is a practice that creates objects and by creating them, determines their nature' (Poster 1982: 149). Foucault insists that discourses constitute themselves or exist in relation to other discourses by establishing with them relations of resemblance, proximity, distance, difference and transformations (Foucault 1972: 44).

This perspective further allows Foucault to put forward the notion of discursive practice. Discursive practice in turn works as a system of formation:

> By system of formation, then, I mean a complex group of relations that function as a rule: it lays down what must be related, in a particular discursive practice, for such an enunciation to be made, for such and such a concept to be used, for such and such a strategy to be organised. To define a system of formations in its specific individuality is therefore to characterize a discourse or a group of statements by the regularity of a practice. (Foucault 1972: 74)

Thus, discourses, in Foucault's work, are ways of speaking about things, of constituting knowledge about an object in one way rather than another through discursive formation. Gutting clarifies the point further by calling 'discursivity' a 'system of dispersion' (1989: 232). By examining discourses on different objects, one can arrive at an understanding of the way these are viewed and dispersed in different fields at a specific point in history. Foucault, by paying attention to the way discourses and discursive practices come into being, has focused on the points at which it becomes possible to speak of a subject. This also allows him to make the link between discourse, subjectivity and power (Dews 1984). This is the contribution of Foucault that Pasquino stresses.

As Pasquino says: 'Posing for discourse the question of power means basically to ask whom does discourse serve?' (Pasquino and Fonatana 1986: 115). Foucault does not reduce discourse to a material or social referent but sees discourse as an effective instance which shows the deployment of power. As Foucault puts it: 'Discourse does not act at the behest of power. It is power' (1986: 147). Discourses do not merely reflect economic or some other sort of power but are instruments of power in themselves. Those who have the right to participate in discourse formation exercise power in this manner by excluding the discourse of 'others' because it is seen as lying outside the rules of discourse formation. Thus, power is made manifest through discourse in the very use of certain statements in place of others.[11]

Foucault's understanding of power as diffuse and located in different discourses, forces any discussion of it to focus on specific fields or issues rather than seeing it as an opposition between those who hold power and those against whom it is exercised. Foucault demonstrates his own method in his approach to the study of sexuality, madness, psychiatry and discipline. In each of these, he identifies those relations of power which are specific to each discourse and shows how what is defined as mad or criminal in medieval Europe, for example, is significantly different to the terms of its discussion in modern times. His study of 'madness' or 'sexuality' is not a study of the subject per se but rather a study of the discourses around which the project is constructed. The deployment of particular discourses in different fields, judicial and psychiatric, for example, in turn allows us to classify people as mad or deviant.

This method then is applicable to all discourse. The following section elaborates how literature too can be seen as discourse.

Literature as discourse Within the field of literature itself, a Foucaultian perspective would state that literature can and should be seen as a discourse which can be submitted to analysis in the same manner as other discourses. In every period, the statements that constitute literature are based on principles of exclusion and inclusion and relate to other statements on the subject. This perspective emphasises a study of literature as an interactive field of 'discourse', where literary discourse acquires meaning only in relation to other social discourses.

Thus, literary discourse, or what comes to be defined as literature, allows us to see how it relates to social power by focusing on what literary discourse includes as its object and how it speaks of it.

This means moving away from readings of individual authors or texts towards a focus on their relationship within the literary field as discourse. This is a move towards examining what is allowed to be said in literary works on different subjects, who is allowed to say it, and how what is said is linked to the wider network of discursive practices. Edward Said has been one of the more prominent critics to employ this method of discourse analysis for a study of literature. Said has concerned himself with a study of power through examining representation (Cocks 1989: 48). In his work on the project of Orientalism (1978) Said shows how the construction of the Orient (in Said's book this term covers mainly the Arab world) is carried out especially within literary discourse which takes the Orient as its subject. The characteristics attributed to the Orient, such as notions of oriental mystique, backwardness, and so on show the power which the Occident has of, first, being able to define the Orient in a particular way and, second, to legitimise these self-same attributes as the reality of the Orient. Said firmly links the task of literary representation to historically specific periods and historically constituted discourses. He further links with Foucault's idea of exclusion and participation in discourse by arguing that literary discourse also has specific criteria of excluding and including audiences. As he says: 'Who writes? For whom is the writing being done? In what circumstances? These, it seems to me, are the questions whose answers provide us with the ingredients of making for a politics of interpretation' (1985: 135).

Discourse formation, in Said's analysis then, is firmly linked to the issue of social power. He argues strongly against the separation of literary studies from its context (1985: 153). In this sense, discourse acquires a relational position between social mores (including gender) and what comes to be defined as the literary text. By examining a literary text discursively, one can choose to focus on different groups of statements depending on the subject on which we focus our analysis. These statements can be related to gender, to race, to class or to notions of beauty and truth. A statement related to gender, for example, can be read discursively to see how it relates to the operation of gender discourse as a whole, thus bringing the analysis of literary works closer to a sociological approach to literature. Whereas liberal feminism believes that the text is reducible to its author and socialist feminists believe that the text is reducible to its ideology, discourse analysis argues that a text is not reducible to either of these two and represents instead an instance of the complex process by which meaning is constructed in society through discourse.

Discourse analysis is ultimately social. It is this social analysis implied in the term which allows us to speak of specific discourses such as that of literature or, as I argue in the next section, even allows us to argue for seeing 'gender' as a discourse.

Gender as discourse: arriving at an operational definition Foucault's approach has been successfully used by feminists to examine precisely those issues which get left out of a more traditional gender analysis (B. Martin 1988). The influence of Foucault on feminism is clearly marked both in the way feminist scholars take up Foucault's notion of a critique of knowledge as objective[12] and also in the way they ascribe to the practice of gender relations a discursive formation. Feminist theory has concentrated on showing how the category 'woman' has been discursively devalued and subordinated to the category 'man' (Braidotti 1989). Feminism has also focused on showing how 'woman's discourse' or women's participation in representation has been excluded and their discourse marginalised. Thus, women have been marginal in the constitution of meaning and, therefore, power (Kurzwell 1986). Taking this as my point of departure, my own understanding of the term 'gender relations' at the level of discourse analysis is indebted to the work of two scholars, Donna Haraway and Jane Flax. Both these writers have been influenced by the work of Foucault and their work is appropriate for my purpose here.

Haraway describes the different attributes that are given to men and women as a 'gender identity paradigm', which in turn is historically and socially specific. Consequently, the different discourses that exist on gender in society function as paradigms which construct women's identity. According to Haraway, the formulations of 'gender' have changed in meaning since the concept was first introduced by feminists. While earlier definitions centred round distinguishing gender as a concept from biological sex, these definitions failed to question the political and social history of concepts that emerge. She argues that the women's movement has constructed women's experience as much as it has uncovered or discovered it. Thus, it is not a matter of recovering true female nature which is socially instead of biologically constructed, or female nature as constructed through women's relation to the modes of production and the organisation of labour in society, but a matter of seeing how gender discourse provides paradigms through which female identities are constructed in different discourses and in different sites (Owens 1985; Haraway 1990).

Jane Flax argues in a similar fashion in her article 'Postmodernism and Gender Relations in Feminist Theory' (1990). Her basic argument is that 'gender' enters into and is a constituent element in all discourses. Above all, it must be understood as a relational term where one constitutive part of the term can have no meaning without the other. As she says:

'Gender relations' is a category meant to capture a complex set of social processes. Gender, both as an analytic category and a social process, is relational ... Gender relations are differentiated and (so far) asymmetric divisions and attributions of human traits and capacities. Through gender relations two types of persons are created: man and woman ... gender relations so far as we have been able to understand them have been (more or less) relations of domination. That is, gender relations have been (more) defined and (imperfectly) controlled by one of their interrelated aspects – the man. (Flax 1990: 45)

Flax's definition of gender relations encapsulates the different elements that need to be examined for a study of gender relations in society. Like Haraway, she emphasises the relational nature of the concepts 'man' and 'woman'. Gender is a social relation that enters into and partially constitutes all other social relations and activities. As a practical social relation, gender can be understood only by close examination of the meanings of 'man'/'woman' in different discourses.

Thus, one could argue that for feminist theory Foucault's work has meant a move towards an analysis of the way categories such as man and woman are presented in different discourses, and of how the power of these representations can be studied in relation to specific sites and issues, rather than posing the problem in terms of a universal female condition. It has stimulated feminism to examine the different ways in which women participate in the production of gender discourses in different historical periods and in different fields. In other words, what has to be analysed is how discourse on gender has the power to produce male and female subjects (Weedon 1988; B. Martin 1988).

This line of thinking has also influenced the work of non-western women scholars who have pointed out that a focus on discourse analysis can also help us to analyse the way in which the experiences of those who do not participate in discourse formation are appropriated. This appropriation occurs in the way women are spoken about in discourse. Thus, the categories 'Third World women' or 'working-class women', for example, are associated with certain defining characteristics. These descriptions are then seen as representing the reality.[13] This criticism can be extended to include the work of western women on Third World women and the work of elite Third World women on other women in their own cultures. Chandra Mohanty, for example, points out the effectiveness of Foucaultian analysis to study the 'construction of Third World women in western feminist writings' (1988).

Posing the issue of power as one which is not divided along two polarities also helps feminists to look at the issue of differences between women. This concept of difference is intrinsic to any understanding of the experience of gender relations in practice. Not all women experience their gender identities in the same way. Instead, their experiences are mediated by their specific historical and cultural positions and are affected by factors of class, ethnicity and geographical location, etcetera. Speaking of a notion of difference, Michelle Barrett points out that difference in a feminist context means 'a more deconstructive model that emphasizes differences within the category woman itself as well as within the specific social existence of woman' (1987: 29).

I feel this notion of difference has to be extended to include not just difference in terms of race and class in material terms, but also a differential participation in relation to written discourse. Thus, even women from the same class – and often women who participate in discourse formations are from the same class – can have a differential relationship to discourse on a given subject. Further, this concept of difference can be a resource, as Sawicki points out, 'insofar as it enables us to multiply the sources of resistance to the myriad of relations of domination that circulate through the social system' (1988: 187). It is these aspects of Foucault's influence on feminism that I find so appropriate for the study of gender discourse through literature in China. It allows me to focus on what underlies or governs the limits of a discourse on gender. In other words, how 'woman', 'femininity' and 'femaleness' get spoken about within the wider social network and specifically within literary discourse. The issue should not be seen as one where one gender was earlier suppressed or non-existent or mis-represented in literature, but rather as a question of seeing how this gender relationship is articulated through changes in different historical and cultural contexts.

Understood in this way, gender relations become not a static un-changed category but a field of discourses on the subject. Further, women remain not merely its victims – suppressed, isolated or even banned by it – but actively participate in its production by helping to construct it, obstruct it and widen its limits. Seen in this light, a discourse on gender relations can constitute itself in two ways: either by trying to hide the actual divisions and tensions in the way gender is linked to a system of oppression and subordination, or by setting forward critical and alternative positions. Thus, discourse as a concept needs to be understood as a multi-disciplinary thematic arrangement which speaks of and defines its objects of knowledge in certain specific ways.

As a final note of caution, I would like to add that feminist attempts at meta-theory do not exist in a vacuum. Foucault's point that power is contained in knowledge also applies to feminist categories. While we need to continue our critique of male domination, we must not romanticise womanhood. We need to be critically aware of the position from which we speak or make theory. We should avoid seeing women as totally innocent, as liberal feminism does, but we should also examine the way we collude with dominant representations of ourselves. We need to be critical of our own responses and see how women actually relate to dominant representations of themselves. This understanding of the way women relate to gender discourse is intrinsic to improving our knowledge of how gender relations operate in society. Further, we need to point out that identity, whether masculine or feminine, is not a *fait accompli*, a given which exists unchanged across time. Instead of asking the question 'what is woman?' – a continuation of the mythification of womanhood – we need to ask how womanhood is defined, created and represented by women and men in specific historical and cultural contexts. And further, how changing these definitions can be an important part of the feminist enterprise.

Differentiating between discourses

While a Foucaultian focus on the discourse on women is an important means of identifying the way social relations of gender are represented in other practices, there is one major problem with Foucault's approach. Although he allows us to formulate the question of power at the level of discourse, his method does not provide us with a means to differentiate between types of discourses. For example, how can we distinguish between a discourse of power and a discourse of resistance? How do certain discourses persist over time and, when they change, how does this change occur? More specifically, though this method helps me identify a discourse on gender in the field of Chinese literature, it does not help me find out how the subjects of that discourse, namely women, participate in it, the point at which women's participation in its production differs and why this is so.

This ambiguity makes it essential to retain a notion of 'domination' and what Cocks (1989) calls 'dominative powers'.[14] While we cannot see this dominative power as held only by one class of people or as vested only in state institutions, the unequal social relations of gender imply that one form of viewing the world and relations to the world have a degree of legitimacy not enjoyed by others. It is this point that has made certain feminists criticise Foucault for only paying lip-service to the notion of resistance. According to them, resistance disappears beneath the absolutely fluid character of power (Balbus 1982; Hartstock 1987).

Although several scholars, including feminists, have attempted to extend and develop Foucault's notion of discourse,[15] I have found the work of Pierre Bourdieu most helpful. My choice is largely determined by the fact that Bourdieu points out how the cultural element is missing in the work of Foucault (Bourdieu 1988) and provides an integrated theory of cultural representation (Ostrow 1981). A focus on the cultural element implies examining the interaction of agents to discourses and therefore to domination and resistance. Bourdieu's method provides a means of analysing women's responses to gender discourse while still locating them within the literary field. Through the use of some of his sociological concepts, we can arrive at an understanding of how people and groups relate to discourses in different fields. While a Foucaultian focus on the operation of discourse and the construction of reality through discourse is important, we need to have a way of seeing how individuals as agents relate to discourses. This is important also for feminist theory.

Feminist theories to date have argued about the subordination experienced by women and about the unequal power relations that exist in society. While it is easy to speak of a dominant discourse, real change is possible only when we know how women perceive their circumstances, at what levels they collude or consent to a dominant discourse and at what levels they oppose or resist its terms.

Bourdieu and the literary field

While Foucault's notion of discourse is useful for examining literature as a specific type of discourse, to understand its practice, Bourdieu provides us with a method for seeing how individuals participate in literary discourse, and what determines their relationship to it.

Writing as a sociologist of literature, Bourdieu examines the way a study of symbolic systems such as literature can be approached. In his article on 'Symbolic Power' (1979), he speaks of how symbolic systems (art, religion and language) can also work as instruments of domination. He sees symbolic systems as 'instruments of communication' which fulfil their political functions by legitimising the social cleavages that exist or, as he says, 'the systems of domination' (1979: 80). He goes on to point out that dominant factions impose and legitimise their domination through different forms of symbolic production (discourses) and with the help of intermediaries who serve their interests (agents) (1988).

Thus, Bourdieu, following the line of reasoning already laid out by Marx, Gramsci and Williams, among others, is linking elements of culture with dominative practices. Unlike Foucault, who seems to be doing away with a notion of domination by seeing power and resistance as diffuse and interlinked, Bourdieu argues that dominant factions exercise power also through the production of discourses on any one subject. Here, he links the practice of discourse to institutional and social domination rather than only to the field of discourse itself. Bourdieu's work at this level seems to build upon that of Foucault. As he himself points out, Foucault has taken from Saussure the notion of the importance accorded to relationships between words and statements and proposed the term 'field of strategic possibilities' (Bourdieu 1988: 542). However, unlike Foucault, who makes the field of discourse itself the explanatory principle and stresses its absolute autonomy, Bourdieu goes on to tackle the issues of agents and institutions by putting forward the term 'literary field'.

The literary field, for Bourdieu, is a 'space of objective relations between positions' (1988). These positions are determined by the function occupied by the agent. As Bourdieu explains in an interview in 1985 regarding his overall project as such:

> I wanted, so to speak, to reintroduce agents that Lévi-Strauss and the structuralists, among others Althusser, tended to abolish, making them into simple epiphenomena of structure. And I mean agents, not subjects. Action is not the mere carrying out of a rule, or obedience to a rule. Social agents, in archaic societies as well as in ours, are not automata regulated like clocks, in accordance with laws which they do not understand. (Bourdieu 1990a: 9)

It is Bourdieu's inclusion of the role of agents that makes the literary field a concept which covers the social relationship between authors, critics, readers, publishers and the literary establishment. Bourdieu points out that in each of these relationships, each of the agents employs the socially established idea he has of the other partner (Bourdieu 1988). Thus, agents accept the differences created by social and symbolic power and express this almost naturally in social interaction. According to Bourdieu, if we focus on the factors of literary production, we can avoid the 'opposition, as strong as it is pernicious, between internal reading and external analysis' (1988: 544). That is to say, a focus on factors of literary production bridges the gap between the literary text and the cultural context within which it is produced. This contextual focus also makes Bourdieu criticise the unquestioned primacy of the author and his genius when it comes to defining art. He criticises earlier theories of literature for their method of study which seeks the explanatory principle of a work in the author taken in isolation (1988: 540). He argues instead for the need to locate a study of literature within the broader field of cultural study. As he states:

Obviously there is no denying the specific determinant exerted by the space of possibilities ... however it is not possible to consider the cultural order as a system totally independent of the actors and the institutions that put it into practice and bring it into existence: if only because there does not seem any way to account for changes in this arbitrarily isolated and thereby de-historicized universe unless we endow it with an immanent propensity for auto-transformations, through a mysterious form of *Selbstbewegung*. (Bourdieu 1988: 543)

He goes on to make the same criticism of the work of Russian formalists who he says, like Foucault, considered only the system of works, the network of relationships between texts (1988: 543). This is an extremely important point and stresses the need to understand the cultural context within which literary discourse makes its appearance. For Bourdieu, any examination of literature implies a focus on the agents who operate within the field and the structure of the field as such. The structure of the field exercises an important limit to what counts as literature and influences the interaction of agents with each other and with the factors of literary production. It also determines what emerges as part of literary discourse.

Bourdieu also distinguishes between discourses of power and dis-courses of resistance within the field of literary and artistic production. According to him: 'Cultural producers hold a specific power, the properly symbolic power of showing things and making people believe in them, of revealing, in an explicit, objectified way the more or less confused, vague, unformulated, even unformulable experiences of the natural world and the social world, and of thereby bringing them into existence' (1990c: 146).

Thus, within cultural practice, agents play a specific role in bringing into existence things which have not been spoken of earlier. Bourdieu goes on to explain that actors within this field may put this symbolic power, which brings things into the open, 'either at the service of the dominant factions or alternatively, at the service of the dominated in the social field taken as a whole' (1990c: 146). Consequently, even within the field of literature, one can distinguish between discourses and link this difference to the social network as a whole, a move which allows us to examine power and resistance. Bourdieu stresses this point clearly when he says: 'The power of naming, in particular of naming the unnameable, that which is still unnoticed or repressed, is a considerable power' (1990c: 149). Hence, agents within the field of literature, in speaking the unspoken in literary discourse, are entering the struggle over the representations of the social world.

Bourdieu is, finally, arguing for the existence of a field which structures the possibilities for agents and their relationship to discourse. The field has its own rules and its own logic. He goes on to point out that the strategies of actors involved in literary or artistic struggle depend on the position they occupy within the field (1988: 545). This position occupied by agents within the field is, in turn, dependent on the social and symbolic capital that they bring with them.

Consequently, using Bourdieu's basic ideas I would like to argue that, for women, their position as agents within the field of literature will be determined by the social discourse on gender. Here the notion of gender discourse must be understood, as this will influence both the perception that women have of themselves as cultural producers and the way others perceive their participation within the field. This notion of field is particularly suitable for the study of women as a group within the field of Chinese literature. I will further discuss the work of Bourdieu in Chapter 3, when I show how access to writing literature in China is strictly controlled by the state-run literary institutions. These institutions exercise control at all levels of the process of literary production, and the space of agents within it is determined by the symbolic power enjoyed by the agent.

The above developments can be seen as important shifts in literary theory with implications for feminist literary analysis. My own approach is based on using the above model in combination with certain elements of feminism. Making a link between discourses and institutions is important because it allows us to see how certain discourses acquire legitimacy because they are officially sponsored discourses. Such a discourse, thus, becomes a reflection of the way institutionalised powers consider specific issues.

Discourses of power and discourses of resistance: the agent's space

As pointed out earlier, Bourdieu criticises Foucault for his inability to explain how systems, whether at the level of discourse or at the level of 'material reality', continue to maintain themselves, and what forces them to change. Unless we are to see discourses as changing through 'auto-transformation', the notion of actors and institutions has to be brought back into the discussion. As Bourdieu says:

> The most resolutely objectivist theory has to integrate the agents' representa-
> tion of the social world; more precisely, it must take an account of the
> contribution that agents make towards constructing the view of the social
> world, and through this, constructing this world, by means of the *work of
> representation* (in all senses of the word) that they constantly perform in order

to impose their view of the world or the view of their own position in this world – their social identity. (Bourdieu 1985: 727)

This social identity, Bourdieu goes on to explain, resides in agents having a sense of their social space. This sense of one's place is arrived at through a process of internalisation and the incorporation of objective structures within which social relationships are lived out.

The above ideas, if applied to gender relations, mean that men and women relate in a specific fashion to each other, premised on their knowing male and female positions and male and female discourse in relation to each other. This would determine the discourse employed by them and the reception and meaning given to their specific discourse. Such a perspective can help us discover the role played by women in the construction of their view of the social world through reading literature. The way women writers represent women characters can then help us identify how women respond to gender discourse in China.

In his attempt to link discourses with certain forms of domination, Bourdieu is following the line of reasoning laid down by other scholars who have attempted to understand how people experience the context of domination.[16] As Joan Cocks points out, no dominant culture is all-inclusive. Instead, it is through the existence of experience not entirely suppressed by dominant culture that we can see domination is at work (Cocks 1989: 64). Dominant discourses, with their specific forms of legitimacy, exist in relation to other forms of viewing the world and social relations. These forms may be residual cultures, or the critical stances taken by different agents within the same field. To arrive at an understanding of resistance, it is essential to retain a notion of 'agency', or people who make critical choices (determined, of course, by specific historical and cultural circumstances), vis-à-vis adhering to dominant discourses. Classical Marxism and structuralism have, in fact, suffered from the negation, so to speak, of the critical consciousness of people by seeing them as either victims of a 'false consciousness' or as determined by structures. I have found the work of Bourdieu very helpful in delineating this relationship of agents to social discourse.

Bourdieu calls the relationship between a dominant view and the resistance to it, a relationship between 'orthodox' discourses, and 'heterodox' discourses. Before arriving at an understanding of what he means by this, it is necessary to discuss those concepts of Bourdieu which help us understand his wider model of analysis. Brubaker points out that Bourdieu has attempted to circumvent the conventional split between an objectivist method of enquiry, where the 'subject or agent' is not considered of any value but is seen as constructed through various social structures, and the subjectivist view of the phenomenologists, where the subject's intention is paramount, by attempting to combine Marx and Weber (Brubaker 1985: 747).

Bourdieu uses the concept of 'habitus', a concept he takes from Weber, and develops it to analyse the relationship between agents and structures. He says:

> The habitus is at once a system of models for the production of practices and a system of models for the perception and appreciation of practices ... As a result, the habitus produces practices and representations which are available for classification, which are objectively differentiated; ... Thus, the habitus implies a 'sense of one's place' but also a 'sense of the other's place'. (Bourdieu 1990: 131)

Habitus works to ensure a 'common sense' through which individuals relate to social structures which are in turn specific to particular types of material conditions of existence. In this light, gender relations do not exist merely at the level of discourse but are lived and experienced by agents. In the case of gender relations this would imply examining women's interaction with them. Bourdieu argues that in order to appreciate a person's actual practical situation in the world, we must see how the meanings of things are actually grasped through the 'active dispositions embedded in the agents' very bodies in the form of mental dispositions, schemes of perception and thought' (1977: 22). Thus, habitus can also be understood as a system of dispositions on the basis of which people arrive at a sense of their relationship to their social environment.

It is this notion of habitus which brings in the cultural element. If the formulation and the deployment of discourses is seen as influenced by the habitus of agents, then a critical examination of the content of discourse can provide us with an understanding of cultural practice as such. What appears as discourse is then linked back to the cultural element from which it emerges.

Thus, when examining a discourse on gender relations, the concept of habitus can be helpful in understanding the way in which women relate and respond to dominant notions of gender relations. Jacques Bidet points out that this concept of habitus 'ensures a mediation between structure and practices' (1979: 203). Bourdieu calls this a theory of practice, 'a product of the dialectical relationship between situation and habitus' (1977: 186).

In the case of gender relations, it would imply that we arrive at a sense of our gender roles through habitus which is in turn mediated by practice. This has important consequences for feminist theory since it is in daily activities that gender relations constantly manifest themselves. As Bourdieu puts it:

> A child constructs its sexual identity, the major element in its social identity, at the same time as it constructs its image of the division of work between the sexes, out of the same socially defined set of inseparably biological and social indices. In other words, the awakening consciousness of sexual identity and the incorporation of the dispositions associated with a determinate social definition of the social functions incumbent on men and women, come hand in hand with the adoption of a socially defined vision of the sexual division of labour. (Bourdieu 1977:93)

Recent work by scholars has noted the use that can be made of Bourdieu's work to understand the relationship of gender with social practice. Risseeuw notes that from a feminist point of view Bourdieu's theory offers several advantages to other approaches which have also attempted to understand the relationship between gender and power (Risseeuw 1988: 184). Along with habitus, she treats his concepts of doxa, orthodoxy and heterodoxy (1988: 184).[17]

These three concepts of Bourdieu help us to understand how discourses are operationalised and used by agents. Bourdieu develops these concepts in his study of how agents take up positions within a structured space or field. Thompson notes: 'The structure of the field is a certain state of the relation of force between the agents or groups engaged in struggle' (1984: 49). Depending on the position of agents within these structures, they would have a differential relationship to discourse on a given subject. It is this differential relationship that is explained by the concepts of doxa, orthodoxy and heterodoxy.

I shall first note the way Bourdieu defines these three concepts. Bourdieu defines doxa as:

> Systems of classification which reproduce, in their own specific logic, the objective classes ... by securing the misrecognition, and hence the recognition, of the arbitrariness on which they are based: in the extreme case, that is to say, when there is a quasi-perfect correspondence between the objective order and the subjective principles of organisation ... the natural and social world appears as self-evident. This experience we shall call *doxa*, so as to distinguish it from an orthodox or heterodox belief implying awareness and recognition of the possibility of different or antagonistic beliefs. (Bourdieu 1977: 164)

Thus, doxa is the self-evident or taken for granted aspect of social relations. Bourdieu goes on to explain that it is this adherence to a doxic relation to the social world which is the absolute form of recognition of legitimacy through misrecognition of arbitrariness (1977: 165). The principles of social organisation and the power relations embedded within them are seen as natural and accepted unquestioningly by agents. Thus, doxa is belief which is taken for granted as 'natural' and therefore forms the unsaid of social practice. Bourdieu goes on to explain that it is in moments of objective crisis that things move out of doxa and become articulated as discourse.

The passage from doxa to orthodoxy and heterodoxy Bourdieu says that it is only when social classifications become the object and instrument of struggle that the arbitrary principles of prevailing classifications can appear as such. It then becomes necessary to undertake the work of conscious systematisation and express rationalisation which marks the passage from doxa to orthodoxy and heterodoxy (1977). Those who in a given field possess the power – economic, cultural and symbolic – have an interest in maintaining the arbitrariness of their discourse. They therefore employ strategies of conservation towards preserving a state of doxa where the established structure is not questioned. As Bourdieu says:

> Orthodoxy, straight, or rather straightened opinion, aims without ever entirely succeeding, at restoring the primal state of innocence of doxa ... it is defined as a system of euphemisms, of acceptable ways of thinking and speaking the natural and social world, which rejects heretical remarks as blasphemies (1977: 169).

Thus, orthodoxy is discourse which tends towards ensuring that the prevailing system of classification remains intact. Here agents make choices of life-style and opinion which adhere to orthodox beliefs and see these beliefs as the correct or natural way to behave. However, Bourdieu goes on to stress that an orthodoxy is founded only in relation to its difference from heterodox opinion. Heterodoxy is, then, those discourses which are critical of the classificatory principles of orthodox discourse and represent the existence of alternative points of view (Bourdieu 1977). They tend towards questioning the doxa and showing the arbitrariness of the classification system of society. Thompson points out that, according to Bourdieu, it is those who are least endowed with capital (material and symbolic) who tend towards strategies of subversion or heresy, and form an heterodoxy (Thompson 1984). Jopke (1987), in his discussion of Bourdieu's method, points out that Bourdieu looks at the formation of groups and the struggles between groups. Related to Bourdieu's notion of struggles between groups is his notion of different forms of capital which locate the agent in the social. As Jopke notes: 'He [Bourdieu] distinguishes between economic, cultural, social and legitimate capital. Thereby he enlarges the commonsense notion of capital as an entirely economic resource institutionalized as right of possession and convertible into money and opens the way to a "general science of the economics of practice" which includes the whole sphere of culture and non-production centred social relations' (1987: 57).

Jopke further clarifies Bourdieu's notion of cultural capital by saying: '"Cultural capital" refers to cultural knowledge as a source of power' (1987: 57). These concepts of social and cultural capital are extremely relevant for the study of women's place within different fields. The importance attached to female participation in discourse formation will, to a certain extent, depend on the social and cultural capital attached to being a woman. In the social sphere, for example, men simply by being born male enjoy a form of social capital and legitimacy denied to women. Women's efforts to accumulate social and cultural capital are thus a real struggle between two social groups: men and women.

Conclusion

Bourdieu's notion of heterodox discourses and his emphasis that orthodox discourses exist only in relation to heterodox discourses give an active role to those who resist dominant beliefs. If the assumptions about the natural differences between men and women are seen as a doxic state of affairs, then women's questioning of this apparent naturalness can force the dominant faction to articulate its position and principles as orthodox discourse. It is only when agents struggle over the legitimation of different ways of viewing social relations that the arbitrary principles of social classification are questioned and move out of doxa. In the case of Chinese literature, it would mean that women writers who create specific types of female characters and call into question different aspects of the 'naturalness' of beliefs about women's social position thus force the dominant faction (the literary establishment in this particular case) to articulate its opinions which hitherto may have been held in doxa. These women writers articulate the previously unsaid and bring a critical discourse on the subject into existence. Dominant discourse, in turn, responds to the works of women writers by evaluating and judging their work. The constant movement of things outside of doxa allows us to understand how struggle and social conflict manifest themselves at the level of discourse. As Bourdieu explains: 'The critique which brings the undiscussed into discussion, the un-formulated into formulation, has as the condition of its possibility objective crisis, which, in breaking the immediate fit between the subjective structures and the objective structures destroys self-evident practicality' (1977: 169).

Thus, women's questioning of the doxa on gender relations would render doxa unstable. Women's own discourse in relation to orthodoxy would help us to examine the different ways women participate in the production of gender discourse. We shall be able to understand if their discourse is the same as orthodoxy or different from it, and allow us further scope to strategise against domination.

This book, then, hopes to combine Foucault's insights into how power relations can be studied through a focus on discourse with Bourdieu's insights into how these discourses are operationalised into different fields and differ because of the active participation of agents. While Foucault's work on discourse theory is intrinsic for a contemporary understanding of what is covered under the term discourse, in terms of using discourse theory in relation to the specificity of the Chinese situation, I use his work in conjunction with Bourdieu's method of differentiating between discourses. This creates a framework for analysing women's responses to discourse on gender by analysing the female characters in specific stories as articulating a specific social discourse and therefore as adhering to specific gender identity paradigms; gender identity paradigms which represent either orthodox or heterodox social ideas on the nature of female identity.

Notes

1. Feminist literary theory today contains an extensive body of work. A major concern of feminist criticism has been the attempt to define a feminist novel or feminist writing. A common idea has been that of 'woman-centred novels'. Michelle Barrett examines this issue in her article 'Feminism and the Definition of Cultural Politics' (Barrett 1982: 57).

2. Jagger (1983), has differentiated between different theories of feminism on the basis of their political affiliations and on the basis of their understanding of human nature. She identifies three major distinctions as liberal feminism, radical feminism and Marxist feminism. Although her work is an excellent point of departure, the eclectic nature of feminist theories today is such that it is difficult to make such sharp distinctions between different positions. In the case of literary theory, for example, there is considerable overlap among feminists of different political leanings. Moi (1985) is, in a sense, following Jagger's model in the distinction she draws between different feminist theories of literature.

3. 'Representation' as understood here should not be seen as only reflecting reality but also a way of constructing, structuring, grasping and knowing the world, a definition which is also used by Berger and Luckmann (1966), Sontag (1977), Cousins and Hussain (1984).

4. Patriarchy as a concept has been criticised both within feminism and within anthropological discourse. Scholars have argued that the notion of patriarchal family structures is imposed on other societies and seen as the norm without

examining the practice of family relations as they exist and change. Patriarchy as a general term common to anthropological studies as a whole has been used by several scholars, for example Rosaldo et al., (1974), Reiter (ed.) (1985), Coward (1983). Gender is a more accepted term these days and was first introduced by Gayle Rubin (1985).

5. Post-structuralist theories are usually identified as those which reject a notion of absolute referentiality and take as their point of departure the notion of 'meaning as being relational'. This type of analysis is closely linked to the changing landscape of social theory, especially in France. Its influence within literary studies has been far-reaching, especially the influence of Derrida and his method of deconstruction which has constituted an attack on notions of the 'centre' in conceptual systems. According to Derrida, centres are privileged signifiers which are elevated or privileged by means of social ideologies. See Culler (1982); see also Eagleton (1983: 127–50).

6. Marx's notion of 'ideology' has spawned an enormous variety of research in different areas and, still today, retains a specific value in analysing cultural representations. In fact, the primary impetus for a sociology of literature approach could be said to have come from Marx. For an excellent treatment of this theme see Michelle Barrett (1979). Several competent studies exist of the Marxist use of ideology for a study of literature. For a good overview of the Marxist classics on the subject, the reader is referred to Dave Lang (1978) and Raymond Williams (1977)

7. In recent years attempts have been made by psychoanalysts such as Sudhir Kakar (1985) to extend psychoanalytic theories to understanding the specific processes at work in other cultures, such as India. Kakar points out the importance of cultural differences with regard to the psychoanalytic development of individuals.

8. The impetus for a reconceptualisation of traditional literary and sociological concepts came from the linguistic theories of Saussure. Saussure understood language as an abstract system consisting of a chain of signs. Each sign is made up of a signifier (sound or written image) and a signified (meaning). These two aspects of signs relate to each other in an arbitrary way, and there is, therefore, no natural or obvious connection between the sound image and the concept that it identifies. The meaning of words then becomes relational and not intrinsic to the word as such. The chief consequence of this for social theory was that other aspects of social life also began to be seen as relational within a system or structure rather than having an unchanging natural character. See Saussure (1974), Ruthven (1984), Pettit (1975).

9. Foucault has convincingly argued that scientific discourse is implicated in the operation of power in society. For a detailed rendering of this argument see Foucault (1972: ch. 6), 'Science and Knowledge'.

10. Discourse theory can also take other aspects as its basic unit of analysis, for example a 'word' or even 'utterance', to use Bakhtin's term (1981). Macdonnel (1986) provides a comprehensive discussion of the way this concept has been used within literary studies.

11. Foucault uses the term 'power' in a radically different way from earlier discussions of the subject. Traditional theories of power have seen it as essentially repressive and disciplinary. Foucault criticises this notion of repressive power and speaks instead of a notion of power as productive (Foucault 1980). Several scholars have written on Foucault and his concept of power: for a general introduction see Dreyfus and Rabinow (1983), also Hoy (ed.) (1986). Cousins and Hussain (1984) also discuss the main features of Foucault's work and provide an excellent discussion of the wider philosophical debates which Foucault draws upon.

12. Feminism's critique of knowledge as objective can, at certain levels, be seen as paralleling the work of Foucault. In the powerful criticism of the 'androcentric' nature of knowledge claims, they add to Foucault's insights by pointing out that not only are knowledge claims not objective but they are male biased. According to Lester K. Ward, who introduced the term androcentric, the androcentric theory is that the male is primary in all aspects, cf. Ruthven (1984: 51).

13. Chandra Mohanty (1991) has done excellent work based on Said and Foucault to analyse the discursive content of the category 'Third World women'. See also Chachchi (1991).

14. Joan Cocks (1989) examines how an analysis of domination and resistance has been carried out by different scholars. She focuses on the work, of Stuart Hampshire, Antonio Gramsci, Raymond Williams, Edward Said and Michel Foucault. It is an excellent treatment of the subject with special value for feminists.

15. In this light, the work of Spivak and the group of 'subaltern studies' also offer a method of analysis. Spivak (1986) examines at what levels oppressed or subaltern groups express their relationship to dominant representations.

16. The work of Marx and Marxist scholars such as Gramsci have also been significant for the analysis of social domination. Marx explains his understanding of the experience of domination as natural through his concept of 'false consciousness', a term linked to his notion of ideology. According to him, people accept the parameters of dominant social discourses because they are unaware of the reality of their exploitation, and are, therefore, 'falsely conscious' about the legitimacy of social relations. Gramsci sees this phenomenon in a wider way by using the terms of 'hegemony' and 'common sense', to analyse the relationship of people to dominant beliefs. Wertheim (1964) has used the notion of 'counterpoint' when speaking of resistance to dominant powers. He also focuses on the way no dominant discourse is completely accepted by a public. See his *East West Parallels: Sociological Approaches in Modern Asia*.

17. Risseeuw (1988) uses the concepts of Bourdieu to put forward a new way of conceptualising and analysing women's daily struggles and experiences. She especially emphasises the strategic responses of women to cultural orthodoxy.

2

One step forward, two steps back: the construction of an orthodox discourse on gender

The previous chapter examined the concept 'orthodox discourse', a discourse which attempts to construct itself as the only correct and legitimate way of speaking about existing social relations. Orthodoxy can, in a sense, be seen as representing a certain cultural continuity with regard to social relations. It is a discourse which, at any given moment, tends towards conservatism and towards preserving the status quo on a given subject. Dominant patterns of social relations are not always maintained by an exercise of repressive power but acquire power by a sort of consensus. Such consensus is based on what Bourdieu calls 'habitus' or the accepted aspect of social relations which structure the disposition of agents. In a sense, all orthodoxy attempts to do is to conserve this state of habitus and maintain a status quo *vis-à-vis* social practice. With regard to gender discourse, for example, changes in the material position of women do not imply that every aspect of gender discourse will change. Certain elements of gender discourse remain in doxa and, mediated through social practice, are accepted by both sexes.

This chapter contains a brief historical survey (largely based on the work of other scholars) of orthodox discourse on gender relations in China. My focus is on that discourse which articulates itself as orthodoxy and maintains itself through institutional practices. Giving a particular slant to the rich material already available on the subject, my intention is to show the continuities that exist in the content, deployment and effects of orthodox discourse both today and in more traditional times. I shall show how orthodoxy on gender relations constructs itself in different periods in relation to the habitus of gender relations. Women's relationship to orthodoxy will be shown as mediated by women's material position, thereby ensuring that orthodoxy never exists in an ideal way even though it attempts to serve this function. It is against the content of orthodox discourse that woman characters in fiction will be analysed.

Orthodox discourse in China today is based on the ideology of

Marxism and its specific vision of male and female roles. I shall argue that this 'new' orthodoxy is in turn based on a more traditional habitus which is specific to China. This is partly because socialist orthodoxy has been imposed upon a more traditional orthodoxy in an authoritarian manner, succeeding in suppressing traditional elements rather than fundamentally changing them. Traditional ideas about women are then pushed underground and operate in a more complex fashion. Here we have a situation where heterodox discourse can turn into orthodoxy when it receives the backing of the state and its institutions.

By the time that the Communist Party of China was formed in 1921, discourse on gender relations had already experienced certain changes. Because of this, the Communist Party was forced to distinguish itself from two other discourses, both of them grounded on different conceptions of gender relations. The first was a more traditional discourse on the position of women, which derived its legitimacy from the Confucian classics. The second was the nationalist and liberal position, which was influenced by western ideas and became popular in China at the turn of the nineteenth century. I will first briefly discuss these two positions before turning to an examination of the way the Communist Party redefines gender relations.

Early orthodox discourse: the construction of a habitus of gender relations

Several scholars have pointed out the inferior position of women in traditional China. Chinese society in Confucian terms was a patriarchal society with strict rules of conduct. The underlying principles or governing rationale were the teachings of Confucius (551–479 BC). The traditional ideal woman was a dependent being whose behaviour was governed by the 'three obediences and four virtues'. The three obediences were obedience to the father before marriage, the husband after marriage and the son in case of widows. The four virtues were propriety in behaviour, speech, demeanour and employment (O'Hara 1945). Education for women was intended to inculcate these virtues. Among the most recommended books of instruction for women were the *Nü jie* (*Precepts for Women*), the *Nü er jing* (*Classic for Girls*) and the *Lie nü zhuan* (*Biographies of Eminent Chinese Women*). All these books were supposed to furnish women with knowledge about how they should conduct themselves in society. The *Nü jie* is attributed to Ban Zhao (AD 1), a famous women scholar and historian. These books gradually became the governing principles for female behaviour, especially among the elite.

All these books stressed the importance of the family for women and their seclusion within the household. Women were denied participation in any of the government or local community institutions. They had no access to the system of examinations through which men improved their social status. Without independent means, a women was dependent on the good will of her husband. In material terms, women were kept dependent by being denied the right to inherit property. Writing in 1946, Olga Lang comments on the total absence of property rights for Chinese women as being almost unexampled (O. Lang 1946). Discussing the reason for women's general degradation in China, Helen Snow makes the same point when she says:

> The distinctive weakness of the position of Chinese women was due to the fact that property could not be transferred by marriage ... A Chinese woman was valuable in her own right only as a hostage or as a source of domestic labor power. She did not exist as a mother in her own right and had no legal control over her children. (H. Snow 1967: 48)

Alongside their lack of property rights, women were controlled by a firmly entrenched system of patrilocal marriages and the related norm of female chastity. This rigid sexual morality was, and remains, a key link in the subordination of women.[1] Particularly in the Sung dynasty (960–1279), with the revival of neo-Confucian ideals, these ideas became even stronger and more widespread (Tianchi Martin-Liao 1985). A combination of these factors ensured that girls were seen only as burdens and temporary members of the natal family. Any investment in a daughter's well-being was considered a waste of money. Women's oppression was, thus, firmly rooted in China's feudal marriage system.[2]

A husband could also repudiate his wife for seven reasons, originally contained in the Li Ji rule of conduct. These were: (1) disobedience of her husband's parents; (2) failure to bear children; (3) adultery; (4) jealousy; (5) loathsome disease; (6) garrulousness; and (7) theft (H. Snow 1967: 50). Such traditional laws served to make women in China extremely vulnerable and forced them to accept the position of subservience accorded to them in traditional discourse (Young 1973; Wolf 1978; Croll 1978).

Another obvious symbol of the confinement and subordination of women was the custom of binding the feet of young girls. This custom is said to have started in the Tang dynasty (618–906), in the later seventh century. The scores of classical poems written about the delicacy of the female foot and the walk that it ensured, testify to the important role played by this custom in terms of norms and standards of female beauty (Levy 1966).

However, in the light of what several scholars have noted, it needs to be stressed that the Confucian ideal of womanhood was mediated by the material position of the women. In general, the pressure and confinement of upper-class women was far greater.[3] Moral codes differed sharply for women of the poorer classes. Although the *Lie nü zhuan* also contains the case history of a poor and virtuous woman whose loyalty and love for her land saved the small kingdom of Wei (O'Hara 1945: 164–5), Wolf points out that peasants could not afford the luxury of secluding their women (Wolf 1978: 161). Women, especially in the southern chinese provinces of modern-day Fujian and Guangdong, often participated in field labour, and certain groups, such as the *Hakka*, were known for not binding the feet of women. This area of China also had a tradition of forming sisterhoods (*jiemei hui*) or support groups of women, including those who had refused to get married (Topley 1978).[4] Thus, these strict codes of conduct were in no way uniform.

Another scholar of Chinese history, Joanna F. Handlin, shows how even among the gentry the Confucian norms of behaviour for women were not rigidly followed. As she says: 'The principles of female subordination and *li* designed to order society, tell us more about how the upper class thought women should behave than how they really did' (1975: 13) Focusing on a sixteenth-century Confucian scholar, Lu Kun, who attempted to admonish women towards good behaviour, she points out that by the end of the sixteenth century a whole range of female behaviour was visible in urban centres. In fact, she sees Lu Kun's admonitions as an attempt to counter the existing situation rather than as a representation of the reality of women's lives or, as Handlin puts it, 'a dialectic between the actual and the real' (Handlin 1975: 15). Such a perspective is useful, for it raises the question of the actual interaction between women and society.

These examples are cited here to show how orthodox discourse is forced to construct itself in relation to a variety of other discourses. It also allows us to look at the means through which women do acquire a certain degree of power and autonomy. Wolf has suggested that within the family women accumulated power over time by building on their 'uterine ties' or ties developed through giving birth to sons. In her later years, it is this close relationship that will ensure that a woman exercises power over her family and over her son's future family and her daughter-in-law. Wolf goes on to explain that women also found ways to exercise power through village gossip, a means by which the community of women could make their husbands lose face (Wolf 1978). Snow also notes that 'gossip' was a weapon deployed very skilfully by women, and in certain cases men were forced to take refuge in monasteries or flee the village to guard their honour (H. Snow 1967: 50).

However, rather than seeing these examples as instances of female power as such, one could argue that this was the only way women could survive an otherwise abominable situation. It does not change women's power relationship in terms of gender relations. They exercise effective power only against their own sex, thereby further ensuring the legitimacy of male power structures, or an acceptance of doxic forms of identification. In fact, traditional folktales abound with stories of tensions between mothers-in-law and daughters-in-law, both of whom seek to preserve and build a power base within the family.

Thus, although it was possible for women to acquire a modicum of power in their old age through having given birth to sons, in terms of discourse, women remained clearly subordinate to men. In her own right, a woman had no power or legitimate position. In the final instance, she remained dependent on the good will of her husband and son. It was this real vulnerability of women that made the 'woman's question' (*funü wenti*) one of the burning issues of late nineteenth- and twentieth-century China, and provided the first instance of an organised and systematic heterodoxy on gender relations.

Repudiating tradition: the emergence of the women's question

Bourdieu argues that in times of crisis (here he implies social, economic and political crisis) prevailing systems of classification become a target of confrontation (1977; 1990). By breaking down objective structures of social relations and their institutions, the basis of prevailing orthodoxy becomes weaker, thus allowing critical opposition to emerge as a real possibility (1977: 169). This is clearly visible in the way gender relations became a field of conflict and a discourse to be contested in early twentieth-century China.

Towards the end of the nineteenth century, large parts of China became part of the Western sphere of interest. The end of the Opium War (1842) had left the country vulnerable to foreign imperialist policies. This period saw the remaining decades of the Qing dynasty, China's last imperial dynasty (1644–1911). The social and political changes that had begun to take place in China radically influenced the urban elite, and the 1898 reform movement saw the plight of women raised as an issue for the first time (Rankin 1978: 39).

Several scholars of Chinese history have pointed out that the issue of women's rights was first raised, though indirectly, by the intellectuals of this period. Their primary concern was nationalist, a natural response to the humiliating defeats that the Qing empire had suffered at the hands of the western powers. Having come into contact with western cultures, these intellectuals were interested in discovering why China had been so easily defeated and what could be done to make it into a strong nation. This nationalism led them to advance a charter of reforms which included improving the position of women (Chow Tse-tung 1960; Rankin 1975; Croll 1978). The main issues taken up by the reformers of this period were footbinding and the education of women.

By the end of the nineteenth century, several anti-footbinding associations had been set up. The custom was castigated as cruel and indicative of the low status of women in Chinese society. Part of the concern of these reformers was that the custom of footbinding made China appear culturally backward in the eyes of foreigners (Croll 1978). The pressure exerted by these reform groups finally succeeded in getting the Dowager Empress to pass an edict in 1902 which requested the gentry to 'influence their families to abstain from the evil practice and by this means abolish the custom forever' (Levy 1966: 20). The main feature of this reform movement, however, is the almost negligible role played by Chinese women themselves. The movement as a whole did not penetrate very far into rural areas and remained restricted to the upper classes even in urban areas. It was only when this demand for 'natural feet' was combined with the demand for women's education that Chinese women were to emerge as reformers in their own right.

Behean, in her research on the issue of early female education in China, notes that Shanghai was in the vanguard of the new movement to establish women's education. Although schools run by missionaries had come into existence a few years earlier, the first modern girls' school was established in Shanghai in 1897, and was associated with the reform movement of 1898. In 1907, an official nationwide system of elementary schools for girls was established and over the years their number continued to increase (Behean 1975: 381).

It is clear from the above that importance was being attached to education as a first step towards the improvement of the position of women. However, it was limited to urban women from a bourgeois or 'respectable' background.[5] This was partially responsible for the 'middle class' and urban nature of the initial feminist movement in China. On the other hand, the importance of female entry into formal education in China is demonstrated by the role played by female students in the various political movements that were emerging. Literacy served as an integrative mechanism for women, allowing them to acquire skills through which they could become self-supporting. It was within the confines of the new schools that the 'woman's movement' (*funü yundong*) first emerged (Croll 1978).

The immediate and most noticeable impact of female education in China was the appearance of a number of magazines or journals for women.[6] Several of these were founded and run by women students who had left China to study abroad. During this period, Japan became a major centre for Chinese intellectuals interested in reforming the customs of their country. By 1907, there were about a 100 Chinese women students in Japan. Most of them were influenced by the patriotic sentiments of the male student community. However, along with espousing patriotism, women also spoke up for female equality (Liv Mei Ching 1988). The first journal to be published in China specifically devoted to women's issues was called the *Funü zazhi* (*Women's Journal*) edited by Chen Xiefen (Rankin 1975). The main focus of all the articles addressed to women was to motivate them to participate in the national movement. That women responded to these calls is evident from the number of women who participated in the anti-Manchu movement, the most famous being Qiu Qin (1875–1909).[7]

After the downfall of the Manchu empire in 1911, China declared itself a republic based on parliamentary democracy. Sun Yat-Sen (1866–1925) was briefly the president of this first republic. This period saw the rapid acceleration of suffragette politics, when several women's organisations sprouted and women started campaigning for the vote. Major cities such as Nanjing, Beijing and Shanghai saw women barricading government offices and demanding the vote (Croll 1978: 66–7). This focus on specific women's demands was different from the pre-Manchu issues which were identified more with nationalism than with feminism. This is evident in the kind of articles appearing during this period, stressing the need for women to become independent persons in their own right (Croll 1978: 82).

The high point of the early women's movement occurred during the May Fourth movement of 1919.[8] Listing the numerous effects of the May Fourth period, Chow says: 'The movement also accelerated the decline of the old family system and the rise of feminism. And above all, the authority of Confucianism and traditional ethics suffered a fundamental and devastating stroke and new Western ideas were exalted' (Chow Tse-Tung 1960: 2).

It is not strange that during this time men were often prominent as champions of women's rights. Many of them, such as Chen Duxiu, Li Dazhao and others who participated in this new culture movement, were to raise the issues of women's subordination in the magazines they edited and in the essays and stories they wrote.[9] Another important indicator of the changing attitudes of the urban intelligentsia on the 'woman question' is the way women characters in fiction were dealt with. This period saw the birth of many young writers such as Lu Xun, Mao Dun, Guo Muoruo, Ba Jin and Ding Ling, to name a few. All of them focus on the condition of women in their works and advocate male–female equality (Hsu 1981). The influence of Ibsen's plays in this period also testifies to the importance of this issue. Ibsen's play *A Doll's House* was translated into Chinese as early as 1918, immediately causing a great stir and leading to the emergence of cases of 'Chinese Noras' (Schwarz 1975; Eide 1985; 1987). Lu Xun later wrote a rejoinder to this phenomenon of China's Noras in an article entitled, 'What Happens after Nora Leaves Home?' (1923). He stresses the necessity to link women's emancipation, with their economic emancipation, as otherwise 'they would only change one cage for another' (Lu Xun 1923: 86). The Chinese Communist Party was to focus on this need for women's material emancipation as the founding principle of its own discourse on the woman question.

It is clear, then, that the objective crisis in China's socio-political life had significant impact on traditional ideas about women. These changes occurred discursively, becoming visible in literature, in politics and in education. The criticism that Chinese intellectuals made of their own culture took the West, and its humanist values of equality, justice and freedom for all, as the point of comparison. Again, this occurred among an intelligentsia whose own relationship to the restrictions imposed by a Confucian orthodoxy was breaking down. The intellectuals of this period were interested in overthrowing all aspects of China's past order. The position of women was only one of the more visible signs of feudalism. Consequently, the discourse that emerged on gender relations was not dealing with a fundamental restructuring of male–female roles as such. Nevertheless, this initial questioning of traditional orthodoxy based on Confucianism was extremely important, for it created a basis for constituting new forms of viewing male–female relations. The early women's movement, although middle class in nature, served two important purposes: it encouraged women to participate in public discourse and it brought the issue of women's subordination to the fore (Siu 1975).

The Communist Party and the women's question, 1921–49

The Chinese Communist Party was founded in 1921. From the very beginning, the Party held a specific idea about the role and participation of women in the revolution. Influenced by the success of communism in the Soviet Union, the early organisers created a bureau specially to take care of women's work. The theoretical basis for the emancipation of women already existed in the form of the works of Marx and Engels. Davin notes that among the best known Marxist texts available in China at this period was Engels thesis that the emancipation of women can occur only with their participation in productive labour (Davin 1975: 363). Along with Engels' texts on the subject, there is evidence to show that translations of works by Clara Zetkin and Lenin were also quoted on women's issues. The underlying emphasis of this position was the need to draw women into productive labour and organise them along class lines.[10]

The leadership of this task called 'woman work' (*funü gongzuo*) was given to Xiang Jingyu.[11] Xiang was of the opinion that envisaging a separate women's movement was a political error and that the women's movement had to be part of the general communist revolutionary movement. The directives regarding women's participation in the Communist Party seemed to have followed a Soviet strategy of assigning the few available female cadres to organising women's groups at the grassroots level. These organisations, among other things, were responsible for holding demonstrations on Women's Day, 8 March. As Leith notes: 'Throughout the twenties, March 8 continues to be a focal point for mobilizing women. By 1926, the movement had grown to such proportions that 10,000 gathered together in Canton, 800 in Hunan' (1973: 53).

Despite the initial success of a communist-led women's movement, a 1926 Party resolution noted that several problems remained. The movement was not really able to penetrate the masses. Many of the volunteers were more romantic than realistic and several of them had problems identifying with their constituents (Maloney 1980). Although the Communist Party succeeded in widening the context of the women's movement, its chief concern remained a focus on class struggle and, therefore, on women workers.

By 1927, the Communist Party had become a force to be reckoned with in urban areas. The Nationalists, encouraged by the imperial powers and its own fledgling bourgeoisie, found it expedient to check this growing working-class movement. They unleashed a white terror of unprecedented proportions during which thousands of communists and their sympathisers were killed (Cheneaux 1968). The centrality of 'gender' as a factor in propaganda is testified to by the vociferous statements made against the alleged attempt of communists to change gender roles and morality. Diamond (1975b) comments on the use Nationalist propaganda of the period made of the woman's question. Rumours circulated about 'naked women' who freely cohabited with men and lacked all morality. Stories were told of communist cadres forcibly cutting the hair of women. Such propaganda was essential to justify the mass executions that were carried out. Cai Chang, one of the women leaders of the period, recalls how: 'More than 1,000 women leaders were killed ... When girls were arrested in Hunan they were stripped naked, nailed on crosses and their noses and breasts cut off before they were killed ... It is actually true that if a girl had bobbed hair she was subject to execution as a communist in Hunan and Canton' (H. Snow 1967: 242).

Among those caught was Xiang Jingyu who was executed in March 1928 (Luo Qiong 1986: 87). Such brutal repression of the early labour movement and the women's movement forced the communists into the hinterland and the countryside became the mainstay of the Party in China. This move was also responsible for changing the face of the women's liberation movement.

In his 'Report on an Investigation into the Peasant Movement of Hunan, 1927', Mao Zedong points out the close link between a struggle against the feudal gentry and patriarchal ideas. This much-quoted paragraph explicitly denounces the system of male superiority in China. As Mao puts it:

A man in China is usually subjected to three systems of authority (political authority, clan authority and religious authority). As for women, in addition to being dominated by these three authorities, they are also dominated by the men (the authority of the husband). These four authorities – political, clan, religious and masculine – are the embodiment of the whole feudal–patriarchal system and ideology, and are the four thick ropes binding the Chinese people – particularly the peasants. (Mao Zedong 1956: vol. 1, 44)

Further on in the same article, Mao stresses the importance of organising women and sees their participation in anti-feudal struggles as part of the process of rural transformation which the Party desired. This particular text of Mao is of importance because it shows both the importance the Party attached to the issue of women's liberation, and the analysis maintained about its role within the overall revolution.

As the Communist Party strengthened its position in the countryside, it instituted several reforms that were to affect the position of women positively and radically. Davin notes that: 'One of the greatest achievements of the Chinese Communist Party has been the change brought about in the lives of Chinese women in the rural hinterland' (1976: 243). Practical policies to deal with the situation of women were first applied in the Jiangxi Soviet (1927–34). These were the land-reform law and the marriage law.[12] These two documents were later to serve as the basis of the laws promulgated in the Yenan period (1934–47). Although constant warfare and generally unstable conditions made the implementation of any policy a hazardous matter, women were granted equality with men at all levels (Davin 1976; Stranahan 1976; Maloney 1980). Davin makes a significant comment when she notes that this was the first time in Chinese history that the 'state became involved in the marriage system by requiring that marriage and divorce be registered with the local government' (1975: 73).

The major focus of mobilisation for women during the 1930s, however, was to motivate them to contribute to the anti-Japanese war effort. Kay Ann Johnson points out that the work among women was felt to be necessary because in many cases women exercised a strong influence on the decision of the male members of the household to join the Red Army. To ensure a successful recruitment strategy, the Party soon realised the necessity of enlisting the support of the whole family (Johnson 1983: 52).

Party policy remained unchanged during the Yenan period (1934–47); Yenan being the place where the communists built their second base after the historic Long March of 1934–35 (E. Snow 1938).[13] The main emphasis of this period was again focused on the anti-Japanese war effort. Several mass organisations were set up mobilise people for the war effort. Separate women's organisations were also set up and special attention was supposed to be paid to women's work. Mao sums up the Party position when he says: 'Women make up half the population. The economic position of women and the special oppression suffered by them not only shows the need felt for revolution but also implies that they represent a force to determine the success or failure of the revolution' (Luo Qiong 1986: 88).

Stranahan quotes unverified Chinese sources to list a figure of about 130,000 women who were members of one or another association. Of these, 70,000 were said to attend meetings regularly and joined in work projects (Stranahan, 1976: 35). Several measures were also adopted to train women cadres and a special school called the School for Women Cadres (Nü Ganbu Xuexiao) was also set up (Price 1975). However, Janet Price (1975) notes that the number of women who actually participated in this and other cadre schools was extremely small and their responsibilities were limited to propagating the tasks outlined by the Party. Nevertheless, great emphasis was placed on women taking the lead in educating children and other women.

Women cadres already familiar with Party policy were trained to set up village cooperatives and women were encouraged to take up spinning, weaving and other such tasks (Davin 1976: 37). In areas where men had been drawn into the army, women were also encouraged to participate in agricultural production (Johnson 1983: 65). Periodic efforts were made to bring women into the political process though, here again, a strict sexual division of labour seems to have existed. There were very few women in leadership positions. Women who did emerge as leaders through Party work were almost automatically assigned to women's work and women's bureaus.

A critical analysis of the early Party position The initial period of the Communist Party's engagement with the 'woman's question' demonstrates the limits of change in gender relations. While the Party attempted to question a traditional orthodoxy, and at this stage the lack of institutional legitimacy gave its discourse the flavour of a heterodoxy, it was unable to question the deep-seated habitus of gender relations. This is specially noticeable in the case of Party policy on intra-family relations. Once the Party had shifted its base to Yenan, its position on the role of women was quite clear. Several directives on women's work pointed out the need for caution and care. Although the fundamental position of the Party – that women's participation in production was the way to female liberation – did not change, caution and unity were the operative words in its dealings with gender contradictions.

This trend became even more pronounced after 1940. As Johnson points out: 'Although official documents established strong principles of reform and thus created potentially powerful legal weapons for reform activists, when actual implementation and actions were involved, clear signs of political conflict and ambivalence arose' (1983: 55).

The struggle for women's rights in marriage and divorce was considered potentially divisive, especially since this affected the very constituents which the Party was seeking to win over. These were the poor and the middle peasants. If the marriage law was actually enforced, in some cases the peasants would lose not only their wives but also their lands. Numerous other incidents document the compromises that the Party made with rural patriarchy and traditionalism in order to further the aims of its 'general revolution'. Women who were interested in pushing forward issues of family reform were seen as divisive and accused of espousing separatism over the interests of the general revolution.

Stranahan records numerous incidents during the Yenan days when women's interests were successively sacrificed in the name of unity and family harmony. Women who came to the women's bureaus with complaints about ill-treatment from the family were, in the 1940s, encouraged not to divorce or create dissension; instead, they were told to go home and attempt to raise their own political consciousness and that of their spouses (Stranahan 1976: 45–6), as well as to be productive and contribute to the general war effort against the Japanese. These and other related actions were proclaimed as the fundamental organisational principles of women's work (*funü gongzuo*) in a circular of the Central Committee distributed in 1943. Johnson describes the position of the Party as being one where it would withhold the right to divorce in the hope that improving economic conditions would also improve the position of women within the family (1983: 68). Cai Chang's words in the early 1940s seem to sum up the position of the Party: 'Our current slogans for work in the woman's movement are no longer "freedom of marriage" and "equality between men and women", rather they are "save the children and establish an abundant and flourishing family so as to cause each household to become a prosperous one"' (Johnson 1983: 75).

The most famous critique of this period is that of Ding Ling (1908–85), the *grande dame* of Chinese letters. Ding Ling came to Yenan in 1937 after having escaped from a KMT prison. She was already famous as a controversial and daring women writer in Shanghai. On arrival in Yenan, she was made editor of the Party's propaganda magazine. Helen Snow recalls that many Party members at Yenan were aghast at Ding Ling's reputation as an avant-garde feminist and by her attitudes towards free love and marriage (H. Snow 1968).

Ding Ling made an open critique of the double standards of the Party on the male–female issue, not only in her stories such as 'When I was in Xia Village' ('Wo zai xiacun de shihour') but also in her article published in the *Jiefang Ribao* on 8 March 1942. According to Ding Ling, women were encouraged to take on new roles as Party activists and yet fulfil their obligations as housewives and remain responsible for the family. The result was that women were faced with unsolvable contradictions and were viewed with contempt irrespective of what they did. As she says: 'they were damned for what they did and damned for what they didn't.' If women did not marry they were ridiculed, if they did, they were criticised for paying too much importance to family matters. She went on to say that male leaders should talk less of theory and more of actual practice. In the end, she made a pointed reference to the discriminatory attitude of the Party. She said that if the opinions she was putting forward had been those of a male leader, they would have been read with great seriousness; unfortunately, being a woman her opinion will probably be dismissed (Feuerwerker 1982: 32). Ding Ling was not wrong in her prognosis. Not only were her opinions and criticism dismissed, she found herself at the receiving end of a great deal of criticism, led by Mao himself (Feuerwerker 1982; Goldman 1971).[14]

Throughout this period women were not noticeable in positions of leadership or decision-making. Though the well-known figures of this time, such as Cai Chang and Deng Yingchao, were at Yenan, and Cai Chang was responsible for women's work, none of them was actually responsible for formulating policy. The narrow Party policy during the anti-Japanese war leads Stacey to call this period the 'time that patriarchy was made more democratically available to masses of peasant men' (1983: 116).

Less scathing critics of the Communist Party have pointed out that it was not necessarily deliberate Party policy to uphold patriarchy. Instead, they argue, the compromises made by the Party regarding the woman's question were a result of the circumstances it faced in its drive to gain control of the Chinese countryside (Davin 1976). In the light of the historical evidence cited earlier, we see a dynamic relationship between Communist Party policy and the practice of gender relations. The early attempts to bring women into communist politics did exhibit a certain radicalism.[15] The Party, in its attempt to construct a policy on women's issues, ignored questions of female sexuality and intra-family relations. It is here that the Party succumbed to a habitus on gender relations. Its members' understanding of social relations was mediated by their sense of habitus, a habitus which for centuries defined a strict code of male–female positions and relations. The understanding of male–female relations continued to be overshadowed by those elements which remained in doxa, and constituted the unsaid, taken-for-granted and therefore 'natural' difference of gender dispositions. It was these 'natural' dispositions of men and women which made the issue of sexual morality and the general sexual division of labour difficult questions for the Party.

On the whole, the period leading up to the liberation of China in 1949 can be characterised as one in which the specific interests of women, and of a revolution in gender relations, were constantly compromised and relegated to become secondary issues. It would be correct to say that the Party lost a great opportunity to effect real change, and had it acted on its own revolutionary laws for female equality, problems that persist today would have been mimimised to a large extent.

Institutionalising a new orthodoxy: women in post-revolutionary China

October 1 1949 saw the establishment of the People's Republic of China (PRC). This victory gave the Party the power to exercise effective control over the limits of discourse formation on most subjects. Through control of the channels of the production and dissemination of information, the Party was able to project its own ideas as the legitimate and correct way of approaching all social relations. It is in post-revolutionary China that we see clear and direct links between an institutionalisation process and the construction of an 'orthodoxy'.

The Communist Party, during its early years, was interested in extending the reforms that had been implemented in the liberated areas to the rest of China. Its policy on women was put into practice with the creation of the All China Women's Federation (hereafter ACWF) in April 1949. In fact, during the period immediately following liberation, great attention was paid to the creation of women's organisations and youth organisations. Their purpose was to ensure that specific sectors of the population could be brought into the mainstream of the revolution. The different types of women's associations that had existed in China prior to 1949 were brought under the umbrella of the ACWF (Andors 1981). Its aims and goals were laid down in the Central Committee circular on women's work towards the end of 1948.[16]

The period immediately after liberation, 1950–53, saw the most radical implementation of the Marriage Law and the Land Reform Law. A series of campaigns via posters and so on were initiated to popularise the Marriage Law which had been proclaimed in 1950. According to Johnson, the basic premise of the campaign was 'the belief that ideological propoganda could succeed in changing traditional attitudes towards women' (1983: 100). Efforts were made to educate and influence mothers-in-law to show them the necessity of supporting the reforms and for improving relationships with their daughters-in-law. However, in no instance was the family as an institution questioned (Davin 1976: 97; Eber 1989).[17]

Considerable effort was put into making divorce more acceptable to the population. In the early stages, when divorce courts were set up at local level, divorces were generally initiated by women and granted on anti-feudal grounds. A 1950 report on divorce claimed that 50 per cent of divorce applications came from those between the ages of twenty-five and forty-five (Croll 1978). Although reform in the urban areas proceeded relatively smoothly, in rural areas it sometimes led to tragic results. There were incidents of women being forced to commit suicide or being killed because they demanded divorce (H. Snow 1967). By the late 1950s, however, the policy of granting easy divorces was changed and social stability again began to be cited as a goal.

Women were also encouraged to participate in production. The new Labour Law of the PRC declared that women were equal citizens and had equal rights to participate in production. Giving women land in their own names was only the beginning of the process of social change.

Since then, the marked improvement in the lives of Chinese women compared to their pre-liberation situation has been acknowledged by most writers on the subject.

However, while the legal and political measures adopted by the PRC definitely created a milleu for female equality, the actual implementation of reform remained uneven. The reforms did not go far enough in terms of changing male–female relations, especially within the family and marriage. Thus, the 'intimate personal' lives of women remained constrained by the ideas of the natural sexual division of labour. Although the number of women involved in factory work and those entering white-collar services rose, the practice of ascribing 'suitable female' tasks to them also increased. Thus women started to dominate in light industry and as junior teaching staff (Andors 1981).

During the land reform period in the countryside, the aim was to bring women into production by giving them land in their own names. However, in many cases the situation remained unchanged because women lacked the necessary skills to till their own lands. The best choice for women seemed to have been to lease the land to their male kin (Diamond,1975a: 26). Croll further comments that since marriage remained patrilocal in nature, women tended to leave their land to their father or brother to manage (1978: 12).

During the first five-year plan, controversy also arose over the role of housewives. It was found that housewives felt socially despised because they did not engage in productive labour. During 1953–57, the press ran many articles on the 'new socialist housewife'. The women's magazine *Zhongguo Funü* (*Women of China*) published articles on dress-making, cookery, childcare, love and other such domestic issues (Davin 1975: 108). The task of politicising housewives was given to the newly created Resident Committees.[18]

It is interesting to note that although the official press tried to legitimise and in places even encouraged women to be, housewives, the question of housework actually being productive labour never entered the debate. As Croll suggests, all the household activities undertaken by women were never quantified or even considered to be productive (1978: 12). Instead, women's status as dependents was stressed and campaigns such as the *Wu Hao* or Five Goods were inaugurated. This was supposed to politicise housework by showing its revolutionary worth. Women were told that they could contribute to society by ensuring that they kept the morale of their working husbands high and maintained harmony in the house (Davin 1976: 169). For working women, on the other hand, the problem remained that of the double burden. Although they had achieved a degree of status and social respect, little attempt was made to handle the contradictions of their position. Efforts to provide social services in the form of crèches and canteens did not change the fact that housework was seen as a female task (Sidel 1974; Stacey 1983).

The initial post-liberation period, for women, was thus, fraught with contradictory demands. The Party was forced to waver from its own ideological understanding of women's liberation as being dependent on participation in what it defined as productive labour, and once again bowed to historical expediency, attempting to shelve the contradiction that occurred in terms of female equality and economic expediency.

The Great Leap Forward: women as labour heroines

The Great Leap Forward (GLF) launched in 1958,[19] and the collectivisation drive in rural areas that followed, saw a revival of the theme of women's participation in production. The GLF envisaged a rapid transition to socialism by mobilising masses of people to contribute to the production of goods (MacFarquhar 1983; Brugger 1981). Andors sees GLF policy towards women as a logical outgrowth of its attempt to mobilise mass labour as a development strategy (Andors 1975: 34). Women were encouraged, both in the rural areas and in the urban areas, to participate in labour.

Initially, women were supposed to take over those tasks which men vacated in order to participate in many small-scale rural industrialisation projects. They were freed from household duties through the creation of community childcare centres and canteens. In many rural areas, grandmothers and older women of the community were encouraged to look after childeren so that mothers could work (Hemmel and Sindjberg 1984). The benefits of female participation in labour were enormous, and many observers have recorded the positive impact that this had on women. According to Sidel (1974), an additional benefit of the GLF was to expand the inadequate healthcare system in rural areas. On the other hand, this drive to encourage women's participation in paid labour also bought certain contradictions to the fore, testifying once again to an unchanged habitus of gender relations.

The most obvious of these was the consistent devaluation of women's labour in the new system of wages in work-points. The maximum number of work-points available was ten. Women on average were never given more than six or seven work-points even where they performed tasks similar to those of men. The explanation put forward for this was that women were not reliable in their work due to the demands of childcare. What it actually showed was a continuing belief in female inferiority and resistance to the idea of women working in the fields.

Tasks consistent with traditional female roles, such as spinning and weaving, were more easily accepted but traditional attitudes to women working in the fields still existed (Davin 1976; Croll 1978; Andors 1981).

In urban areas housewives were encouraged to join urban communes and neighbourhood committees. These in turn organised weaving co-operatives, shoe-making cooperatives, stitching cooperatives, home-based food processing and the running of community canteens. Women were also asked to undertake jobs being made available in the light industrial sector because men were being drawn into other work. Women, especially older women, were also drawn into the service industry, such as child-care. This period saw an increase in childcare facilities and kindergartens available to working women, especially in state-run factories (Chan 1974; Davin 1976; Andors 1981).

When analysing the rhetoric on female liberation that emerged during this period, Andors comments that the measures which were conducive to women's emancipation were incidental to the policies being implemented. The goal of rapidly creating socialist institutions and of catching up with the West raised the issue of conflict between women's equality and socialist construction. Andors's reading of the situation also holds true if we examine the fact that policy changes after the Great Leap Forward rescinded many of the measures that had been used to encourage participation by women in wage labour. The cuts appeared first in the welfare services, such as rural crèches and canteens.

The period 1963–66 saw the reinstitution of the household as the fundamental social structure. The early 1960s exhibited a great deal of ideological confusion regarding the role of women. The traditional view of a woman's place within the household received both tacit and overt support during the Socialist Education Movement (1962–65). Although the resurgence of feudal ideas, such as the giving of dowry, arranged marriages, and discrimination against women in the workplace, was recognised by the ACWF, in contrast to earlier periods where concrete material policy measures had been adopted, the post-GLF period saw the whole issue as one of education and propaganda drives (Diamond 1975a).

The major conflict concerned women's primary responsibility in the period of socialist transition: were they to be dependents and helpers of their spouses or revolutionary and productive activists (Andors 1976: 101)? This conflict became more apparent because women were already visible in the field of production and a few had even emerged in leadership positions. Sheridan (1976), in an examination of the background and lives of young women leaders in China, notes that most of the women who had achieved political and social status in China and had been appointed members of the National People's Congress (NPC), were women workers who had risen from the shopfloor through a demonstration of skills in the production process. As Sheridan points out, the histories that she deals with show 'the interlocking of several roles – political roles, family roles, and roles as workers' (1976: 60). Thus, in reality, women were constantly occupying multiple roles. In fact, what we notice is the addition of a new role for women – that of worker – on top of their existing family roles.

The Cultural Revolution, 1966–76

The onslaught of the Cultural Revolution in 1966[20] and the large-scale disruption that it brought to aspects of family and social life, also saw the disbanding of the All China Women's Federation (Croll 1977). Strong criticism was directed at the editors of the magazine *Zhongguo Funü* (*Women of China*), pointing out that during the early 1960s they had over-emphasised the role of women in the family while downplaying their role in production. Another source of criticism was that the 'class perspective of women' had been ignored in discussions of women's roles.

The period from 1966 till the downfall of the Gang of Four in 1976 saw a renewed emphasis on women's role in production and their participation in politics. The ideological stress was laid on being Red rather than expert (Schurmann 1971). Politics was seen as more important than economic construction, and a heightened political consciousness was demanded of everybody. This created targets of criticism on the basis of class background, and intellectuals were often the main target of attack (Robinson 1971; Thurston 1988). The most significant campaign to concentrate on the role of women in society was the Anti-Lin Piao and Confucius Campaign (Pi Lin Pi Kong) of 1972. It began with a critique of Lin Piao and was later extended to include an attack on Confucian moral values. The campaign, directly attributed to Jiang Qing, the wife of Mao Zedong, named Confucian feudal values as the ideology of the oppressive ruling classes. A number of 'Confucian statements' were attibuted to Lin Piao who was then cast in the role of chief villain. Several derogatory statements he had made about women were criticised, and the occasion was used to campaign for female equality (Croll 1977).

Under the general guidelines of opposing discrimination against women, women and youth groups at local levels held meetings and implemented educational campaigns to fight the old attitudes towards women. Some of the specific issues raised concerned discrimination against women at work and the failure of men to participate in housework; even the issue of encouraging matrilocal mariages in order to undermine the patriarchal family system was raised (Croll [ed.] 1974). As the campaign progressed, newspapers and periodicals carried articles which featured examples of women who proved the fallacy and biases of feudal discourse. These women were held up as role models and communist heroines (Croll,1977; Johnson 1983: 194–207). Interestingly enough, it was this campaign, coinciding with the heyday of the women's movement in the West, which led to claims of 'patriarchy kowtowing in China' (Stacey 1979). The Chinese women's movement was cited as an example of the superiority of the socialist system where women's rights were concerned (Eizenstein 1979; Weinbaum 1976). However, with the downfall of the Gang of Four following the death of Mao Zedong in 1976, policies have again changed in China. In typical fashion, so have the new role models being presented to women.

Re-emphasising femininity and motherhood: the post-Mao years

The economic and political changes that have occurred in post-Mao China have affected all levels of Chinese society and have led to the emergence of new guidelines and directives for women.[21] Although the ideological underpinnings of women's roles remain grounded in the previous notions of female equality, there is a striking difference today between the much publicised ideology of equality and the practice of female subordination. The new policies introduced by the Chinese government under the name of the 'Four Modernisations' have once again brought the contradictions between the issues of female equality and the government's goals to the fore (Davin 1988).

The main policy change of the post-Mao period has been the introduction of the 'household responsibility system' in rural areas and the 'industrial responsibility system' in urban areas (*ziren zhi*). In tandem with this, free trade zones have been opened in coastal areas (Feuchtwang et al., [eds] 1988; Saith 1987; Andors 1988; Crane 1979)[21] and the production of what are called 'sideline products' (such as pig-breeding, weaving, poultry, silk-breeding) has also been encouraged. It has also been noted that women are mainly responsible for sideline production in rural areas (Croll 1983; Andors 1981). The result of these measures has been the rise of new rich peasant families.

In urban areas, reforms have placed a greater emphasis on productivity. Incentives and bonuses have been introduced to encourage workers (Christianssen 1989), and managers of enterprises have been given greater powers: they now have the right to hire and fire workers and to dock pay for unproductive work (Pieke 1991). All these measures have been encouraged under what is called breaking the 'big rice pot (*da guofan*), a system of guarantees under which all workers, irrespective of performance, had a right to an average wage (Leung-Wing-yue 1988).

Women's contributions to the programme of modernisation have been outlined in Party directives to women's organisations and in journals specifically addressed to women (Jiang Tingsheng 1987). The repudiation of Cultural Revolution policies has meant that the ideological emphasis on confronting feudal attitudes towards women which were highlighted in the anti-Confucian campaign, have all been put on ice. Images of women which encouraged them to enter new avenues and emphasised their roles as labour and peasant heroines who could do all that men could do are a thing of the past. Today, there are new issues and new ideas regarding what women should expect under socialism.

The reconvened All China Women's Federation took over its old task of propagandising the aims of the Party *vis-à-vis* women. As in previous years of Party policy on the woman question, women are first and foremost called on to do their duty by working for socialism (Chang Jiaqin 1988). The Fifth National Women's Congress, held in 1983 and attended by about 2,100 delegates, laid down the tasks of the women's movement for the next decade. A major policy document published in the aftermath of the conference emphasised women's roles as mothers and within the family. Women are seen to be responsible for childcare and the ideological care of the younger generation. Further, the lack of reference to any sharing of these tasks between men and women ensures that women remain primarily responsible for childcare. However, the document also stresses the government's commitment to defend the rights of women and children.

Along with this assumption of women's responsibility for childcare, comes renewed emphasis on the campaign of the Five Good Family (*Wu Hao Jia*), in contrast to the importance placed on women's productive roles in earlier times. Though women are simultaneously encouraged to participate in productive labour, both roles are stressed as equally contributing to socialism. This echoes the 'socialist value' that was placed on the work of housewives in the early 1950s (Croll 1983).

Besides childcare, women also remain largely responsible for housework. A recent study of family life in urban China notes that women perform more than 70 per cent of all household labour. This naturally limits their access to job-training and other avenues for increasing their skills. In an interview with a journalist from *China Reconstructs* a working mother compares herself to a juggler: 'Catching the "ball" of her work for the country's socialist modernisation and snatching at the second ball of running a household' (Tan Manni 1980: 19).

This is corroborated by evidence from an extensive urban survey carried out in selected cities in which Whyte found that women do most of the cooking, cleaning and childcare (1984: 224). Though the government has shown a constant awareness of this fact, the modern solution is to encourage the production of consumer goods such as washing machines and refrigerators which will lighten the domestic loads of women (Robinson, 1985: 44). Although domestic appliances certainly make life easier, women's responsibility for these tasks does not change. Mao Zedong's often cited comment that washing machines do not liberate women has today been turned on its head.

The continuing double burden caused by an entrenched sexual division of labour leads to inequality in other spheres. Dalsimer and Nisnoff note how the policies introduced in post-Mao China have created conditions which impose sex-differentiated roles on women in production (1984: 32). Women find themselves forced into the service sector and into teaching. In 1982, women workers dominated in the broad fields of cotton textiles, finance and trade where they formed 60 per cent of the labour force; they made up 50 per cent of the total labour force in light industry (Women of China 1983: 8). In 1990, women made up 37.6 per cent of the total employed in China. Out of this, only 20.5 per cent are employed in administrative jobs in the state sector (Pei Qing, 1992: 20). Overall wages and material benefits to workers used to be higher in the state-owned sector. This sector also has subsidised services such as transportation, housing, schools and health-care facilities. Dalsimer and Nisnoff note, for example, that at the Changchun automobile factory, a state-owned enterprise, a dozen nurseries were provided whereas the embroidery factory in the same city with a 90 per cent female labour force only had a modest childcare centre on top of the factory (1984: 27).

Apart from sex segmentation in different types of industries, there is sex discrimination within industries as well, especially as far as wages are concerned. While men are distributed throughout the eight-grade wage scale in the factories, women are more often found in the lower grades. In the Dalian ship-building works for example, one woman was reported at grade 7 and another at grade 5, while the other women workers were clustered in the lower grades (Dalsimer and Nisnoff 1984: 25). A similar bias seems to be occurring in the allocation of bonuses. A *Workers' Daily* commentary, 'Attention Should be Given to Unequal Rewards between Men and Women', reported that after smashing the big rice pot, discrimination against women had again surfaced: 'For example, women workers have the same, or even a greater workload than their male counterparts, but when it come to allocating bonuses some people would say, "she is after all a woman and cannot compare to her male comrades"' (Leung Wing-Yue 1988: 85).

Leung Wing-Yue also notes that sexual discrimination exists in the workforce organised on a leased-out or subcontracting basis. She quotes a Chinese survey which found that over 60 per cent of redundancies caused by economy drives in factories during the second half of 1987 were of women (1988: 86). The same bias is reflected in the recruitment, training and promotion of women cadres (*China Daily*, May 1983, p. 3).

The chief reason given for discrimination against women is the fact that their household duties often make them neglect their jobs. Further, women's right to paid maternity leave also influences management decisions. These attitudes have become even stronger in recent years because most factories now enjoy the right to hire and fire employees. In certain cases, discrimination has been so acute that even graduates from Beijing University have been refused jobs. These incidents are a startling demonstration of how protective legislation for women can become a cause of discrimination against them. As Tan Manni points out: 'Labour protection benefits for women often push them into unfavourable positions' (1983: 23).

Such acts of discrimination are also leading to the re-emergence of an argument which had been previously discredited in China. This is the demand that 'married women' return home and give up their jobs in favour of men. An article in *China Reconstructs* quotes some husbands as saying: 'Send our wives home and subsidise us with their wages. Then we are freed of household chores, we can do better at our jobs' (Tan Manni 1983: 23). Some working mothers echoed this demand and said: 'I think I should give up my own career for the sake of my husband and family' (Tan Manni 1983: 23). Ideas such as the above represent a desire on the part of women to revert to older forms of habitus and show the way dominant values work through consensus and acceptance rather than by force.

However, it is interesting to note that the All China Women's Federation has come out strongly against the raising of such demands. It has pointed out the necessity for women to continue working and has reiterated the links between women's liberation and their participation in production. The Tianjin Women's Federation carried out a survey among working women which noted that the tasks women needed most help with are childcare and shopping. Of the 1,000 women interviewed, 797 wished for help with shopping (Tianjin Women's Federation 1985: 100). This is not surprising since a large urban population makes shopping a fatiguing task at the best of times (1985: 19).

The report's solution is to mobilise surplus labour in urban areas to help out with these tasks, but this solution does not try to end the tradition of women being primarily responsible for household work and childcare. Though the mobilisation of surplus labour, in most cases other women, would alleviate the immediate problems, it would in no way undermine women's responsibility for these tasks. Evidence from urban areas suggests, however, that domestic service in cities has become the major reason for women's migration to urban areas. In most cases, these are women from under-developed provinces such as Anhui. The existence of domestic service in China shows that this practice enjoys the support of the state.

Along with active discrimination in the job market and education, other forms of exploitation of women are also now prevalent. Women are victims of sexual harassment and physical violence. In recent years, the Chinese press itself has carried cases documenting the gravity of the problem (Dai Qing and Luo Ge 1988). Prostitution and pornography have become rampant in urban areas and numerous rackets dealing with the abduction, buying and selling of women have been exposed (Pearson 1989).

The lives of rural women have also been affected by the household responsibility system. To mobilise female participation, cases of individual women who have made a success of sideline activities and become rich were also publicised. Although certain families and women have become rich, evidence that patriarchal practices have resurfaced in rural China is available from several sources. Female infanticide, much publicised in 1983–84, is only the extreme form of this tradition. The *People's Daily* of 23 March 1983 carried a letter from twenty-three women from Anhui province who had all suffered because of giving birth to baby girls. The letter describes how they were abused by their husbands and not allowed access to contraceptives until they gave birth to a son. The women write: 'We cannot understand why 32 years after liberation, we women are still so heavily weighed down by such backward feudal concepts ... We long for a second liberation.'

The official press in China has typically blamed feudalism as the cause of such practices. More critical analysts have seen the re-emergence of this practice as tied to the way state policy has indirectly colluded with feudal ideas. The twin policies of the rural household responsibility system and the one-child family-planning policy are partially to blame (Croll 1983). Evidence suggests that reversion to the household as the main unit of rural production has led to peasants strongly desiring sons. This demand for labour conflicts directly with the government's one-child policy. Since a daughter is seen as a source of labour which is lost to the family on her marriage, women who give birth to girls are maltreated, and baby girls are killed. Croll notes that in some places the ratio of baby girls to baby boys was 1:4 (1984a: 20). In 1990, women formed 48.4 per cent of the total population as compared to 48.7 per cent in 1982 (Pei Qing 1992: 20), showing the impact of female infanticide during the intervening years.

Croll also points out the danger of women's labour disappearing under that of the 'household' in rural areas. Despite the many success stories quoted in the Chinese press, she adds a cautionary note:

> Current policies returning production to the household are marked by the near ommission of any substantive analysis of the household and the relations of production and exchange within it. In the absence of such discussion which defines the distribution of labour and rewards within the household, it is likely that the gender hierarchy will be reproduced in production and the individual contribution of women be camouflaged by the family wage. (Croll 1983: 126)

Women's labour may also be intensified now that they are expected to work on sideline occupations, help with agriculture and take care of the household's basic needs (Hopper 1984).

However, it should be pointed out that the ACWF has made certain efforts to combat the most overt forms of discrimination against women. It has carried out educational campaigns among women and has tried to popularise women's rights through an emphasis on the law. Fran Williard, for example, notes that compaints about mothers-in-law, humiliation by husbands who had mistresses, arranged marriages, physical and mental maltreatment, financial non-support and other forms of inequality were aired at tables managed by women lawyers and Federation members (1985: 14). Again, one notices that the problems as such have not changed despite decades of propaganda and favourable legislation. They are the problems against which women fought at the turn of the century.

While, on the one hand, the ACWF champions the equality of women, on the other hand, it also contributes to dominant notions of female roles and images. The way the Federation has dealt with the issues of 'love and marriage' is a case in point. *Women of China*, the official magazine of the ACWF, has devoted considerable space to issues of love and marriage. Since marriage is seen as the aim of all women, to be 'left on the shelf' is considered a state to be pitied. Consequently, it is seen as the duty of social organisations such as the Women's Committees, the Neighbourhood Committees and Youth Organisations to arrange opportunities for young people to meet and get married. Marriage bureaux have also been set up to serve as officially sanctioned matchmakers. While marriage is seen as a natural way of life, the requirements of what counts as an eligible spouse have changed. These reflect the increased consumerism that is visible in urban areas (Tan Manni 1983: 12).

Another significant change in post-Mao China has been the encouragement given to consumerism through the means of advertising. Chinese cities today are littered with advertisements related to household goods from washing machines to tape recorders. As in other countries, advertisements in China use female models, and posters of smiling women standing in front of well-stocked fridges are commonplace. Alongside this, fashion and cosmetics have become important and the hairdressers' and beauty parlours are always full. Such trends mark a significant departure from the ideas of frugality and simplicity that China tried so hard to propagate earlier. They also reveal the resurgence of older notions of femininity, proving that a change in economic or political relations does not automatically imply a change in the way an orthodoxy on gender relations incorporates elements of long-standing cultural tradition.

Another aspect of post-Mao China that needs to be stressed is a remarkable fluidity in the opinions and discourses on the question of women. Harriet Evans, in a study of how popular magazines available in China deal with the sex-gender issue, notes: 'Sensationalist, macho and violent stories, printed ostensibly to teach a moral lesson, are found alongside advice to young mothers about how to calm babies who cry too much' (1989: 12). She further notes that other semi-official magazines such as *Women's Forum* (*Funü luntan*) tend to discuss more topical issues like marriage problems and love matters and give advice on how best to handle these (Evans 1989: 12). These discussions represent a new emphasis on the more traditional nature of female roles in China today. They also represent a range of possibilities that have emerged with the loosening of Party control over publishing.

Though there has been a definite rise in conservatism on the question of women, hitherto unknown feminist voices have also been heard. Several women within the ACWF itself have taken consistent stands against the resurgence of sexism. They have pointed out that for women to be able to compete with men, they need access to job-training facilities and scientific knowledge. As a report by the Anhui Provincial Women's Federation says:

> Lenin once pointed out that the working class should seek its own emancipation, as should working women. We feel that the same can be said of women becoming capable and qualified people in every field. Provided they

are determined to break through the confines of conventionalism, work with persistence and diligence, and overcome obstacles in their path, women can certainly make something of themselves. (Anhui Provincial Women's Federation 1985: 33).

The report then goes on to list subjective and objective factors behind the subordination of women. It also demands that more women should be accepted as cadres in the Party. It points out that, at the provincial level, women form only 23.2 per cent of cadres and the figure decreases sharply among senior ranks. Women account for only 7.2 per cent of cadres at the county levels and 6.2 per cent at the prefectural bureau level (Anhui Provincial Women's Federation 1985: 35).

Despite such efforts on the part of the Federation, post-Mao China is a place where conventional ideas about women have resurfaced. As usual their problems have been subordinated to the immediate policy aims of China. The contradictions that are beginning to emerge between the gender-specific interests of women and the modernisation programme are expected to get worse unless an attempt is made to redress these trends.

Conclusion

An analysis of Chinese policy towards women, and the shifts and changes in the issues that are perceived as women's issues, shows that the crux of the problem has remained the contradiction between women's reproductive roles and their participation in wage labour. While the Chinese Communist Party has constantly expressed support for female liberation, this support has been conditional on women's specific interest not conflicting with the overall interests of the Party. The persistence of 'feudal' values about women imply that economic liberation, though an important necessity for female liberation, is not sufficient in itself.

China's case demonstrates that gender relations remain an aspect most resistant to change. The rigid sexual division of labour upon which a habitus of gender relations is built is not only hard to change, but is tenaciously maintained despite changes in economic circumstances. In China one of the most fundamental beliefs remains: that of women's natural role as mothers and providers of the emotional and nurturance needs of their families. As shown, although the status of women in China has changed enormously, this automatic assumption continues to receive tacit support from the government. Their domestic responsibilities and their reproductive roles are seen as aspects which make women different from men, a biological difference which is seen as imbuing them with 'natural' characteristics.

The difficulty in change at this level is what has drawn me to use Bourdieu's ideas of habitus and doxa as notions which can help us better understand the complexity of gender relations. In the Chinese case, we notice that patriarchal arrangements of gender relations based on the old 'biology is destiny' argument can exist in an uneasy alliance with even the most radical of discourses. This implies that these beliefs remain unquestioned because they are unrecognised. A socialist orthodoxy constructs itself by accepting a traditional habitus of gender relations and allowing these elements to remain in the realm of doxa. Even when it is recognised that discrimination occurs because of the conflict generated by women's dual roles, there is little, if any, attempt made to bring the issue of men sharing in these responsibilities on to the agenda.

The persistent sexual division of labour and the failure to alleviate the domestic burden of women has merely resulted in the addition of new roles on top of women's previous roles, rather than a redefinition of male and female roles, resulting in the exhausting double burden faced by women. The government's limited efforts towards dealing with the specific demands faced by women justifies the charge made by feminists that the policies of socialist states towards women are constantly subordinated to the productivist goals of these states. An analysis of the continuing forms of female subordination, and the way in which socialist policy itself condones male–female inequality, is postponed. Every time the issue emerges from doxa, a new orthodoxy is constructed around it by emphasising one or the other role of women rather than attempting a fundamental restructuring of gender relations. This constant displacing of the woman's question is often hidden by the formal equality that women have acquired, and behind the accession of women to previously unconventional occupations (Molyneux 1981b: 36).

A historical analysis of the Chinese case shows us that only those elements of gender relations were criticised which directly furthered the cause of the socialist revolution as the Chinese saw it. It is in this selection of certain issues that the unequal power relations between the sexes manifest themselves. Although the Party broke down the institutional power of the old patriarchy through land reform and the guarantee of legal equality to women, gender conflict is never allowed to emerge because the Party's discourse remains a new discursive alignment of old elements. It shows us the passage from doxa into orthodoxy.

The Communist Party, especially in the rural areas of China, first confronted feudal ideas about women in China as an heterodoxy, challenging a Confucian orthodoxy with its discourse of female equality. In the Chinese case it is interesting to note that the Party recognises the importance of ideological change, in fact it positively emphasises it, but it refuses to touch certain aspects of gender relations. These are the sexual division of labour and the consequent belief that women are naturally suitable for certain tasks. That is why the mobilisation of women for tasks which are a natural extension of their familial roles is no contradiction.

This is not an attempt at a deliberate policy by the Party. The Chinese case demonstrates that although the 'wider limits' of the discourse on women are extended, certain elements remain behind. This also allows us to form an alternative hypothesis to that of Stacey and others who argue that the Party as such is patriarchal. Further, if we see discourse on gender as premised on those areas which the Party does not see as real contradictions, we can also understand women's own support and participation in the ranks of the Communist Party. They not only actively propagated the Party line but also believed in it. Like the Party, they were convinced that the contradictions between their gender-specific interests would be detrimental to the goal of national and class liberation. It is this aspect of Chinese policy on women that allows us to say that the new orthodoxy on gender relations is a curious mix of patriarchy and socialism, where the tensions between women's productive and reproductive roles remain unresolved. It also shows us the importance and power of discourse and the role that discourse plays in the mystification of the material subordination of women

Another significant aspect of socialist rhetoric on gender relations is the protectionist discourse within which state support for female equality is couched. Women are constantly identified as those who need to be 'protected', on par with children. Women's rights are enshrined in the constitution as a gift of the Party rather than as something won by women through struggle and because women deserve to be equal. This discourse of protectionism has been visible ever since the woman's question first appeared as a necessary part of a charter of social reform. The stalwarts of the early reform movement are all men, with the exception of a few token women. In the socialist phase of the revolution, those women who emerged as leaders were automatically assigned to female tasks, which were seen as secondary to the overall goals of the revolution. This protectionist discourse of the Party is also what made it suppress the more radical and independent discourses which emerged within the women's movement during the period of the May Fourth movement of 1919. The Party cannot afford to allow competing discourses, which link questions of female subordination to intra-family relations and pose the problem as a contradiction between the interests of men and women. This would undermine the Party's legitimacy as the arbitrator of social relations.

The structural subordination of the ACWF, as a mass organisation for women, is another natural consequence of this protectionist bias. Women are identified as dependents who cannot look after their own interests. This protective strategy serves a double function, for it also ensures that women who do act in their own interests outside the avenues provided for them, are successfully marginalised and discredited as divisive. The need for an independent women's organisation is removed if the Party constantly proclaims to support and protect the interests of women. Whenever this protectionism offered by the state and its organisations fails, the Party blames feudal ideology rather than examining the limitations and drawbacks of its own strategies and policies. Feudal ideology, in other words, becomes a convenient scapegoat for the tensions that emerge when the gender interests of women come into conflict with state policy.

Because of the Party's compromises at various levels, and the way women are defined as dependents, power relations between the sexes have changed very little over time. At the material level, women remain unequal to men in all areas of social life. At the level of discourse, this inequality is hidden behind an ideology of equality. Any analysis which seeks to examine the position of women in China, then, has to start with debunking this myth of equality which is maintained by orthodoxy. The ideology of equality through state protectionism ensures that the emergence of an independent women's organisation which will consistently champion women's rights is an uphill task.

While orthodoxy and its contents can be examined through the way the state presents its position on the woman's question, we also need to find a way of assessing what women make of these representations of themselves, and how they represent themselves in alternative ways. Women throughout different periods have responded to the demands made on them in different ways. While many have accepted the demands uncritically, others, as exemplified by Ding Ling, have tended to look critically at their position in society. The post-Mao years, with the loosening of control at various levels, further demonstrate that the state does not have a monopoly on the production of a discourse on women. Though it attempts to construct an orthodoxy, in practice, several discourses coexist.

This heterodoxy, in the Chinese case, contains different discourses: some seek a return to a position that existed before the CCP came to power and are echoes of conservative ideas about women; others seek radically to question all elements of a traditional and socialist orthodoxy. While the former justify and support discrimination against women by seeking to contract the limits of change that have occurred, the latter seek to widen the limits of discourse. Orthodox discourse, thus, can, as Bourdieu points out, at best be an imperfect attempt to re-create a doxic situation. In other words, an attempt to construct an orthodoxy on any issue implies first of all the necessity to do so. It is a response to the tensions that exist within any social situation.

Strands of heterodoxy can also be spotted in different places. Within the Women's Federation, for example, there has been a growing acceptance of the existence of female subordination rather than pretending that the problems of women have all been taken care of. Although the ACWF is structurally limited in its propagation of female equality, it has highlighted and criticised incidents of blatant discrimination against women. Independent women's voices have also been heard through university student groups such as the Guangdong University students who have started a journal specially devoted to publicising cases of discrimination against women. Some of the more critical women writers are also part of this more independent critique of gender relations. A few women's studies programmes have also been set up in universities (Shen Zhi 1987).

In the final analysis, discrimination against women can be eradicated only if what is taken for granted about male–female relations is questioned; not by a revival of an earlier conception of male–female relations, as is happening in China today, but by a radical questioning of their relation. It is this apparent fit of women's natural roles with their objective circumstances that seems to provide a motif of continuity within the changing discourse on Chinese women.

Notes

1. Control over female sexuality is not peculiar to China alone but has been identified as a fundamental part of most cultures. For a theoretical discussion of gender and sexuality from a cross-cultural and historical perspective, see Ortner and Whitehead (1981).

2. The role played by patrilocal marriages has been examined by several scholars. In the case of China see, Freedman (1970).

3. This feature of feudal society leads one to argue that dominant or orthodox discourse in pre-capitalist societies attempts to control only those it classifies as its 'representatives'. The adherence to morals and values is, in fact, one of the bases on which the upper classes distinguish themselves from the general mass of the population.

4. While sisterhoods are a positive and successful example of resistance to social pressure, they existed only in the south of China. For many young women the only means of resisting forced marriages was suicide, a very common happening in traditional China. See Wolf (1978).

5. Croll has an interesting quote to prove the class bias of these early reformers. She quotes from the prospectus of one of the schools opened by a number of wealthy merchants: 'In opening schools for girls we are reverting to the illustrious custom of the three dynasties. In order to open up the intelligence of the people, we must certainly make women free and afterwards customs can be changed ... It is the intention of the school to make no distinctions of rank but since in the future, pupils from the school will be leaders and teachers in other schools, only respectable families will be admitted' (Croll 1978: 52).

6. See Liu Mei Ching (1988) for details about the content of women's journals in Japan during this period.

7. Qiu Qin is often seen as the heroine of this period. She came from a gentry family, with liberal parents. She divorced her husband and left her children in order to study in Japan. There she came in contact with members of the Tong Menghui, an association set up under the leadership of Sun Yat-Sen, later the president of republican China in 1911. Qiu Qin participated in their activities and in 1906 returned to China to work and propagate revolution. She was arrested and executed by the Manchu government in 1909 when she and her co-conspirators planned the assassination of a high official (Croll 1978: 65).

8. The actual incident that started widespread demonstrations all over China was the protest of 4 May 1919 against the enforcement of the Versailles Treaty, from which the movement draws its name.

9. As early as 1916, Chen Tuxiu suggested that a new family system was essential if women were to be liberated. The magazine *New Youth*, of which Chen was editor, ran regular columns on the subject from 1918 onwards. See Chow Tse-tung (1960) .

10. The leaders of the communist movement in China accepted the analysis outlined above because by the early 1920s women workers had emerged in large numbers in the urban areas of China. Further, Honing (1986) in her study of women textile workers in Shanghai points out that women were severely exploited and worked long hours under miserable conditions.

11. Xiang Jingyu was the only woman in the first politburo of the Chinese Communist Party. She studied in France with Zhou Enlai and returned to China in 1922 to participate in Party work. She was one of the few women who were part of the decision-making apparatus of the early Communist Party. She was appointed director for women's affairs by the Party in 1923. Xiang's personal position on the priorities for organising women was largely influential in deciding the direction of the early women's movement. She was especially against the early feminists, regarding them as middle-class women attempting social charity. This prejudice against feminists was to continue and the word 'feminism' (*nüxing zhuyi*) came to be seen as pejorative. See Leith (1973).

12. The Soviet Land Law of 1931 provided for the distribution of land among hired hands, labourers and peasants regardless of sex (Stranahan 1976: 21). This

was an historic landmark in China, for before this women had never had the right to inherit property. The second important piece of legislation in this period was the promulgation of the Marriage Law in 1931 (*Zhonghua Su-wei-ai gong he guo hunyin tiaoli*). This law listed three basic principles: free choice of marriage, legalisation of divorce and the position of children. See Delia Davin (1976).

13. Edgar Snow's (1938) accounts of his travels to Yenan provide an excellent account of the kind of conditions which existed in Yenan at that period. He records that the position of women in China was much lower in the Shanxi provinces. The custom of footbinding still prevailed and thousands of women were sold and bought during the famines of the 1920s and 1930s.

14. In today's light, it is interesting to note that similar critiques have been made by female guerrilla fighters from Cuba and Zimbabwe. Women recall that on their return to 'normal' life they were seen as 'strange, loose women, while the men were welcomed back as heroes of the revolution'. See Molyneux (1981a).

15. A good example of the radicalism of certain of the women's organisations during this period is documented in William Hinton's *Fanshen* (1966), a history of how revolution and liberation occurred in the Long Bow village. Hinton records the steps that the local women's organisation took against those men and mothers-in-law who continued to mistreat wives. He records how the 'eat bitterness' (*chiku*) campaigns worked in practice. One of the young members of the village women's committee speaks up in a public meeting and denounces her husband's ill treatment of her; this in turn leads to other women speaking about their experiences. Hinton's record, however, also shows how Party representatives always tried to link the oppression suffered by women to their class oppression. The contradictions between the sexes were seen as a direct result of class relations and, as such, 'non-antagonistic contradictions'.

16. The circular evaluated the experience of women's work in the liberated areas and pointed out the shortcomings that had existed. Commenting on the central task of women's work, the circular stated: 'The orientation of woman-work in the liberated areas should still be based on mobilising and organising women for an active part in production. ... In the first place women must be given equal rights and position with men, and in the countryside get and keep an equal share of land and property and learn to look upon labour as glorious' (Davin 1976: 203).

17. After the law was proclaimed, a survey of marriages in the rural countryside listed the different types of marriage as following: free marriage, arranged marriages where the couple were allowed to meet each other before the marriage, and arranged marriages where the couple had no choice. Of these three forms, free marriage, where the couple married by their own choice, was both the least common and the ideal that the Party encouraged (Davin 1976: 96).

18. These Resident Committees were an important link in the Party's attempt to control all aspects of social life. They were in charge of health and sanitation in the community and were known to provide advice in situations of domestic conflict (Davin 1976: 168).

19. The Great Leap Forward was a campaign launched in 1958 at the behest of Mao. It was the first large-scale attempt by the Party to collectivise rural

landholdings under the famous commune experiment. For details on the campaign and its effects, see MacFarquhar (1983).

20. The Cultural Revolution was launched in 1966. Its main aim was to attack what Mao termed the revisionist and rightist tendencies within the Party. He specifically called upon students to attack the leadership. Called the Red Guards (*Hongwei bing*), students from all over China participated in mass campaigns against the top leadership. For details on the movement as a whole, see Robinson (1971).

21. Post-Mao China has witnessed major changes in the organisation of social and economic life in China. For details on the policy changes initiated in this period, see Feuchtwang et al. (eds) (1988).

3
The literary field and women writers

This chapter examines how literary criticism attempts to analyse and classify the works of women writers. Such an examination can help us identify how literary discourse constitutes the subject of women's literature (*nüxing wenxue*). In doing so it incorporates elements of orthodox discourse on gender. It is these elements that show the 'discursive alignment' (to use Foucault's term) on the basis of which discourse on a subject is deployed in different fields. Here one can see how the difference between what are socially perceived to be male and female characteristics become a crucial factor in distinguishing a female literature.

The criticism of women writers has to be placed not only within the context of an overall discourse on gender, but also within the context of the specific character of the literary field in China. Although we can use categories of comparative literature, it becomes important to stress that the literary field (that is, the creation, publication, dissemination and criticism of literary works) in China is different from that in the West. The principles on which the world of literature and art is organised in China define the wider boundaries within which literary criticism can address the issue of women writers. In China, for example, the institutions of the state[1] construct a specific vision of reality by using a specific type of discourse to represent it.

In China, it is the Party which exercises this function and represents orthodoxy, becoming the guarantor of legitimacy, possessing a *symbolic power*, 'a power to create things with words', as Bourdieu says in his article 'Social Space and Symbolic Power' (1990b: 138). Bourdieu stresses the importance he attaches to the categorisation of people into groups as a way of reproducing social divisions. These social divisions are not simply those based on class; they are also made and deployed in other ways. People are categorised and catalogued into data, which in turn feed into policy and politics, on the basis of group characteristics of race, gender, class, education, location and so on. Thus, a struggle over the systems of social classifications, the processes through which we arrive at group characteristics and the effects of these characteristics is a necessary struggle. As Bourdieu says: 'to change the world, one has to change the ways of making the world, that is the vision of the world and the practical operations by which groups are produced and reproduced' (1990b: 137).

In this sense, the creation of gender identities, or women as a group, will follow the same logic as that of the creation of other groups. That is, it will bring in certain ways of categorising women and their representation, and set in motion a process through which identities are created. It is this power 'to create groups', which is one of the major aspects of symbolic power (1990b: 137). Bourdieu goes on to explain that this symbolic power consists first of: 'a power of conserving or transforming present classifications when it comes to gender, nation, region, age and social status, a power mediated by the words that are used to designate or to describe individuals, groups or institutions' (1990b: 137).

Here again we see the important role Bourdieu gives to discourse and to those who have the right to participate in discourse formation at the symbolic level. Symbolic power can, then, be seen as giving legitimacy to certain discourses and to the discourse of certain agents. This, as Bourdieu tells us, resides in the right which the agent has through the acquiring of symbolic capital. Again, the actual mechanisms which guarantee symbolic capital may be culturally specific. While educational qualifications may be an important element in one culture, kinship or caste may be more important in another. The varying degree of power enjoyed by different people in the same field depends upon the degree of legitimacy enjoyed by an agent. This in turn may be linked to the social and cultural capital of the group to which the agents belong. It is here that gender becomes an important category. The gender of an author, the fact of being male or female, equips an agent with a specific type of symbolic capital. Thus, the discourse of an agent in a field is linked to social power.

The second condition that guarantees the success of symbolic power is that the vision of social relations, the idea of society reproduced in discourses, in the naming of groups, and in the construction of identities, is close to or corresponds with social practice. Both produce each other simultaneously, so to speak. It is this relationship with 'reality' which brings in the habitus of social relations, the common-sense vision of the characteristics generally attributed to existing groups, characteristics which not only determine the way groups are spoken of, but also structure, to a large degree, the dispositions of the agents who comprise the group. Bourdieu says: 'In fact ... a group, class, "gender", region, or nation begins to exist as such, for those who are part of it and others too, only when it is distinguished, according to one principle or another, from other groups, that is, via cognition and recognition' (1990b: 138).

While Bourdieu highlights the important role played by the state and its institutions in the process of 'world making' (1990b: 137),[2] he retains a notion of conflict and resistance where this process is questioned not only by disfranchised groups but also by other members of society who compete to impose their own vision of the social world. Symbolic struggles are real struggles over the legitimation of different world views. It is these struggles that show up different positions as orthodoxies and heterodoxies and allow us to examine both how groups such as *nüzuojia* (group of women writers) are attributed with specific categories, and how those categories are challenged and/or reinforced at the objective and subjective level by agents, in this case women.

The following discussion will analyse how the literary field in China operates through institutions which have been created by the state to monitor it. It is important to retain this perspective of linking discourses to an institutional basis when studying the field of literature and the discourse on women writers as a group within it.

The fundamental principles of literary criticism in China

Since the establishment of the People's Republic of China (PRC) in 1949, Marxism, Leninism and Mao Zedong Thought have formed an orthodoxy within literary discourse in China. Even before the Chinese Communist Party came to power, the literary theories of the Soviet Union had become popular in China and became the 'official' position of the Party regarding literary production long before 1949.

By the mid-1920s, literary circles in China had already begun debating the question of links between literature and revolution and the majority of writers were to come increasingly under the influence of Soviet literary theory as it came to be introduced into China. By 1931, the League of Left Wing Writers had been formed in Shanghai under the leadership of Lu Xun (1881–1936). The basic thesis of Marxist literary analysis, as it developed in the Soviet Union, was that literature was determined by economic factors and represented the ideology of the ruling class of any epoch, in this case capitalist society with the bourgeoisie as the ruling class.[3] Socialist literature thus had a dual purpose: to criticise bourgeois society and to help in the creation of a new socialist ideology.[4] Several writers were to play a dominant role in disseminating and popularising Marxist literary thought in China. Among these, the names of Qiu Qiupai and Lu Xun have often been prominent (Pickowicz 1980).

In terms of literary style, this meant an emphasis on Socialist Realism, which had become the officially approved style in the Soviet Union by the mid-1930s. According to Boorman, the most succinct definition of Socialist Realism was given during the first All Union Congress of Soviet Writers in August 1934:

> Socialist realism is the basic method of Soviet literature and literary criticism. It demands of the artist the truthful, historically concrete representation of reality in its revolutionary development. Moreover, the truthfulness and historical concreteness of the artistic representation of reality must be linked with the task of ideological transformation and education of workers in the spirit of Socialism. (Boorman 1963: 17)

In China too, Socialist Realism became the foundation of attempts by the Party to lead writers.[5] Literature was supposed to serve the interests of the peasants and the soldiers and workers. Mao states this clearly in his talks at Yenan. The importance of Mao's talks for an understanding of modern Chinese literature cannot be over-stressed if we are to carry out a fruitful investigation of contemporary Chinese literature (Mao Zedong 1980: 6). Mao's 'Yenan Talks' have to be read within the wider framework of the New Culture Movement begun after the May Fourth Movement of 1919 (Chow Tse-tung 1960). Held to commemorate the sixth anniversary of the death of Lu Xun in May 1942, these talks have become the grand referent on which Marxist literary criticism in China is supposed to ground itself.

Mao attempts to lay down ways by which the 'right' literature could be identified. He further goes on to identify the four problems to which literary works must address themselves. These are questions relating to position, attitude, audience, work and study (Mao Zedong 1980: 58; all further references to the talks are from this edition, translated by B. McDougall). In terms of position, the policy was to identify with the broad masses. In terms of attitude, the question to ask was, who should be praised and who should be criticised? The question of audience was, for whom should literature be written? And the question of work and study was intended to deepen an understanding of the laws of historical materialism and learn from the masses (pp. 58–9).

The political content of Mao's talks has been the aspect most highlighted by western readers of Chinese literary criticism. D. W. Fokkema, for example, points out those aspects of Mao's talks which focus on the explicitly subordinate position of literature to the class struggle and he highlights some of the contradictions that exist in the text and which confront Chinese writers in practice (1980: 160). Fokkema links his criticism of Chinese literary theory to an examination of some of the shortcomings of Marxist literary theory on which it bases itself. Similar sentiments are echoed by other western scholars of Chinese literature who point out that the subordination of literature and art to politics is not only contrary to the spirit of art, which is supposed to be based on freedom, but is also detrimental to artistic quality (Hsia 1961).

Some scholars, however, have pointed out other elements contained in the talks. Holms, for example, has highlighted those aspects which focus on the necessity of popularising literature among the people. He points out that Mao's talk at Yenan also paved the way for a greater emphasis on populism and that this policy led to a turn away from European models which had dominated Chinese literature since the May Fourth Movement towards national Chinese forms (Holm 1984: 279). Along with an emphasis on national or popular forms, artists were called upon to learn from the masses so that they could truly reflect the consciousness of the people in their works by becoming a part of the masses. As Mao himself puts it:

> Revolutionary Chinese artists and writers ... must go into the midst of the masses of workers, peasants and soldiers; they must go into the heat of the battle for a long time to come, they must go to the sole, the broadest, the richest source to observe, learn, study and analyze all men, all classes, all kinds of people, all the vivid patterns of life and struggle and all raw material of art and literature, before they are ready for the stage of processing and creating. (p. 70)

This statement by Mao is a criticism of intellectuals who, he felt, lived in an ivory tower and spoke in a language opposed to popular usage.

Bonnie McDougall has also examined the artistic criteria that Mao puts forward in his talks. These, she feels, were influenced by more traditional Chinese literary concepts which 'seem to rest on an under-lying conception of poetry as the paradigm of literature and art generally' (p. 11). Whether Mao's Yenan talks had only a political or both a political and literary function, they set the political and artistic agenda for the future of literature in China. In other words, they became the ultimate source of legitimacy for all artistic work.

Since the establishment of the People's Republic, the ideological content of literature and its relationship to politics entered a new phase, one where renewed emphasis was placed on the important part played by literature in the overall project of socialist reconstruction and the propagation of a new revolutionary ideology. Literature was seen as a reflection of reality, an idea taken over from Lenin,[6] and writers were supposed to create positive images of life under socialism and help in the creation of a 'new democratic civilisation'.

This position is best represented by Zhou Yang (1908–89), who wrote prolifically as both a literary critic and a literary theoretician. He was one-time Minister of Culture, Vice Chairman and Chairman of the All China Writers' Federation and was largely responsible for setting China's policy on art. Zhou Yang occupies an extremely interesting position within Chinese literary history. During the early 1930s he was one of the members of the League of Left Wing Writers but he was opposed to Lu Xun's degree of tolerance and advocated a strict subordination of content and style to political need. During the Cultural Revolution, Zhou Yang spent ten years in prison.

In his *China's New Art and Literature*, Zhou Yang spells out his own position regarding what is literature: 'The fundamental difference between literature and art on the one hand, and other forms of expressing ideas on the other, is that literature and art use images to express thought; without images there can be no art, and images can only be taken from life' (1954: 16).

Statements such as the above represent a direct continuity with the project of Socialist Realism and Lenin's theory of reflection reworked through Mao's Yenan talks. In fact, Zhou Yang was the major critic who attempted to use the yardstick of Socialist Realism to measure literary works on a large scale. In his address to the second All China Writers' Federation (1954), Zhou Yang emphasised the importance given to 'realism' in Mao's Yenan text. Going on to specify what he meant by Socialist Realism, Zhou Yang says: 'Socialist Realism should be seen as a dynamic force ... It requires our writers to familiarize themselves with the new life of the people, portray the advanced characters among them and reflect their new thoughts and emotions' (1954: 29).

Along with an emphasis on realism, the literary orthodoxy stressed the importance of 'positive characters'. Writers were expected to create role models which could be emulated by the broad masses. In her study of the creation of positive characters in Chinese fiction, Tsai Mei-hsi points out how the heroes or heroines were always depicted as ardent revolutionaries whose first and foremost duty was to the success of the revolution and obedience to the Party. These larger-than-life heroes became even more stereotypical during the Cultural Revolution, when the few model operas and stories were being created under the express guidelines of Jiang Qing (Tsai Mei-hsi 1975).[7]

While several western critics have justifiably attacked the 'ideological' content of Chinese literature (Hsia 1963: 114), there is an attempt among them to reduce all the complications and contradictions that were actually part of the literary world of China to this one fact. As Huang puts it:

There is no denying the element of propaganda in Chinese literature. But the definition of propaganda by the Chinese is remarkably different from what we understand by the term. The Chinese term *hsuan-chuan* suggests publicizing and spreading, and is closer to the Western term of mass communication. What has not been seen and accepted is that Chinese communist literature is also art. A serious communist novelist performs a dual role, as artist as well as propagandist. (Huang 1973: xi)

The Chinese case makes it clear that any literary work has to be placed within the system of its own specific literary field and has to be understood within the way literature is described and organised in a specific historical and cultural context. Despite the strict regimen of control exercised on literary production, writers in China have been able to achieve a certain standard of quality which makes it possible to study literary works as part of the larger social discourse operating at any one given time. As Perry Link cautions in speaking of a 'system' of literary control in China, we must not see it as 'fixed standards that writers, editors and readers can confidently follow' (Link [ed.] 1983: 2). Thus, although the Party played a dominant role, especially during the 1930s, artists and writers responded to the appeal of Marxism, spontaneously influenced by the real situation in their country.

At another level, the changes in the political line of the Party have always influenced the criteria set for the evaluation of literary works. Often these changes have been sudden and unforeseen, catching a lot of literary workers unawares as in the anti-rightist campaign of 1957.[8] Merle Goldman points out that these shifts in policy have been determined in large part by internal economic and political factors and sometimes by international events (1971: 2). It is actually on the basis of these changes that historians of Chinese literature have periodised modern Chinese literature into that of the Great Leap Forward, the Culural Revolution and post-Mao.

Before turning to the specific context of post-Mao literature, within which the issue of women writers is located, it is important to have a general idea of how Party principles are put into practice through its various literary organisations.

The organisation of the literary field

Although the relationship between literature and politics in China is not straightforward, it cannot be denied that the Party exercises a certain control over all aspects of artistic and literary production. This is done mainly through the various literary organisations and associations that are sponsored by the state. Analysing the organisation of literature in

China, Perry Link points out that the primary rule of literary control is that literature must support the current political leadership. He identifies five important groups which play a significant role in this function. These are readers, writers, editors and publishers, critics and the top leadership (Link [ed.] 1983: 2). He goes on to explain: 'By top leadership I mean literally the highest levels ... By critics I mean officials whose job it is to analyze literary works and if necessary, to criticize authors according to the political criteria of the top leadership ... By readers I mean primarily urban readers' (1983: 2).

This definition of literary control in China is extremely useful in classifying and understanding the workings of the system and also in being able to collect material regarding the different categories. Most studies of Chinese literature have concentrated on looking at the factional struggles within the field and have focused on representative periods and personalities. Bady is quite correct in pointing out that more work needs to be done on the socio-economic organisation of literature in China. We know very little about the material conditions under which artists and writers live (Bady 1981: 646).[9] In the event, the following discussion should be seen as pointing towards those areas which we should study. Despite the paucity of information, it soon becomes apparent that the organisation of the literary field is an important anchor for orthodox discourse.

The All China Writers' Federation In China, becoming a writer is not only a matter of personal taste or personal choice. All writers in China have to belong to some form of literary society or organisation which functions as their *Danwei* (work-unit).[10] The first systematic organisation for writers was set up in July 1949 as the All China Federation of Literary and Art Circles (*Zhonghua quanguo wenxue yishu jie lianhehui*). A separate union for Chinese writers (*Zuojia Xiehui*) was set up in 1953. This writers' union is at the apex of the structure of literary organisations in China. The Federation was set up as a mass organisation[11] and given the responsibility of implementing literary policy. It was designed to function as an umbrella organisation for all national-level writers' and artists' associations, research societies and branch federations of writers and artists. At present there are ten member organisations in the Federation. The Chinese Writers' Association, is one of the ten. The others are organisations for different aspects of the arts, such as music, theatre, visual art and so on. I was told that there are fifty-eight major research institutions concerned with literary research. These are mostly attached to social science academies and universities (Thakur 1991).

The constitution of the Federation lists eight articles and the first stresses the importance of close links with the Party's line and objectives. Thus, among the several tasks of the Federation, one is to encourage the study of Marxism, Leninism and Mao Zedong Thought and to work with strengthening the relationship between the Party and writers. Theoretically, it is also supposed to protect writers' freedom to a certain extent (*China Handbook for Literature and Art* 1983: 116–17). This is the perspective stressed by the Party. As Hu Qili, a senior Party leader, said in his address to workers in the art and literary circles: 'The aims of literature should correspond with the aims of the Party and Socialism. This aim is to diligently reflect greatness of our times and use the principles of socialism to educate the masses' (1986: 2). Hu Qili goes on to criticise critics and writers who have been advocating absolute freedom of expression without keeping in mind the social effects of the works being produced (1986: 5).

Apart from these directly political tasks, the Federation also attempts to foster research and literary exchange with foreign artists. It organises conferences, seminars and other forums of literary discussion and exchange and is responsible for the various literary prizes awarded every year, the most famous of which is the Mao Dun prize. The Federation also publishes several major literary journals, namely the *Wenyi Pinglun* (*Literary Gazette*), *Renmin Wenxue* (*People's Literature*), *Shikan* (*Poetry*) and *Minzu Wenxue* (*Ethnic Literature*). Local branch associations also publish monthly journals and there are altogether more than sixty association journals throughout the country (*China Handbook for Literature and Art* 1983: 118).

Apart from its political function, the Federation also serves a practical function. It is work-unit for its members; thus, it is, in effect, an employer. It provides salaries to all its members and is in charge of guaranteeing them basic amenities such as housing, coupons, health facilities and so on. The Writers' Federation personnel can be divided into three separate groups: cadres or administrative personnel, writers and critics. The Federation has its own publishing house and literary translators. Within each section, there are specialists and ordinary members, part-time and full-time members. In fact, the whole organisation can be seen as a huge corporation which attempts to exercise monopoly control over all aspects of literary production and the management of the literary field.

The Bureaucrats or **Ganbu** Cadres form the basic administrative group within all Chinese organisations. Very little specific information is available about how the system of nomenklatura works in China (Lieberthal and Lampton 1992). Lieberthal divides China's cadres into six clusters. These are: (1) economic bureaucracies; (2) propaganda and education (this includes the cadres of the Writers' Federation); (3) organisational and personnel; (4) civilian and coercive bureaucracies; (5) military cadres; and (6) CCP territorial committees. He, however, points out how difficult it is to get access for research within these organisations (Lieberthal and Lampton 1992: 2–3). Schurmann cites a 1954 definition of the word 'cadre' (*ganbu*) as: 'Persons who work in state institutions or a department of production, capable of unifying and leading the masses to carry out Party and government policies and directives, to implement duties and programs promptly under the leadership of the Party and higher level government institutions, are cadres' (1971:165).[12]

It is a fairly well-known fact that the number of cadres in each department is large. According to an article published in the *China New Analysis* in 1988, there were some 27 million people who can be defined as cadres. Among them 350,000 work in the judicature and the legal department, 10.8 million in education, culture and hygiene, and over 4 million work in the administration services of the state (p. 9).

The cadres of the Writers Federation are almost always graduates of literature or other fine art departments. The organisational structure is very much like that of all organisations in China, the only difference being that these bureaucrats deal with writers and artists. This means that their functioning, salary scales, criteria for promotion and so on are all on par with bureaucrats working in any government department. However, I have been able to find little on the actual decision-making structure, but overall policy-making obviously lies with the Party. As scholars of Chinese politics have often pointed out, in China, as in other state-socialist societies, the functions of the Party and state overlap with real power in the hands of the Party (Saich 1981).

Regarding the recruitment of cadres, a booklet published by the Writers' Federation in 1983 has the following to say: 'The work of recruiting and training cadres of the writers federation has to be done in accordance with the directives of the Central Committee of the Party. Its main elements are recruiting younger and better educated members, with professional training' (1983: 121). This is in line with the overall reform of the administrative services. The Federation has a committee with one Chairman and several Vice Chairmen. It also has a leading group recruited from among writers, critics and senior Party functionaries. This committee is expected to meet at least once every six months to take policy-related decisions. It was this committee which was in charge of revising the constitution of the Writers' Federation. This is obviously a very important committee and appointments to it are both political, in the case of critics and bureaucrats, and based on personal fame, in the case of writers.

The main power of the *ganbu* lies in the clout they can exercise in terms of all sorts of selections. From housing to picking out delegates for a trip abroad, the cadre is an essential part of this literary organisation. Ideological and Party work is also carried out by the cadres. It is their job to see that all the writers who are members periodically attend sessions on ideological work and, since 1989, in the aftermath of the student movement, there has been renewed emphasis on ideological training. Sessions were held throughout 1990 on the collected works of Deng Xiaoping. The study of Mao's Yenan talks was also reintroduced. The *ganbu* can be taken as the direct representative of the Party. Of course, the individual influence of the members will differ depending on their position within the service and the informal symbolic capital they have.

The writers Writers form the main part of this organisation. According to an interview I carried out in November 1990, there are no fixed criteria for writers to be accepted as professionally attached to the Federation. Several broad criteria are used. The first is that writers must have had a major impact within the literary field. Apart from this, they have to be introduced by two people who are already members of the Writers' Federation. After this, membership is approved by a selection committee. Becoming a member of the Federation is like becoming a member of a club; it is a place for making contacts and essential if one wants to travel anywhere.

Once accepted, a writer is placed in one of three categories. Category I is usually reserved for the old group of writers such as Bing Xin and others of the same generation. Writers such as Gu Hua, Wang Meng and Zhang Jie, a group of middle-aged but nationally well-known writers, also get category I. This is the most prestigious category and writers in this top grade have enormous freedom in determining their schedules and work conditions. Category II contains mainly middle-aged writers and some younger authors who have become famous over the last decade. Category III is the largest in terms of numbers and contains all the younger generation of writers, most of whom started writing after the fall of the Gang of Four in 1976. The different categories work as a system of promotion and are linked both to the number of years members have been been writers and how famous they have become.

The provincial-level writers' associations are more flexible, and a famous writer attached to a provincial organisation can often exercise more control over his or her work and time. For example, Zhang Kang-kang, whom I interviewed in 1988, said she preferred to remain a member of the Heilongjiang writers' association because it was less bureaucratic.

The salary scales of writers vary considerably. While writers in categories I, II and III earn about 300 yuan per month, those in category I start between 140 and 200 yuan ($70–100). Writers also earn an extra 10–12 yuan for every 10,000 words that they produce. Along with this, writers can also earn money from the sales of their books.[13] It is this tenure track system of being an artist which makes the organisational structure of the Writers' Federation so different. It also works as a social security system in that a writer is not dependent on being productive to earn a living. The cadre of the Writers' Federation considered this a superior system because, according to him, it meant one could concentrate on art rather than becoming a commercial artist.[14] On the whole, writers are the most vulnerable members of the literary organisation and take considerable risks if they choose to confront the limitations of the Party regarding the content of literature.

The two writers whom I interviewed in Beijing were members of the Writers' Federation. When asked about their opinion of the Federation, both writers pointed out that it was essentially a bureaucratic organisation whose main function was to exercise control over writers. However, they also pointed out that it was essential to be a member of the Federation, since that meant being able to write full-time. One of them said that since the suppression of the pro-democracy movement of 1989, some of the writers had stopped cooperating with the Federation by refusing to attend its gatherings and by not submitting new work to be published. Both also pointed out that the individual prestige enjoyed by a writer often influenced the attitude of the Federation.

Apart from the salaried writers who are attached to the Federation, there are amateur writers in China who attempt to combine their writing with other jobs. They can submit their work directly to magazines, where editorial policy determines whether they will be published. The main responsibility of editors is to ensure that published works support and help the Four Modernisations. It is difficult to make an assessment of this group bcause of its unorganised nature. However, professional writers often start as amateurs before the quality of their work makes them eligible for membership of the Writers Federation.

The critics Critics are recruited to the Federation in much the same way as writers, and often work for the various journals published by the Federation. The job of literary critics is two-fold: (1) to carry out literary criticism and research; and (2) to translate Party policy into literary theory. One of the guidelines set out for critics is a comment made by Deng Xiaoping in 1981 which says: 'The main task of literary criticism under the guidelines of the Eleventh Party Congress is to develop a literary criticism which takes the spirit of communism as its base and attempts to develop a socialist spiritual civilisation. They must vigorously oppose negative tendencies such as class exploitation, petty bourgeoise sentiments, individualism, anarchism and revitalise the Party's spirit' (1981: 489). Thus, even in post-Mao China, the task of literary criticism remains firmly rooted in the Party's Marxist framework.

In general, critics can be said to play the most important role in terms of implementing the Party's policy and actually making use of the principles of Mao Zedong Thought to analyse literary works. Their work represents orthodox discourse, and their position within the literary field has often been one of legitimating the demands of the Party. This has created friction between writers and critics so that criticism has not been taken seriously by writers who, rightly so, have seen it as a political weapon.[15]

Critics can also be attached to university literary departments and may be honorary members of the Federation. They have more freedom for research and, since 1976, access to inter-university exchanges at the international level. Post-Mao China has witnessed great interest in literary theories other than Marxism. Of these, Freudianism or psychological criticism was the most popular. Articles on deconstruction and structuralism, and so on have also appeared.[16]

Gu Xiang, one of the critics I interviewed in China, pointed out to me that there had always been two strands within the literary field: one represented by Zhou Yang and the other by Feng Xuefeng and Hu Feng. While Zhou Yang, as pointed out earlier, represents the Party's position, Feng and Hu argued against the Party's attempts to set strict Marxist criteria to judge literature.[17] However, it needs to be stressed that 'official criticism' still bases itself on Marxist literary theory although there have been attempts to re-evaluate its heritage. This re-evaluation of Marxist theory is occurring within university departments as well. The two Beijing University critics I interviewed pointed out that criticism of cultural revolutionary literary principles has also implied a re-evaluation of Marxism as such, a point which will be further taken up in the next section. They also pointed out that the degree of freedom varied from association to association and from place to place. Thus, for example, criticism coming out of Beijing was considered orthodox in comparison to that coming out of Shanghai. This is reflected in the greater use made of Western theory by Shanghai critics.[18]

Publishing and readership Publishing houses in China, as in other erstwhile socialist countries, have always been an area strictly controlled by the state. The Publications Administrative Bureau, under the Ministry of Culture, was set up in 1950 and all private publishing houses were abolished by 1956 (Nunn 1966: 14). Publishing houses were asked to specialise on the basis of subjects and areas, rather than compete against each other. Detailed annual planning takes place regarding the number of titles that may be published in each field. Nunn notes, for example, that 'planning reports are required on a formal, quarterly and annual basis from the publishing houses' (1966: 19). The largest publishing and distributing house in China is the Xinhua Publishing house, which has branches and outlets throughout the country. The 1984 China Publishing Year Book (*Zhongguo Chuban Nianjian*) gives the total figures for the number of publishing houses and number of books published for the previous thirty-five years. In 1984 there were 330 publishing houses all over China. Of these 140 were national and 190 regional publishing houses. Apart from this, there were twenty-five publishing houses attached to universities (1984: 2). However, approximately 60 per cent of publishing takes place in major cities like Beijing and Shanghai.

Regarding the total number of books and journals published in China, the figures available are shown in Table 3.1.

Table 3.1 Books and journals published in China, 1950–84

Year	Total	New Titles
1950	64,086	408
1956	25,439	16,751
1966	6,967	4,596
1978	8,941	7,594
1984	29,346	22,007

Source: *Zhongguo Chuban Nianjian* (1984: 4).

However, books do not make up a large per cent of this total. In 1984, for example, only 5,661 books of literature were published. For the same year, only 13.1 per cent of all published journals were to do with literature (*Zhongguo Chuban Nianjian*, 1984: 5).

Although there has been a certain loosening of rules and regulations in the post-Mao era and one notices the systematic increase in publishing since 1978, the government has consistently sought to control publishing outlets and to define policy for publishing. The 1983 *China Publishing*

Year Book carries a special article on the responsibility of publishing houses. As the article says: 'China's publishing industry is completely different from that in capitalist countries. It is led by the Party and its task is to publicize Marxism, Lenininsm and Mao Zedong Thought and popularize science, thereby enriching the cultural life of the people' (1983: 2). Thus, a writer's or critic's freedom is clearly constrained by the strict rules governing the publishing industry.

All publishing houses are dependent on the state-controlled supply of printing paper. Although several small publishing houses have emerged in the post-Mao era, these have concentrated on the publishing of popular or pulp fiction, largely in the form of magazines and periodicals, which include articles on fashion, love stories, humour and so on. In short, they are modelled on the kind of popular journal available in Hong Kong and the West. The government has recently attempted to control these publishing houses in an attempt to control the spread of what is called 'yellow literature' or literature with a pornographic content. Printing or publishing work which is not officially approved by the Party can mean imprisonment, revocation of a licence to print and fines.

Apart from the control exercised over the logisitics of supply and printing, editorial policy for various journals also functions as a mechanism of control. A report of a conference of editors quotes the editor of *Wenyi Bao* (*Literary News*) criticising other editors for publishing too many articles concerned with Western literary theory. This, he felt, was a blind following of fashion (Chao Zhong 1988: 5). Others criticised the commercialisation of art and spoke in favour of effective policies to control wayward tendencies in the publishing world.

A word about the readership in China. Eighty per cent of China's population still resides in the countryside. Among them, the rate of illiteracy is still comparatively high. According to this logic and on the basis of surveys carried out by Chinese researchers in rural areas, peasants view film as the greatest form of entertainment, followed by the traditional and local forms of entertainment such as story-telling and the traditional opera. For example, the most popular journal throughout China in 1983 was the film magazine *Dalin Dianying* published from Shanghai which sold more than 6 million copies (*Zhongguo Chuban Nianjian*, 1983: 157).

Perry Link, in his survey of the reading public of Guangdong city, points out that even though the choice of reading material available to the public is varied and easily available through local lending libraries, reading involves only the 'minority who have the time, inclination, and ability to read anything beyond the occasional sign or poster' (1985:

226). Link, however, points out that, despite this, the very size of urban populations in China ensures that fiction remains comparatively popular. Examining the statistics of a public library he found that 74.95 per cent of the books borrowed were fiction (1985: 227).

Relations between the various groups On the basis of the above, a fairly clear picture emerges of the overall restrictions under which literary production in China operates.

The main issue which determines the relationship between the different members of the Writers' Federation is the policy of the Party. In the final instance, it uses the power at its disposal to control all aspects of the field. This power is based on its capacity to define and limit the object of literature and to control the engagement that individuals can have with it. Its power, in this sense, is essentially coercive. However, one thing that detracts from the monolithic image of Party control is the existence of informal networks of relationships based on familial or class lines. It is here that Bourdieu's notion of symbolic capital is important. He has convincingly demonstrated that informal channels or the formation of elites and cliques are central to the functioning of all forms of organisations. These are channels based on kinship ties, educational elites from the same university and, of course, political patronage. On the whole, these informal networks balance the changes that occur due to Party policy, ensuring a degree of continuity. On the other hand, if the fate of a political leader changes within the higher echelons of the Party, those under his patronage may also suffer adverse consequences.

Although there have always been writers and critics who have questioned this literary control, they have paid a heavy price for their choice (Goldman: 1971). The period of what is largely referred to as post-Mao China until the suppression of the student movement in June 1989 did exhibit a loosening of state control and can be seen as one of those periods in communist China's history where writers were able to use the space provided for new ways of expression and for exploring new subjects. The questioning of Party policy on social and political issues, which was encouraged by the senior Party leadership, also paved the way for writers and artists to raise problems with the organisation and political control of the literary field in China.

Literature in the post-Mao Era 1976–88: struggle with orthodoxy

The post-Mao period in China is the specific background against which discourse on women writers emerged. It has been a period of dramatic policy changes and shifts in perspective. This has affected not only the economic and political organisation of China but also its arts and literature. Among western scholars of Chinese literature, post-Mao China has been seen as a period of liberalisation and experimentation in both form and content. Among Chinese intellectuals and writers and artists, there has also been a sense of expectancy and excitement. This is reflected both in the kinds of fiction which started appearing in post-Mao China and in the reassessment of earlier literary theory and debates on the basic character of literature and its role and function in society. Chinese critics have analysed the history of post-1949 Chinese literature and divided it into three stages. The first stage spans the period before the Cultural Revolution; the second stage covers the ten years of the Cultural Revolution; and the third stage covers the period since the eleventh Party Congress of 1978 (Chen Huangmei [ed.] 1981).

The literary policies of the Cultural Revolution and the left line (*zuo de yingxiang*) came under sharp attack from writers, critics and Party ideologues, and the official Party policy on literature was once again declared to be that of 'letting a hundred flowers bloom and a hundred schools of thought contend' (*Baihua qifang*). This trend of liberalisation was further emphasised during the fourth Congress of Writers and Artists held in October–November 1979.

During the conference writer after writer spoke out in favour of greater liberalisation of the arts and literature. This message was put forward by Zhou Yang, then the Vice Chairman of the Writers Federation. It reflects the great change both in Zhou Yang's own position and in Chinese art and literature in general. After giving a reading of the history of Chinese literature in the last thirty years, Zhou Yang went on to stress: 'We must not regard Marxism–Leninism–Mao Zedong Thought as unchangeable dogma but as a guide to action. We face many new circumstances and new problems unknown to the writers of Marxist classics, Comrade Mao Zedong included' (Duke, 1985: 35).

This very open questioning of Party standards and principles would have been impossible during the life of Mao. At the theoretical level, a major forum was held in Beijing in 1982. Organised by the All China Federation of Literary and Art Circles and the Literary Research Institute of the Chinese Social Science Academy, the symposium on Mao Zedong Literary Thought attempted to formulate a new perspective on literary theory and to reassess the significance of Mao's Yenan talks and other writings on literature in the light of current changes.

This theoretical questioning of old clichés and the attempt by the Party to set a new direction for literature and art were accompanied by the increased publication of stories that developed a critique of Chinese society at several levels. The first few years after 1976 saw a huge rise in the type of fiction which came to be dubbed *Shanghen Wenxue* (Scar Literature). This was essentially a literature of exposure directed against the excesses of the Cultural Revolution (Gallick 1982).[19]

Goldblatt (ed.) (1982) points out that the literature and art of the period 1979–80 soon went beyond being simply a critique of the Cultural Revolution and the Gang of Four, and writers started to focus on the more deep-seated problems of socialism. Favourite themes of this period were a critique of bureaucratism and corruption. Duke calls this the Neo-realistic critique and he sees it as stemming from that element among Chinese intellectuals which has always considered itself entrusted with a mission and a 'serious concern for society and principled demand for social justice' (Duke 1985: 96).

In fact, it has been pointed out that this is the main dilemma confronting the writer in China under socialism. For, if the writer adheres to her/his conscience and exposes the problems of life under socialism, she/he runs great personal risks. Even more than fiction, the genre of *Baogao Wenxue* (Reportage Literature) has focused on the darker side of life in socialist China.[20]

At the stylistic level, too, there have been major changes. The aspect most highlighted as being new to China is the emergence of Obscure or Foggy Poetry (*Menglong Shi*), the use of the 'stream of consciousness' and the attempt to explore the psychology of characters. As Leo Ou-Fan Lee says: 'after the fall of the Gang of Four, a number of writers – both the middle-aged generation of the newly rehabilitated "Rightists" and a younger generation of "non-official writers" in their twenties and thirties – are beginning to pay renewed attention to style' (1985: 161). Although criticism and the literary establishment allowed the publication of such works, the official Party focus by the end of 1980–81 was already turning towards re-emphasising the role played by literature in positively influencing society. Articles started appearing which spoke of the way literature could serve the programme of the Four Modernisations initiated under Deng Xiaoping.

The 1980s saw two major campaigns which focused directly on the question of liberalisation in the arts and literature and attempted to reinstitute Party control over literature. These campaigns were initiated by the propaganda department, with its major theorists such as Deng Liqun and Hu Qiomu, and were intended to get rid of spiritual pollution and other harmful cultural phenomena that had emerged in China. Such trends in literature were put down to the influence of bourgeois liberalism and were followed by critical articles in all the ideological magazines. As an influential *Guangming Ribao* (*Guangming Daily*) article states: 'In recent years, there has emerged the theory of socialist alienation which is an erroneous philosophical and social trend' (16 December 1983). Such a perspective is also stressed by other Chinese critics. Liu Jianjun points out that art and literature should reflect the spirit of their times. Going on to explain he says: 'The spirit of a time means representing its historical advancement ... the spirit of my country's present time is to reconstruct, reform and build' (1984: 4).

Another issue at stake was the use of 'humanism' as a philosophical criterion for the purposes of literary creation and analysis. The debate was sparked off by the publication of Bai Hua's *Kulian* (*Bitter Love*); Dai Houying's *Ren a Ren* (*People Ah! People*) was attacked on similar grounds (see Duke 1985). Both these books were criticised for blurring the issue of class consciousness and for painting entirely negative pictures of China's revolutionary history (G. Yang 1985: 513). The criticism of the depiction of alienation and humanism in literature, along with the criticism of Obscure Poetry, heralded the start of a general ideological tightening up in the field of literature and art which became even tighter after the student movement of 1989.

Although writers have experimented with form and content, literary criticism in China remains didactic in nature, still adhering to the theory of Marxist literary criticism. Because the official Party line continues to see literature as a reflection of society and of the class struggle in society, literary criticism retains its capacity to control writers for their political standpoint. At an analytical level, one is forced to agree with Fang Zhenwang when he says that judging all artistic work to see whether it is politically acceptable means that problems in criticism inevitably arise (1988: 715).

The criticism of women writers has to be understood within this context of socialist literary criticism. In the rest of this chapter, after a short historical introduction, I shall examine the basis on which similarities are being drawn between women writers. For the sake of clarity, the main arguments being offered by Chinese critics have been placed into two groups: those that address the question of the content of women's writings, and those that attempt to assess the literary style of women writers.

Nüxing Wenxue or the discourse on women's writing

Post-Mao Chinese literature is also significant for the emergence of a number of women writers whose works have attracted critical acclaim both within and outside China. The very term, 'women's literature' (*nüxing wenxue*) has excited lively debates in literary magazines and journals in China. The criticism of specific women writers has also increased significantly. It is in the definitions and analysis of women's writing that we can see the discursive workings of orthodox gender discourse. In China, coupled with the strong limits within which the literary field as a whole operates, the way a discourse on women's writing is articulated becomes an important indicator of how the Party and its institutions would like to control the subject.

Historical Background In classical China, women writers were never considered a serious part of the established literary circles. Except for a few anthologies and poems by women which received critical appreciation, the poems written by women were more popular in tea-houses and with professional story-tellers (Prusek 1974). In fact, in classical China, the only woman writer who achieved a degree of critical acclaim and recognition was Li Qingzhao (1084–c.1151). She is said to have been an extremely versatile writer who had mastered the techniques of various literary forms. The limited participation by women in the field of literature is not surprising if we keep in mind the position of women and the discourse on gender relations which existed in traditional China. However, women, especially of the upper classes, often had access to education and were cultivated in the appreciation of poetry. Widmer points out that in seventeenth-century China, upper-class women participated in literary clubs (1989: 1).

The short history of modern women writers in China can be divided into three stages. The first voice to be heard was that of Qiu Qin (1879–1907). Also regarded as China's first feminist and woman political activist, Qiu Qin wrote revolutionary and political poems, besides writing about her own life. Women writers first appeared as a group during the years directly following the May Fourth Movement (1919). This was mainly because women had access to education during this period but also because of an influx of new ideas about the position of women in society. Women had become a subject of discourse on which people took positions and articulated opinions. Concern about the sufferings of women was a major theme in the literature of this period.

The major women writers of this period, influenced by the radical spirit of the May Fourth Movement and the emerging influence of communism, were, among others, Ding Ling, Xiao Hong, Cao Ming, Chen Xuezhao, Li Pozhen and Feng Zi. Their works dealt essentially with the emotional changes that were occurring in the lives of women; the conflict faced by women raised within a traditional ideological mould to be dependent upon the male members of their family; and the new demands and aspirations being voiced by the educated youth of both sexes. According to Feuerwerker, one condition which made this possible was the questioning of old literary techniques and the jettisoning of the classical language of literature led by veterans such as Chen Duxiu and Hu Shi (Feuerwerker 1975). They not only portrayed the aspirations and demands of the new, educated Chinese urban women, but also exposed the suffering and exploitation of women bound by traditional ideological and social structures.

The representatives of this period are generally considered to be Xiao Hong and Ding Ling. Goldblatt, who has translated some of Xiao Hong's work into English, says of her work: 'In thematic terms, Xiao Hong generally deals with the plight of women from the deprived classes; her stories are almost invariably tragic and do not offer much hope for change' (Goldblatt 1982: 2). Xiao Hong's work focuses on women as the victims of an oppressive and unjust society. Hers is a literature of exposure designed to move people to take action.

Ding Ling (1908–1995), on the other hand, has always featured strong and independent women characters, especially in her stories situated in pre-liberation China. She became especially famous for her story 'The Diary of Miss Sophie' ('*Shafei nüshi de riji*'). Written in 1928 and located in Beijing, it describes the sexual desire and love of a young girl. The explicit description of female sexual desire caused a stir even among the liberated avant-garde of Shanghai. She also gained a measure of success in 1950 when she won the coveted Stalin Prize for her depiction of land-reform in *The Sun Shines on the Sangan River* (*Taiyang Zhaozai Sangan Heshang*). Feuerwerker, in her excellent book on Ding Ling, points out that the political constraints on literature in post-1949 China ensured that Ding Ling's literary output was not as prolific as in her earlier period (Feuerwerker 1982). She became the victim of the politics of China, paying for her outspokenness and independent opinions. In 1957 she was branded a rightist and spent the next twenty years in remote rural areas, where she was effectively banned from writing until her rehabilitation in 1976.

At the time of the founding of the All China Writers' Federation in 1949, thirteen women were members. This number rose to fifty-six in 1966 (Wei Junyi 1986: 9). According to the *Beijing Review*, in 1986, out of 1,000 members of the Federation 235 were women. (p. 18). Although a number of women writers appeared in the first seventeen years after the establishment of the People's Republic of China, their influence in terms of creativity and quality was far less than that of the pre-liberation writers. This can be partly attributed to the uncertain political and ideological restraints under which writers were expected to work.

During the 1950s and 1960s, the more prominent women writers were Yang Mo, Zong Pu and Ru Zhijuan, the latter two having regained popularity since the fall of the Gang of Four. Yang Mo became famous with her novel published in 1958, *Song of Youth* (*Qingchun Zhege*). Set against the backdrop of the student movement of the early 1930s, the novel traces the life of its female protagonist and shows her gradual politicisation and identification with the left movement in China. The book is well written and deals with a complex theme sensitively. It also shows a woman taking a radical step because she chooses to risk her secure life with her husband and venture into the uncertainties of political life. Nevertheless, her independent choices are dictated by her political cause.

Zong Pu focused on a similar theme in her short story, 'Red Beans' (*'Hongdou'*) (1961). It features as its protagonist a young university student who is in love with the son of a factory owner. It traces her gradual politicisation under the influence of a girlfriend who is a member of the Youth League. In the end she refuses to marry her boyfriend and leave the country, choosing instead to stay behind and serve the cause of the revolution. Zong Pu was dubbed a rightist during the Cultural Revolution for this story because she chose to focus on a love story rather than on the issues of class struggle.

Ru Zhijuan became famous in 1958 for her story 'Lilies' (*'Bai Hehua'*) which describes the work of a young woman as an army nurse during the civil war in China.

The third, and most recent, group of women writers in China emerged after the fall of the Gang of Four (1976). Influenced by the radical upsurge of feeling opposing the Cultural Revolution, this new group of women began to explore the reality of 'being women' in the China of the 1970s and 1980s. Most of them are young and started writing only after the Cultural Revolution. A survey of the backgrounds of 100 women writers, based on the bibliographical data provided in *100 Women Writers* (*Yibai nü zuojia*), shows that more than 60 per cent of these writers were born in the 1950s and are members of the Writers' Federation. The rest are attached to various literary magazines or artists' associations. Not surprisingly, they are also largely graduates from Chinese language or literature departments. Li Xiaojiang points out that women writers of the post-Mao period are essentially intellectual women and can be divided into two groups. The first are those who graduated before the Cultural Revolution but could not write due to the political situation; this is the generation born in the 1950s. The second group consists of the younger generation or those who were students during the Cultural Revolution and went to the countryside (Li Xiaojiang 1988: 283).

An initial survey points to eleven women whose work is being analysed and discussed as examples of women's literature. These writers were either previously considered unimportant or have recently emerged as writers for the first time. Among the former are Ru Zhijuan and Zong Pu. The new writers are Zhang Jie, Shen Rong, Zhang Kangkang, Zhang Xinxin, Dai Houying, Dai Qing, Wang Anyi, Shu Ting and Tie Ning.[21]

Though this criterion – the number of articles dealing with their works – cannot be taken as a judgement on 'good' writers, since the more controversial writers such as Yu Luojin are simply ignored in most cases, it is helpful in raising some questions about the yardstick used for assessing the works of women writers in China. What are considered to be the main characteristics of women's literature? What types of works are being upheld as positive or negative? What is the purpose and impact of such specific criticism? By taking specific examples, the appropriateness of Chinese literary categories can be assessed along with a consideration of why a particular text is considered negative or positive.

The subject matter of women's literature Despite enormous differences between the works of women writers, several Chinese critics have attempted to study women writers as a specific group. One similarity easily distinguished in the works of women writers is their choice of subject matter, which is seen to centre around family, love, marriage, the emotional life of individual characters and the ordinary little things of daily life. Wu Daiying, a well-known critic of women's writing, sums up their work by saying that it deals with 'small subjects, small people and small things' ('*xiao ticai, xiao renwu, xiao shijian*') (1985: 13). She demonstrates her point by citing as examples Ru Zhijuan's 'Family Affairs' ('*Jiating Shi*'), Zhang Jie's 'Love Should not be Forgotten' ('*Aishi puneng wangji de*'), and Chen Rong's At Middle Age (*Rendao Zhongnian*). All these stories have women as the central character and deal with topics that are intimately linked to the lives of women, such as love, family life and the conflict between family and career.

This aspect is also highlighted by other critics. As Xie Wangxin puts it: 'One of the most significant contributions of women writers today has been their serious perusal of the theme of love, the logical and historical exploration of this popular sentiment' (Xie Wangxin 1985: 77). Zhang Jie is seen as a forerunner of this exploration with her 'Love Should not be Forgotten', as is Zhang Kangkang with her 'The Rights of Love' ('*Ai de quanli*'). Xie Wangxin goes on to point out the different motifs of love stories written by women. Lu Xinger in her 'Beautiful

Structure' ('*Meili de Jieguo*') and 'Married Life' ('*Jiehun Shenghuo*') says that love, not marriage, is the most sacred of all bonds, and it is precisely love which becomes a 'beautiful structure' between two people. Shen Rong, in her story 'Wrong, Wrong Wrong' ('*Cuo Cuo Cuo*'), opposes idealism in love and tries to show that for love to be successful it must correspond to China's reality. Wang Anyi searches for 'pure love', whereas Zhang Kangkang in her 'Northern Lights' ('*Beiji guang*') opposes the commoditisation of love. Xie Wangxin ends his discussion by saying: 'These women writers try to show the desires of Chinese women who want equality and independence in feelings, careers and love' (1985: 80).

A similar reading of the overall content of women's writings is made by Cheng Wenzhao when he examines the 'contemporary consciousness' (*shidai yishi*) of women writers. He sees women's writing as an expression of their historically-determined consciousness and therefore as an expression of their material position in society. It is on this basis that he sees women's fiction as concerned with issues of love and marriage (Cheng Weuzhao 1987: 120). Sun Shaoxian makes a similar point when he relates the evolution of the theme of marriage in women's literature to the way in which the custom as such has changed in society. He points out that women's discussion of this subject has to be linked to their demands for 'free marriages' and that throughout history this has always been an important demand of the women's movement (Sun Shaoxian 1986: 95).

As well as love and marriage, women writers are said to take youth as one of their subjects. As Shen Ying says: 'They show particular sensitivity in dealing with the lives of youth' (1984: 22). The stories of Zhang Kangkang, such as 'Tower' ('*Ta*') lend themselves to this reading. It describes the confrontation of youth with the aftermath of their Cultural Revolution experience.

It is also acknowledged that some women writers are attempting to deal with broader, more socially related topics, but they are considered as being better equipped to deal with 'smaller themes'. Wu Daiying says that Zhang Jie's 'Heavy Wings' ('*Chenzhong de Zhibang*'), which deals with China's recent economic reforms, is 'not as good or strong as her other writings such as 'Love Should not be Forgotten' (Wu Daiying 1985: 15). Lu Wencai also points out: 'Women's literature has been identified as almost synonymous with a literature concerned with marriage problems and a search for the right man [*hunyin wenti xunzhao nanren*]' (1989: 157). While this is seen as inevitable given the material position of women, it is also cited as the cause of their inability to break into the tradition of 'great literature' (Yi Qing, 1987). Ren Yiwu expresses a similar sentiment when he says: 'In general one can say that men's mentality has made the wider issues such as man's relationship to nature, to reality, to history the concern of male writers; women's mentality has made women writers concern themselves with daily life, small details, friendship, love, family, things that interest women' (Ren Yiwu 1988: 116).

Though critics such as the above reflect a traditional bias in limiting discussions on love and marriage by defending them as 'narrow subjects', Wu Daiying contradicts this claim. She cites the example of Shen Rong's *At Middle Age*, which, though 'small', depicts the experience of a whole generation of intellectuals.

While the scope of women's writings is seen as narrow and limited by a number of critics and therefore to be dismissed, other critics tend to be patronising and argue that women's preoccupation with topics such as love and marriage is inevitable, since this represents the reality of their experience (Zhang Weian 1982). Chen Huifen points out that one has to recognise the effect of patriarchal society (*nanxing zhuantong*) on women themselves: they are unable to escape the limits of its customs and its demands. On the other hand, we must support their efforts to move beyond the narrow confines of their lives (1987: 14).

There are some voices defending women's writings against charges of narrowness. Shen Ying puts it aptly when she says: 'One should not assume, as some colleagues do, that women writers deal only with family tales. They have also described the foundation of society and the human subjectivity with great sensitivity' (Shen Ying 1984: 24). In terms of content, women writers are also seen as ideal commentators on the experiences of the women's movement in China. Official criticism has attempted to place the work of women writers within the history of the Chinese women's movement and socialist construction. The changes in the images of women presented in the writings of women since the May Fourth period are seen as a chronicle of the women's movement in China. As Wang Youjin says: 'The understanding of and discussions regarding the women's movement in China and its expression in literature has been an important contribution of women writers' (1985: 17–18).

The issues raised by women writers are thus seen as a reflection of their reality. Further, the increase in the number of women writers is seen as related to the level of their historical and cultural development (Jin Zhiyu 1986: 26). Ma Naru makes a similar reading of the changes in the three generations of women writers. She sees the focus of women writers changing from the May Fourth Movement to today. During the May Fourth, she points out, the focus was on women's self-realisation and on young intellectual female protagonists who confronted traditional feudal values. The period from the revolution in 1949 till the death of Mao, she sees as one where all writers, irrespective of sex, focused on social problems and on external issues. The post-Mao period is again characterised as one where women writers are returning to a focus on issues of self-realisation (Ma Naru 1987: 92).

Yan Ping makes a similar distinction between three periods of women's writings. He distinguishes between women writers of the May Fourth; women writing from 1940 to 1970; and women writing in the post-Mao period (1989: 16). In the first period women writers are seen as representing women's desire for love as mothers and wives; in the second period, they concern themselves with how they can serve the nation and be socially productive; in the final stage they are concerned with how to make their personal and private lives compatible with their social roles (Yan Ping 1989: 23). Other critics also see the basic concern of women writers as being a desire to 'discover one self' (*renshi ziji*) (Chen Huifen 1987: 8).

The partial role of women writers of the pre-liberation period was to promote examples of what women in China could become or do. Stories depicted both the exploitation of women and the positive changes they would experience once they were willing to throw in their lot with the socialist revolution. After liberation, this official role of writers became even more pronounced. Writers were expected to create positive heroes who could be emulated in real life. Women writers and images of women in literature, were likewise, supposed to inspire women to accept new role models (Hsia 1963).

Tsai Mei-hsi points out that if a single theme can be discerned throughout the fiction which deals with women before 1978, it is that women characters, depending on their class background, are all ardent supporters of the revolution and the leadership of the Party. She points out how women as revolutionary mothers and as revolutionaries in their own right were supposed to represent the positive characters in fiction (Tsai Mei-hsi 1975: 210).

The rise of women writers today is seen as reflecting the economic, political and spiritual gains of socialism (Yu Yan 1985). Though the position of women in China has changed significantly for the better since 1949, the expectations that women writers will show the way to their less 'conscious' sisters still persists. Xie Wangxin points out: 'Though women have been provided with constitutional guarantees, some of them remain ideologically backward, the main task of the women's movement thus remains consciousness raising' (Xie Wangxin 1985: 86).

We have already noted how love, marriage and related issues are seen as natural themes for women and how the demand for changes being made within these social structures is considered as positive. As long as women do not deviate from their traditional role of nurturing and loving and continue to search for this elusive love and beauty in their prose and poetry, reflecting their beautiful spirits in beautiful language, there is little negative criticism apart from the claim that their subject matter is not deep enough.

However, negative criticism appears when more radical images of women are presented. This criticism is directed against a specific type of female character, the woman as virago (*nüxing xionghua*), and against western-style feminism (*xifang nüxingzhuyi*) (Hai Ronghua 1989). Lu Wencai points out: 'several critics have expressed apprehension at the appearance of female characters in the women's fiction of this period who are viragoes or tough and strong women' (1989: 159). Women who possess *xionghua* go against the normal expectations of womanhood in China, and thereby form an heterodoxy. Zhang Qing represents this orthodox perspective in his analysis of *nüxing xionghua*. He points out that 'masculinisation' (*xionghua*) is most visible in the women characters of certain writers: 'Masculinised women [*xnüxing xionghua*] are those characters who contradict the ideas we have had for centuries of women as soft and emotional, pliable and dependent, patient ... all the things that make women beautiful' (Zhang Qing 1986: 40).

Thus, women characters who are depicted as going against female nature are castigated and held up as negative examples. In this aspect, literary criticism continues to follow the tradition of outlining 'good' and 'bad' characters. Dai Jianping points out that two types of women characters can be traced in women's writing from the May Fourth Movement onwards: one is those who are in the phase of self-realisation (*ziwo guannian*) and see liberation as being part of this; the other is those who see women's liberation as being tied to social liberation (Dai Jianping 1987: 42). This article takes the Marxist perspective in critic-ising women characters who aim only at self-realisation.

This use of traditional moral criteria to judge the content of women's fiction is most glaringly obvious in the case of Yu Luojin's *A Winter's Fairy Tale* (*Yige dongtian de tonghua*) (1978). The novel contains a woman character who is twice divorced and has a love affair with a senior Party cadre. She is described as immoral, individualistic and as contravening the spirit of socialism.[22] Thus, one notices that an orthodox discourse on gender relations is used as the basis for classifying the content of women's writings. The way women are supposed to live their lives, and the ideas associated with the correct position of women in China, act as strong determinants of the way the content of women's writing is analysed. A similar use of orthodox discourse can be noticed in the way a female writing style is identified.

Femininity and female writing   The content or the specific focus and scope of women writers is not the only criterion used to distinguish male from female writing. Women's writing is also considered distinctive on the basis of its creative and artistic style. The works are considered new and beautiful and replete with poetic metaphors and subjective imagination. One critic says of women writers: 'Their works are not merely poetry, but like a beautiful and lively tune, with a hint of sadness – a dream-like tune' (Li Ziyun 1987a: 15).

Veteran writer Cao Ming makes a similar comment when she says of Zhang Jie's story 'Children of the Forest' ('*Cong shulin li lai de haizi*'): 'The forest, the mist, is dream-like, ethereal' (Wu Daiying 1985: 15). Zong Pu's work excites the same sort of comment from different critics, who liken her descriptions to paintings. Wang Anyi is also seen as having this style. Shen Ying says: 'Her character Wen Wen [a young girl in the story 'Gentle Drizzle' ('*Yu shasha*')], comes through to us through the sound of dropping water, revealing the purity of the spirit of youth which still hasn't been destroyed (1984: 37). This search for beauty seems to be read as an escape from the harsh reality of the lives of women.

Wang Fuxiang, another critic, accepts the criterion of women's more frequent use of poetic metaphor to distinguish them from male writers. He says: 'Women's literature uses more beautiful metaphors and exhibits a certain delicacy in the choice of words' (1984: 16). An article in the *Guangming Daily* (7 November 1989) says the same thing when talking about the works of Shen Rong, Zong Pu, Zhang Kangkang and Zhang Xinxin. Where as Shen Rong's writing is described as sensitive (*ming-gan*), Zong Pu's is refined, cultured (*wenya*) and delicate.

Other critics have pointed to the stylistic breaks with traditional literature which characterise the works of women writers, especially the use of stream of consciousness and a focus on the psychology of the protagonists. Both extravagant praise and criticism have surrounded the discussion of these facets, from statements such as, 'They are breaking down traditions in much the same way as our earlier writers Lu Xun, Guo Muoruo' (Xie Wangxin 1985: 21), to, 'Stream of Consciousness and other psychological explorations of women's mind are not necessarily a new female realism and nor should they be praised as such' (Wang Fuxiang 1984: 16).

Zhang Kangkang, Zhang Xinxin and Zhang Jie are generally considered to be the leading female exponents of the stream of consciousness style (*yishi liu*). The fact that women use this style of expression more often than men leads one critic to call it 'female realism' (*nüxing xianshi zhuyi*) (Wu Daiying 1984: 39). Another critic says of Zhang Xinxin's style: 'She follows the pattern of associations that arise unbidden to the surface ... it is like a box within a box, related yet unrelated' (Dan Zhen 1985: 122). Zhang Jie's style is seen to contain a mixture of stream of consciousness and romanticism in the stories published before 1980, and to constitute a form of critical realism in the stories published after 1980. (Xu Ping 1988).

In dealing with realistic motifs and character presentation (an important critical and value judgement in the tradition of Chinese socialist realist criticism), women writers are generally considered to be lagging behind men (Xie Wangxin 1985: 83). Among all the women writers, only Shen Rong is praised for her ability to handle themes which depict overall reality, not just women's subjectivity and position. Because of this, some critics say: 'In her outlook of life and breadth of vision, she possesses the characteristics of male writers' (Xie Wangxin 1985: 82). Her story *At Middle Age* is praised for its realistic technique and context rather than for romantic idealism. She is also said to combine socialist realism with the technique of modern short stories. In the final analysis she is seen as continuing in the tradition of Chinese literature since the May Fourth period, a combination of classical Chinese literature, western models and proletarian writing (Zhang Weian 1982: 18).

Another distinctive aspect of women's writings is considered to be their subjectivity (Xu Ping 1988). Women writers of the 1930s and 1940s, from Ding Ling to contemporary women writers, have all been seen as writing essentially in the subjective style. Prusek points out the dominance of the subjective style of narrative during the formative period of modern Chinese literature: 'There can be no question that subjectivism and individualism, joined with pessimism and a feeling for the tragedy of life ... are the most characteristic qualities of Chinese literature from the May Fourth Movement of 1919 onwards' (1974: 13).

The subjective tradition is a kind of narrative which proceeds from personal experience and reproduces merely a partial aspect of reality, for example in the form of diaries as in Ding Ling's 'The Diary of Miss Sophie'. Jin Zhiyu also identifies subjectivity as being present in the works of women writers from the West (1986: 27).

The creative force behind the women writers today also includes their emotionalism and their belief in the superiority of feelings over reason (*Qingsheng yuli*). Wang Xiaoying is quoted by Wu Daiying supporting this: 'I feel emotions are far more honest than reason so I always follow the flow of my feelings' (Wu Daiying 1985: 16)

Even when specific differences among women writers are acknowledged, their subjectivity is seen to have much common ground. Wu Daiying says: 'Their inner sensitivity and its specific artistic form can be attributed to women's specific psychological build-up' (1985: 13). The focus of women's writings is seen as emotion; the feelings and reactions of the individual characters in their relation to the world. One critic sums this up: 'Over all we can say that emotions are the most important factor in their art. All works of art reveal some emotions but in the works of women this emotionality is more pronounced' (Cheng Wenzhao 1987: 121).

This focus on emotion and beauty is seen not only as the source of women's creativity, it is also seen as the chief source of their popularity. Coming out of the Cultural Revolution, these works are seen to replenish people's emotions and to help them achieve a balance. They are also seen as part of the overall softening (*ruanhua*) visible in recent literature (Huang Mei 1989). Exhausted by a constant and deadening exposure to the erstwhile 'political literature', coupled with the intense emotional experiences of the Cultural Revolution, a focus on feeling was bound to be popular. 'Women writers have opened up a beautiful new world for us and helped to purify people's hearts,' sums up Li Ziyun (1987b: 15). Their work, apparently, moves people to tears. Shen Ying says: 'Most of them possess what the French humanists have called women's natural beauty, and have tried to show ways of making this life more sweet, tender and worth believing in' (1984: 21).

This predominance of emotionalism in women's writings is seen as natural and understandable, but at the same time it is also the main weapon used to denigrate their work. Women are seen as creatures of sentiment. As Wu Daiying says: 'In life it has been proven that whether women are daughters, mothers or wives, their love is stronger than men. This imbues their writings with feelings. But this emphasis on feeling leads them to individualism and does not allow their context to be deep enough' (Wu Daiying 1985: 15). Such a perspective is not new and certainly not new to China. Not surprisingly, the pronouncements of Chinese critics can be seen as belonging to what Margaret Atwood calls the 'Quiller Couch syndrome' in western literary discourse: 'This phrase refers to the turn of the century essay by Quiller Couch, defining "masculine" and "feminine" styles in writing. The "masculine" style is of course bold, forceful, clear, vigorous etc; the "feminine" style is vague, weak and tremulous' (Atwood 1986: 76).

Thus, we see that Chinese literary criticism, in its attempt to group women writers together, emphasises certain features of their work. Underlying this is a wider discourse on gender. The next section argues that these general features are grounded in a specific understanding of women's nature whether as determined by biology or by their material conditions.

The deployment of a discourse on female nature From a general review of what constitutes the content and style of women's literature, it is not hard to see that the conceptual basis for reading specific aspects of femininity in women's writing in China centres round discussions of the essential female nature, a discourse which also underpins the discourse on gender in society as a whole. Whether it is women's quest for beauty or their emotionalism, both are explained by the biological and psychological differences between the sexes. Wu Daiying's article carries the most detailed discussion on this topic: 'Because women are psychologically and physiologically different from men, they are different in their outlook and responses to society. On such a basis we can divide literature into male and female' (1985: 13). She quotes a diverse set of authorities, both Chinese and western, to support her claim. She draws attention to studies in dream analysis by western psychoanalyists such as Freud, which say that men and women dream differently, and use language differently. Accordingly, the 'space' of women's dreams is smaller. Women's dreams take place generally in a familiar environment, whereas men's dreams occur in much more varied settings (Wu Daiying 1985: 14). Emotionality is seen as a natural facet of women's make-up. Sarah Ellis, Jung and even Hegel are quoted to show that strongest emotions are expressed by women. Such arguments are also given in support of her thesis that women are more emotional and sensitive. As she says: 'Men love to fight, are more outgoing, women are softer, and more oriented towards their feelings' (Wu Daiying 1985: 16).

Wu Daiying sees this difference not only as natural but also as essential, for, without it, 'women would not be women'. She quotes Li Tachao and Lu Xun as her Chinese authorities who at one time or another commented on the difference between the sexes; especially Li Dachao who says: 'men have autocratic characters which need to be balanced with women's tranquil beauty and emotions, to preserve the order of nature' (Wu Daiying 1985: 14).

Ren Yiwu's article also makes the same assumptions. He points out that 'from the biological and psychological point of view we know that women as a group have a specific consciousness [*yishi*]'. This he goes on to describe as sentimental, soft and tender. As he says: 'Under the pen of women writers, women's sensitivity, tenderness and latent sentiments come alive … in the depiction of the characters, we feel as if we are entering the minds of women' (Ren Yiwu 1988: 115).

Chen Huifen makes the same point about women's nature and cites psychological evidence which states that biology determines women's psychology. Thus, women are good at some things and men at others. This link between physiology and psychology is also seen to determine women's use of language (Chen Huifen 1987: 9).

Other critics, such as Guo Xiaodong, do not use biology to argue about the specific nature of women. Instead they see this nature as related to material developments in society. Speaking of the phenomenon of 'masculinised women' (*nanxinghua de nüxing*), he says these are women who have achieved equal status with men in terms of education and social prestige but they are caught in a difficult situation for they experience a loss at the emotional level (Guo Xiaodong 1988: 15).

The argument of essential femaleness is also at work here; women's problems occur because they enter a male world. Thus, the changing character of women is a result of social changes in their roles. Zhao Fusheng, writing on the same subject, believes this is a problem specific to intellectual women who are no longer satisfied with traditional relationships with men. He points out that they are single women and often lonely (Zhao Fusheng 1986: 4–5). As he puts it: 'A feeling of loneliness is the inevitable result of women who in their road towards liberation break down traditions, but still retain a certain nostalgia for traditional attachments because they are unable to find anything new' (Zhao Fusheng 1986: 11).

Strong women characters in the stories of Zhang Jie and Zhang Xinxin are criticised for going against nature, among other things. Thus, these women characters, essentially described as lonely, intellectual women, are to be pitied not emulated. They are not necessarily representative of womanhood; rather they are 'masculinised' women.

Although the majority of critics have confined themselves to this rather limited essentialist perspective, in recent years (1986–87) there have been literary critics who have attempted to criticise this functional division into male and female literature. In the past few years, the discussion of women's literature has been influenced by feminist literary theory from the West and serious research is being carried out within universities on the topic.

The articles by Kung Haili (1986) and Kang Zhengguo (1988) are a case in point. Kung Haili's article introduces certain concepts of western feminist literary theory such as the ideas of Virginia Woolf. It gives a short history of the western women's movement and reviews the ideas developed by Kate Millet in her book *Sexual Politics* (1971), pointing out how she develops the use of gender as a category for analysing fiction. However, the author makes no attempt to use any of these concepts to analyse women's literature in China. Kang Zhengguo's article uses the work of Toril Moi to introduce prominent American feminist literary critics such as Elaine Showalter (1977; 1985), Cheri Register (1980) and Mary Jacobus (ed.) (1979). It is essentially a review of western theories rather than an argument in favour of using these theories to read women writers in China. Lin Shuming's article 'Feminist Criticism in China Today' (1990), is more radical in this aspect. She notes the growth and influence of feminist literary criticism and points out that 'although there are several writers and critics who do not like to call themselves feminist writers or critics, nevertheless, today we find that it is a major trend within literary criticism' (Lin Shuming 1990: 36–7). She sees the influence of feminism in the preoccupation of women writers and critics with a search for discovering the essence of 'woman'. As she puts it: 'society has men and women but not "woman", it is this search for "woman" that makes feminist criticism' (1990: 37). She points out how, in China as in the rest of the world, the category 'human' (ren) denotes men (1990: 37). Thus, a focus on women is the beginning of a feminist criticism. Courses are also being taught in Comparative Literature departments at major universities such as Shanghai and Beijing.[23]

Li Ziyun is another prominent literary critic who has attempted to point out how certain women writers manage to go beyond what is being described by literary discourse as women's literature. She takes the examples of Zong Pu, Shen Rong and Zhang Jie to show that their works go beyond those which depict only female consciousness (*nüxing yishi*). She feels that a distinction needs to be made between the way in which the term women's literature is used in present-day China and the way it is used in the West. As she says:

> I want to stress here that the use of the term *nüxing wenxue* [women's litera-ture] is different in China than in the West. The Western term stresses that we must analyse women's history by taking as our point of departure women's self-consciousness and those emotions which are specific to women. In China, the women's literature I speak of describes how material and ideological causes determine women's subordination. (Li Ziyun 1987b: 13)

Elsewhere Li Ziyun points out that one of the main concerns of women writers has been their focus on the problems that arise between a couple when they both want to pursue careers. She says this desire on the part of a woman is seen as going against tradition and reflects the unchanged attitudes regarding women and their social position (1987a: 8). On the one hand, her article grounds itself in a Marxist perspective by stressing the material and ideological causes of women's subordination; on the other hand, it uses this perspective to make a relevant critique of essentialism. It is a critique of attempts to see women's writing as limited because of their 'feminine natures'.

However, even though Li Ziyun argues that certain women writers are able to move beyond the limitations of their gender, she still accepts the basic argument that, in general, women's writing is influenced by their gender. A good woman writer, according to her, is one who is able to disassociate herself from the historical limitations of being a woman and begin to address other questions in her works, rather than focusing narrowly on the female condition in China.

Sun Shaoxian's book *Nüxing Zhuyi Wenxue* (*Feminist Literature*) (1987) attempts to take up the issue of women's literature at a more serious and historical level. The book claims to look at the topic from a new perspective. It touches upon sociology, history, psychology and language studies in order to discover something about female literature. Sun Shaoxian comments that critics in China have tended to study the question of women writers either to ascertain something about female consciousness (*nüxing yishi*) or to determine its comments on the issue of female liberation (1987: 2–3).

Sun Shaoxian makes an important distinction between 'female literature' (*nüxing wenxue*) and 'feminist literature' (*nüxing zhuyi wenxue*). According to the author: 'Feminist literature is that which irrespective of sex takes as its subject matter the female condition in a patriarchal [*nanquan zhuyi*] society. Whereas women's literature is that which is written by women' (1987: 4). According to this thesis, women do not have a natural capacity to write a feminist novel, nor can they all deal with the complexity of female characters; indeed, some male writers have tackled this issue very sensitively, particularly Lao She and Ba Jin.

Sun Shaoxian distinguishes his own analysis of the position of women within a patriarchal society from that being put forward by what he identifies as the more extreme positions within the western, especially American, women's movement. According to him, they preach that women are absolutely different from men and that men are going to lose their power to women. He sees such a position as ahistorical and idealist (1987: 134). As he says:

> Society is made up of both men and women. Although patriarchal culture is a period of female subordination, it is nevertheless a historical stage of human society ... Therefore women should not continue to be dependent on men but they should also not try to replace patriarchy with matriarchy. The way forward has to be to create a culture for both sexes [*xuangxing wenhua*]. (Sun Shaoxian 1987: 130)

Sun's final message for women, therefore, is cautionary and articulated within the wider limitations of his own Marxist conceptual basis. Although he attempts to relate the issue of women's literature to the historical context of China and examines the way in which patriarchal culture serves as an important determinant of women's literature, he refuses to deepen his critique to include the political context of the PRC. No attempt is made to examine Marxist literary theory in China to see how it determines the way in which the works of women writers are perceived and what questions get asked of the works. Despite their limitations, Li Ziyun and Sun Shaoxian's work represents a great improvement on the analysis of most Chinese literary critics who address the question of women's literature by making simplistic assumptions about female nature and female consciousness. It is also interesting to note that both authors go to considerable trouble to distinguish their analyses from those of the western women's movement. This distancing represents the overall domination of Marxist terms of analysis on most questions, be they literature or the women's movement.

Li Xiaojiang's book *In Search of Eve* (*Xiawa de Tansuo*) (1988) also attempts a more sophisticated reading of women's writing in China. Her book is also interesting because it is published as part of a Women's Studies series (*Funü yanjiu congshu*). Like Sun Shaoxian, Li places the work of women writers within the specific historical context of China. She examines the effects of traditional cultural values on the representations of women and links the changing image of women in literature to their material circumstances. She further stresses that the depiction of women writers in fiction by women has been an important boost to Women's Studies in China (Li Xiaojiang 1988: 240).

On the whole, it is noticeable that there are few women literary critics engaged in the study of women writers. Xie Wangxin (1987) points this out and lists only five who have had an impact in this area. These are Li Ziyun (*Shanghai Wenxue*), Liu Siqian (Henan University), Wu Zongyi (Beijing Teachers' College), Shen Ying (*Tianjin Wenxue*) and Chen Meilan (Wuhan University) (Xie Wangxin 1987: 149). This paucity of women critics is what makes me hesitate to break down the criticism directed against women writers into 'male' and 'female'. As my earlier discussion shows, essentially all work of criticism is determined by the context of the Chinese literary field and reflects a general discourse on gender in analysing the work of women writers. Women critics are also confined by this broader limitation and should not be seen as occupying a special place because of their gender.[24]

Conclusion

Any discussion of the criticism of women writers in China has to be placed within the wider framework of the specific way literary production is organised in China as a whole. The governing principles of literary theory in China are based on the way Marxist literary theory developed in the Soviet Union. In effect this has resulted in an overall subordination of literary production to the political goals of the state. The practice of literary criticism in China has also been specifically oriented towards ensuring that the literary works produced corresponded to the political and ideological requirements of current Party policy. In short, the specific organisation of the literary field forms the wider limits within which discourse 'as an activity of writing and reading' can take place. This also holds true for the way gender discourse is treated in literature.

Turning to what is being specified as *nüxing wenxue* (women's literature), we have seen that it serves as an interesting example of how literary discourse is constructed around a specific theme or subject. It also demonstrates how certain tools of feminist literary criticism can help us show that literary criticism, when directed towards women's texts, does not premise itself on so-called objective criteria but is implicated in a whole network of gender discourse.

In China, the rise in the number of women writers, with their special focus on the lives of women, has meant that the literary establishment is forced to take a position on their writings and establish criteria for understanding and analysing their work. Its first task, as we have seen, has been an attempt to group women together on the basis of identifiable characteristics. It is these underlying characteristics that show us the role played by gender discourse when it comes to speaking about women. In the Chinese case, we notice that the underlying arguments for a supposedly female-specific literature are grounded on assumptions about the nature of women. What is effectively being spoken of is not simply women's literature but the category woman itself; a category which gets meanings attributed to it discursively. The wider, social meanings attributed to female nature and women become the crucial determining elements of their writing.

At the theoretical level, Chinese criticism of women writers is hampered by two fundamental problems: the limitations imposed by Marxist influence on its own critical tradition, and its inability to move beyond generalisations and platitudes. The overall importance of being politically correct hampers the possibility of radically different analyses of women's fiction. Here again we see that two discourses intervene to form the basis for an analysis of women's fiction: one is the discourse of Marxism and the other is the discourse of a socially and historically constructed femininity.

The above aspects of gender discourse are visible in China for two reasons: (1) it is rare for women to appear on the literary scene in such large numbers, so there is no tradition on which critics can draw in order to make comparative conclusions; (2) Marxist literary criticism, which forms the conceptual basis of literary criticism in China, does not offer a theory of women's literature, so the critics are forced to look elsewhere. The subordinate position of gender discourse in China does not allow official critics to engage in feminist criticism. Instead, they turn to essentialist theories of women's nature to substantiate their claims that there is a 'women's literature'.

Criticism within such narrow parameters has always plagued women writers and in China today it works as a double-edged sword. On the one hand, it has provided women with a niche from which to express themselves. This is demonstrated by the increasing number of women writers and the increased attention that is being paid to their work. On the other hand, such stereotyped assumptions serve to limit the areas open to women writers, while also denying the importance of the problems that they expose in their stories. Their attempts to redefine notions of love and marriage are dismissed as non-serious subjects and reflect the bias inherent in Chinese society, of a public and private sphere.

The positive and negative criticism of certain works gives us an inkling into the way in which the Chinese ideologues would like the question of women's liberation and equality of the sexes to be handled. The question naturally arises, what is the response of women writers to the critics' assumptions and are any alternative readings of female fiction possible in post-Mao China? Further, what are the differences between women writers in China and on what basis can these differences be spelled out? This aspect of difference among women writers becomes an important area of enquiry because it has so far been largely ignored. It also allows us to debunk the myth of a female literature and helps specify the way criticism of women writers reflects and links up to a wider discourse on gender in society.

Part II examines the different responses of women writers to gender discourse in China through analysing the female protagonists in four stories.

Notes

1. My purpose here is not to engage in a debate about the role and function of the state, except to point out that China is a one-party communist state. For a comprehensive understanding of the subject, see Held (ed.) (1987).

2. Symbolic power for Bourdieu is ultimately tied to the institutions of the state where one can see 'in the state the holder of the monopoly of legitimate symbolic violence. Or, more precisely, the state is a referee, albeit a very powerful one, in struggles over this monopoly' (1990b: 137)

3. Bonnie MacDougall (1972) points out that in the early 1920s Marxist theory was only one of the theories being discussed. The most popular of the Soviet theorists were Lunacharsky and Plekhanov. Both these writers stressed the sociological nature of literature as a tool for social change. See Craig (ed.) (1977).

4. There were several debates during this period about what constituted a socialist ideology. For an understanding of the Chinese case, see Selden (1971) and Schram (1973) Both books provide an overview of Maoism and the ethics which Chinese Party members were supposed to cultivate.

5. For an excellent discussion of the debates ranging around the issue of Socialist Realism and socialist literature in the Soviet Union and the impacts these debates had on Chinese literary policy, see D. W. Fokkema (1965).

6. Lenin's theory of reflection stresses that literature should be a mirror of society. In his article on Leo Tolstoy (1908), Lenin points out how 'Tolstoy is original, because the sum total of his views, taken as a whole, expresses what is precisely the specific features of our revolution ... Tolstoy's views are indeed a mirror of those contradictory conditions under which the peasantry had to play their historic part in the revolution' (Lenin 1977: 348).

7. The subordination of literature and art to politics was taken to an extreme during the Cultural Revolution. Several writers, such as Lao She, committed suicide, while Zhao Shuli died in prison and Ba Jin was placed under house arrest. Only five model operas, praised by Jiang Qing in 1967, were allowed to be performed. These were: (1) *Raid on the White Tiger Regiment*; (2) *Taking Tiger Mountain by Strategy*; (3) *Sha Jia Bang*; (4) *The Red Lantern* (5) *On the Docks*. For further details about Cultural Revolution literary policy, see D. W. Fokkema 1991: 594–611.

8. The anti-rightist campaign was launched in 1957–58 at the behest of Mao Zedong. Essentially it was a campaign against intellectuals, writers and artists who questioned the Party's use of Marxism as the only correct way of understanding literature. Merle Goldman (1971) provides an excellent historical study of the various occasions when non-conformist intellectuals questioned the Party's monopoly over art. For an understanding of the politics of the anti-rightist drive, see her ch. 9, pp. 203–42.

9. Bady (1981) focuses on the financial renumeration of writers in China. His article, however, does not attempt to analyse other aspects of Chinese literary organisations.

10. *Danwei* is the Chinese term for a place of employment. For an

understanding of the *Danwei* system as it functions in contemporary China, see Pieke (1992) especially his chapter 'The Structure of Urban Society', pp. 113–72.

11. Mass organisations are organisations designed to represent specific social groups such as trades unions and women. Although non-Party members are part of these organisations, essentially they represent the interests of the state.

12. Also see Barnet (1967). For an analysis of post-Mao China and the bureaucratic apparatus, see Lieberthal and Lampton (1992).

13. Bady (1981) gives a table showing the amount of money earned by certain writers. He distinguishes between their salaries and royalties (*gaofei*). In the case of well-known writers, royalties can be extremely high. On p. 653, for example, he shows how writers such as Ba Jin earned up to 229,000 yuan in royalties.

14. Shen Rong and Zhang Jie, whom I interviewed in November 1990, did not see the system of writers being employed by the state as negative. Instead, Shen Rong pointed out that in the West an artist is also not completely free since he is dependent on the market.

15. Wang Meng, in an interview with Wang Gang, also stresses the limitations of official criticism. As he puts it: 'In the past we had a special type of Chinese criticism. This was offhand comments by Party leaders which came to be seen as the last word on the subject' (Wang Meng and Wang Gang 1989: 7).

16. Wang Ning, a professor at Beijing University, has been at the forefront of introducing western literary theories into China. See Thakur 1991: 62–9.

17. Hu Feng and Feng Xuefeng both questioned the Party's imposition of Marxist theory as a dogma during the 1940s and 1950s. Goldman (1971) gives an excellent account of the activities and basic theories being propagated by these two literary figures. The important role played by Hu Feng and Feng Xuefeng on the one hand, and Zhou Yang on the other, was also stressed by Gu Xiang, a critic of the Writers Federation whom I interviewed in November 1991. He also pointed out that the role of Zhou Yang as the guardian of literary doctrine and policy was fundamental until his downfall during the Cultural Revolution. After the Cultural Revolution his position became far less doctrinaire. He came out as one of the most prominent champions of 'humanism' during 1982–83.

18. Two staff members of Beijing University, Dr Zhang Jingyuan and Zhang Yiwu (interview at Beijing University, November 1990), both stressed that contemporary criticism is the most difficult to engage in since Party policy on literature tends to fluctuate. They attested, however, to the new openness and expansion within the field of literary criticism as such.

19. The initial stories dubbed Scar Literature after the short story of Lu Xinhua, 'The Wound' (*'Shanghen'*) (*Wenhuibao*, 11 August 1978), were all concerned with the suffering of the masses under the erroneous policy of the Cultural Revolution, a trend actively encouraged by the new leadership of Deng Xiaoping.

20. Liu Binyan and Dai Qing have been at the forefront of this type of literature. Their reportage on conditions in China have consistently depicted the dark side of life. Dai Qing has focused on the conditions of women. See Liu Binyan (1988) and Dai Qing and Luo Ge (1988).

21. In my interview with Wang Ning, he mentioned the names of other writers who are beginning to attract critical attention, such as Ge Fei and Can Xue.

22. Yu Luojin is currently living in Germany. She left China in 1985 because of the kind of criticism her novel received. I acted as interpreter to Dr E. Follath, journalist for *Stern* magazine in 1983 when he interviewed her. At that time she seemed very aware of the fact that the attacks against her reflected years of prejudice regarding the role of women in society.

23. Several courses in Comparative Literature in universities such as Beijing and Shanghai now teach contemporary western literary theory. Zhang Jingyuan, for example, teaches post-modern literary theory, including the work of Derrida, Foucault and Said, at Beijing University. I was told these courses are very popular.

24. Western readers of Chinese literary criticism have also commented on the significance of the increased literary output by women writers. See Wakeman and Yue Daiyun (1983) and Gerstlacher et al. (eds) (1985).

PART II

Responses to Gender Discourse

4
A methodology for character analysis

The second part of this book examines how women relate to orthodox discourse. How do they respond to the group characteristics that are attributed to them? In other words, what is their understanding of their own position? Keeping in mind that my enquiry is located in the field of literature, I propose to answer the second question by turning to the work of women writers and examining the way they participate in a discourse on gender. I found many stories of great interest, several of which I could have used to comment on the social relations of gender. My final selection was based on identifying those stories by women writers which contained distinctively drawn women characters who could be assessed against the expectations of the dominant discourse. I wanted to show how the works of selected women writers can be read in a manner which helps to reveal an orthodox gender identity paradigm and how certain other stories can articulate an alternative or heterodox gender identity paradigm.

My focus on character analysis is largely determined by the fact that Chinese criticism, when addressing the work of women writers, tends to comment on the type of female characters being portrayed in fiction. The limits imposed by the specific organisation of the field of Chinese literature, and the constant privileging of Social Realism as a style, have meant that realistic characterisation remains a strong part of the novel. This attempt at a reflection of reality, even if not seen actually to reflect reality, is mediated by a discourse which links itself to social discourse more closely than, say, a post-modernist novel.[1] It is this mediation through discourse that allows us to see how women characters are constructed and how they relate to the social context. In effect, this mediation through the use of discourse constructs the identity of the agent, in this case, the female characters in the novellas to be discussed.

What is a character?

Before speaking about the relationship a character has to discourse, it is important to specify what is meant by the term 'character'. I have turned largely to the work of narratologists to arrive at an idea of what is meant by 'character' and its relation to the text as a whole. In the analysis of fiction, narratology as a method points out that one can focus on different elements of the narrative; for example, focalisation, narrative structure, the position of the narrator, the position of the author, or the characters in the story (Bal 1985; Chatman 1978). It is not my purpose to engage in a detailed discussion of character theory.[2] Instead, I will briefly state the way character analysis has been carried out in literature and then discuss the specific use I have made of the term. My own approach is based, first, on abstracting the character from the narrative as a whole, and, second, relating it to its specific discursive context.

Broadly, there are two different approaches to the study of literary characters. The first is the realist approach which sees characters in fiction as being similar to people. In other words, a character is attributed with the same characteristics as a human being. This approach tends to emphasise the mimetic aspect of a character and it is this idea which underlies Forster's famous distinction between 'round' and 'flat' characters. While round characters are seen to be 'individuals', the flat characters are considered mere 'types' (Forster 1927). When studying literary characters, round characters can be analysed from a psychological perspective. Another important trend in the realist approach to character analysis has been the examination of the morality of a character. Characters are 'good' or 'bad' depending on the morality of their actions (James Hughes 1986: 134). Mieke Bal makes a similar point when she notes: 'the description of a character is always strongly colored by the ideology of the investigators ... consequently what is presented as a description is an implicit value judgement' (Bal 1985: 82). Thus, character analysis means bringing into the open judgements based on our social ideas of how specific characters should behave.

The second broad approach, represented by structuralism and semiotic theory, sees characters as inseparable from textuality and words; they have no reality outside the text (Rimmon-Kenan 1983: 33). Rimmon-Kenan points out that several theorists have stressed the textual nature of the character. Among these, the structuralist method of Greimas, with his focus on 'actants', has been of enormous importance. According to Greimas, the character and literary texts as such possess no mimetic value. Character is essentially subordinate to or defined by action. This perspective as Chatman, among others, points out, is influenced by the approach put forward by the Formalists such as Propp (1968).[3]

Although not without value in terms of providing an alternative tradition to mimetic readings of the character, the subordination of character to mere action or textuality provides us with no means of relating a work of fiction to the social context, the main idea that I was interested in exploring. Semiotic theory, like that of Eco, uses the notion of 'codes' to speak of this link. I have chosen not to deal with it here, because it would have meant entering an entirely different methodological frame.[4]

The approach put forward by Shlomith Rimmon-Kenan offers a promising way out of this problem. Rimmon-Kenan takes the view that character analysis must not be seen as fixed but as dependent on the nature of the narrative as such. Accordingly, while some forms of narrative may not have much to do with characterisation, in other types of work the character dominates (1983: 35–6). This approach is suitable for the kind of stories chosen here. All of them use a strong focus on characterisation, as pointed out earlier; that is, characters rather than events dominate the narrative.

A more independent place for character analysis is also advocated by Chatman, who argues that although characters do not have 'lives', readers endow them with 'personality' to the extent that 'personality is a structure familiar to us in life and art' (1978: 137). He goes on to say: 'A viable theory of character should preserve openness and treat characters as autonomous beings, not as mere plot functions. It should argue that character is reconstructed by audience from evidence announced or implicit in an original construction and communicated by the discourse, through whatever meaning' (Chatman 1978: 119). He points out that this reconstruction by the audience is done by focusing on 'character traits' within the narrative, where a trait is seen as a 'relatively stable or abiding personal quality' (1978: 67). Further, he stresses how a different set of traits may change through the course of the narrative. These sets of character traits, thus, have to be seen as a 'vertical assemblage intersecting the syntagmatic chain of events that comprise the plot' (1978: 127). The character traits are assembled from the text by focusing on different aspects through which characterisation is carried out. Here, Chatman's definition also brings in the role played by the reader or audience in attributing meaning to the original construction because the audience relies upon its knowledge of the trait code in the real world (1978: 125).[5]

Mieke Bal (1985) also points out that it is on the basis of certain data that a character becomes predictable within a frame of reference. This limiting of the possibility for the character to be other than what it is, is used by the reader to locate the character in terms of predictable social criteria. As Bal points out: 'In terms of predictability, the character's age, sex and profession create certain expectations regarding the character's predictability' (1985: 84). Like Chatman and Rimmon-Kenan, Bal also sees the characteristics which accumulate to form a whole as what presents us with the image of a character (1985: 85). A character's relevant characteristics can be put together by selecting what Bal calls a relevant semantic axis. Again, like Chatman, she sees the selection of relevant axes as determined by the ideological position of the reader (1985: 86).

Thus, narratologists advocating an independent analysis of characters in the narrative, essentially focus on identifying the character through the assembling of traits, which in turn are based on the selection of the reader. The audience, in identifying certain traits and then naming them, is making use of social classifications and social forms of naming. When readers reconstruct a character, they are not relying only on literary conventions but on their knowledge of the world as such. It is at this level that the work of Foucault on discourse, with its much wider application, becomes relevant. The use of discourse theory can help bring another focus to character analysis; it can help us locate the character within a universe of discourse. This universe of discourse links the character in the narrative to its historical and cultural context. Instead of seeing the character as representational or non-representational, it can be seen as constructed through the use of specific discourses which can also be recognised as social discourses. While some discourses may emerge as lying closer to dominant ways of viewing the world, others may fall closer to a critical or heterodox way of looking at the world, thus giving us an idea of the way in which discourses circulate and interact.

My starting point was to show how literature is also a specific type of discourse. A literary text does not stand alone but is implicated in a web of relationships that make up a universe of discourse. Similarly, a character in a literary text can be identified as relating to one discourse or another. This perspective vindicates the insights developed by Bakhtin years ago in his study of the novel. Bakhtin puts the problem so clearly that it is worth quoting him at length. Writing in 1934-35 on 'Discourse of the Novel', Bakhtin says:

> The speaking person in the novel, is always, to one degree or another, an ideologue and his [*sic*] words are always ideologemes. A particular language in a novel is always a particular way of viewing the world. One that strives for social significance ... action is always highlighted by ideology, is always harnessed to the character's discourse (even if that discourse is still only a potential discourse), is associated with an ideological motif and occupies a definite ideological position. (Bakhtin 1981: 334)

Although Bakhtin uses a different terminology, his point is that all language is contextual. Thus, my argument stresses that, rather than subordinating character to the plot as some structuralists and formalists tend to do, character analysis must also concern itself with examining the ways in which a character is assembled and what discourse is brought out in its analysis. In reconstructing a character, we can analyse the character's discourse on a given subject by relating it to social discourses on the same subject. The selection of which discourse to follow through will form the relevant semantic axes. Here, discourses such as those of race, class and gender would emerge as some of the different discourses along which a character is reconstructed or assembled. As new discourses and new discursive alignments come into play, our readings of literary characters also change and new elements are brought to the fore.

Thus, a character can be viewed as a composite of different, and even possibly conflicting, discourses linked to the social network. A character retains a certain representational quality. It is not representative, in the sense that it is the same as a person, but it is representational to the extent that it reflects certain social discourses and operates within a specific universe of discourse.

Whereas a traditional mimetic approach focuses on the psychology of the character, an approach using discourse would locate the representational moment in the way the discourse of the character relates to the social discourse. Not what it thinks and why, but how it is located, looked at and looks; in other words, the discourse on the character, both within literary criticism and within the text as such. Characters do not cross the boundaries between fiction and the world in a literal sense but reveal the articulation of different discourse formations within the text.

Since my purpose is to assess how women represent and are represented against orthodox gender discourse, my analysis attempts to reconstruct the character in terms of the type of discourse it reflects on the issue of gender relations. Here the empirical world of gender relations is mediated through a specific focus on gender discourse. Again, I turn to James Hughes when he says: 'character is a relational term. The kind of character used will be determined in its main outlines by the form of the discourse universe the character must inhabit' (1986: 135). It is this universe of discourse which I shall attempt to point to in my own specific readings of the four female characters chosen for analysis.

Reconstructing the character

Apart from the theoretical problems associated with character analysis, we still have to deal with the way a character should be assembled from the text. It can be reconstructed by what Chatman (1978) and Bal (1985) call assembling the character traits that are dispersed through the text. These traits are directly presented by the character when it speaks of itself or through the eyes of a third party, either the narrator or the other characters in the story. According to Bal, there is another possibility, which is through the actions in which the character is depicted. While I shall follow this method of initial identification of the character, the steps will not be demonstrated in the analysis. Instead, for the sake of coherence, the character will be presented keeping in mind the purpose of the analysis or the reader's starting point. In other words, I shall reconstruct the character to demonstrate the existence of a particular gender identity paradigm.

Since the purpose of my analysis is to arrive at a sense of the character's relationship to gender discourse, we can identify or reconstruct the character by focusing our reconstruction on those aspects through which women's identity is constructed within the text and by focusing on those character traits which link the character with a discourse on gender in society. Here, three levels can be identified against which the character is assembled. I have made the following breakdown:

1. The character's setting in the story, i.e. the objective circumstances and limits within which the character is textually placed. These are the markers of the character and determine its possibilities. They form the setting of the character within the narrative.
2. The character's relationship to other characters which appear in the narrative. This will be done by focusing on the discourse of the character on others and other's discourse on the character.
3. The responses to and understanding of the various events and actions by the character. That is, the development of the character. This will allow us to examine the context of the character in relation to discourse on gender. We will be able to show how the character in its development ultimately represents a particular discourse on gender relations or a particular way of viewing male–female relations.

It is through an examination of these aspects that we can arrive at an understanding of the character's position with regard to gender discourse. These aspects are dispersed through the text and should not be seen as fixed. In fact, changes in them can help us arrive at the way the character's relationship to discourse may change and develop.

I shall use Bourdieu's concepts discussed earlier to assess the types of relationship which the characters being analysed have to a discourse on gender relations. These can include a sense of relating to their discourse universe by identifying with orthodox discourse or by taking positions which lie closer to a heterodox discourse. It is here that we see the way characters reflect a view of their world and a view of their position within the world determined by their setting. While not confusing character with agent in the real world, I shall attempt to show that a process of gender identification and construction of femininity can be seen at work even in the portrayal of female protagonists. This process reveals the gender discourse of the character.

The function of the author

While the character can be abstracted from the text through a focus on character traits, it needs to be pointed out that the character is ultimately a textual construction attributed to an individual author.

In analysing the position of the author, Foucault is again useful. He has written about what he calls the 'author function' in discourse. He points out that the author's name 'permits one to group together a certain number of texts, define them, differentiate them from and contrast them to others' (1984: 107). Thus, essentially, the author serves a classificatory purpose, allowing us to group different texts under one name. This in turn allows us to contextualise the text in terms of historical and cultural factors.

Accordingly, the role of the individual author is not what is important in terms of literary discourse; rather it is the kind of place enjoyed by the 'author function' which is of importance. Foucault sees the 'author function' as linked to the points at which society holds the individual responsible for the production of certain discourse. It attributes an author function in terms of 'ownership'. That is, the author is the owner of the text and has rights of publication and withdrawal. The author function also serves as a point of control, by making an individual responsible for certain discourses articulated in the text.[6]

Thus, for the purposes of this book, I see the role of the different authors whose stories are being analysed as belonging to the author function. Here, the gender of the writers chosen becomes important, not their individual lives. Since literary discourse sees authors who are women as writing differently from men, the gender of the author becomes an important criterion of classification. Specific characteristics are attached to this classification. A whole way of literary analysis is implied in this differentiation of texts on the basis of the gender of the author. As discussed in Chapter 1, feminist literary criticism has pointed out the way the works of women writers have been treated in the past. Further it has developed new ways of reading this difference, and today we can speak of feminist literary criticism which has its own methods and theories. Feminist literary criticism uses this classification of gender difference and attributes a new meaning to 'gender' as serving a specific type of author function.

What becomes important in the case of Chinese women writers in terms of the author function is the gender attributes that operate once a text is acknowledged as written by a woman. It is the 'common characteristics' of women writers, as shown in my discussion of literary criticism in Chapter 3, that show us the operation of gender discourse and influence the works of critics when they read women writers. In my method, thus, it is the gender of the author which is the important reason for selecting the particular texts, rather than the specific psychology or motivation of the individual writer. In dealing with the author of the various texts, I am not relating the text to the author, only identifying the gender discourse tied to the author being a woman and in placing the text within the historical and cultural context of China.

Notes

1. Aleid Fokkema (1991), in her comprehensive study of the character in post-modern fiction, points out that there is no single definition of postmodernism. Instead she says: 'Texts belonging to the postmodern canon display a firm distrust of language' (1991: 15).

2. Several excellent introductions to the subject of narratology exist. I have relied largely on the work of Chatman (1978), Bal (1985) and Rimmon-Kenan (1983). They provide an excellent introduction to the practical use of the tools of narratology.

3. Propp (1966) with his interest in the structural aspects of the study of narratives, focuses on fairytales. He points out that the characters found in fairytales can be reduced to their basic functions. His work influenced the study of characters in other genres of fiction as well. Chatman (1978) comments on Propp's work as being largely representative of the Russian Formalist tradition.

4. A. Fokkema (1991) has used Eco's semiotic theory as the basis for developing her understanding of the function of character within the text. She uses the model of codes that Eco develops to speak of character. She first expresses the idea of the character as a 'sign'. As she puts it: 'The codes that operate in the construction of the character sign determine the nature of this sign' (1991: 73). She sees most codes as 'conventions of representation'. Although I found her work extremely persuasive, she works with an entirely different body of theory to mine, showing the wide range of possibilities that exist while focusing on character analysis in narrative fiction.

5. Chatman (1978) also makes use of Eco's basic model of the different types of codes against which a character can be assessed. He focuses on the 'trait code', for example, as one of the literary conventions which guide the work of characterisation and character analysis.

6. Speaking specifically of the function of the author within literary discourse, Foucault points out that the way in which the author has been described within western literary discourse is strongly influenced by 'the manner in which Christian tradition authenticated (or rejected) the texts of an author'. He goes on to say that modern literary criticism continues to use the same way of defining an author (Foucault 1984c: 110–11). Thus, the tradition of 'authentication' forms a basic principle of the author function. Within the field of classical Chinese literary criticism, 'authenticating' texts and especially poetic verse have played an important part. The biographies of the lives of poets and writers form a major part of classical literary studies. See the introduction by Idema (1991).

5

Orthodox responses to gender discourse

Female characters in two novellas have been chosen for analysis in this chapter. These characters will be shown as representing an orthodox gender identity paradigm, to reintroduce Haraway's term, along which men and women identify. This gender paradigm works as a discourse within which women's identity is constructed through the narrative. This process of the construction of the character and the identification of character traits will be shown to correspond to the way orthodox gender discourse constructs women's identities. The characters should not be seen as reflecting reality; instead, they will be used to illustrate the role played by discourses in the construction of a gender identity paradigm for women.

To identify one gender paradigm as 'orthodox' and the other as 'heterodox', I shall briefly restate the use I have made of Bourdieu's theory of reproduction, on which this classification is based. Bourdieu points out that we arrive at an understanding of our social positions in life, of which gender identities are an important aspect, through the use and acceptance of certain forms of behaviour which, in turn, are grounded in a cultural habitus. However, these apparently natural divisions, such as between the sexes, are accepted only in a quasi-perfect state. In actual practice, social divisions are sites of struggle, struggles which are reflected in the conflict that arises over the systems of social classification and representation. Thus, different discourses which try to explain the social world compete for legitimacy. Here, orthodoxy becomes discourse which attempts to ensure that a particular system of classification and particular ways of representation remain intact and adhere to the dominant forms of social practice. For example, in terms of gender relations, when women are spoken of, or speak, a particular nature and practice is attributed to them. Orthodoxy succeeds also because it has institutional means at its disposal.[1]

In China, one notes that orthodox discourse on women, against which the female protagonists will be assessed, describes women as naturally emotional and self-sacrificing. Further, their primary identifications are described as lying within the family and marriage. This apparent naturalness of women's roles is also taken over in the characterisation of women in fiction by both male and female writers because neither sex escapes the limits through which human beings acquire a sense of their social identity.[2] For the character to be recognisable to its readers as a woman, she has to possess those characteristics which mark her as a 'woman'. This is the function of gender discourse.

My analysis of female protagonists in the fiction of women writers demonstrates that women are not only defined by discourses, but make use of the same discourses in the way they articulate a certain gender paradigm in their construction of a fictional identity. This use of gender discourse by women is the point at which their interaction as agents can be specified. Women exercise their agency through the selection they make from the different discourses that speak of gender relations. In their own discourse, they contribute towards constructing and changing the world through the work of representation.[3]

In the two women characters discussed here, an orthodox gender paradigm will be brought out. The first is the character Ouyang Duanli in the novella *Lapse of Time* (*Liushi*), and the second is Lu Wenting, the character in the novella *At Middle Age* (*Rendao Zhongnian*). Although the two characters are located in different types of social circumstances, they both represent ways of seeing which are closer to a dominant discourse on gender relations. The first reflects an unchanged habitus of gender relations, where the traditional separation between male and female spheres remains unchanged. The second represents an attempt to change specific aspects of gender relations and institutionalise a new socialist orthodoxy on gender relations.

A traditional gender identity paradigm: Ouyang Duanli in *Lapse of Time*

Wang Anyi is one of the better-known younger women writers of post-Mao China. She has achieved considerable fame for her short stories and is acknowledged as a writer of enormous potential and talent. She started by writing children's stories at a very young age. Today, however, her stories deal with a wide variety of subjects and provide an unusual glimpse into contemporary Chinese society. Several of her works have been translated into English. Wang Anyi wrote the novella *Liushi* (*Lapse of Time*) in 1981.[4]

The context of the story *Lapse of Time* describes a family living through the Cultural Revolution, 1966–76, and is located in Shanghai.[5] The head of the family is the father who has been classified as a capitalist because he was a factory owner. He has a wife, two sons and a daughter. His eldest son, Wen Yao, his wife Duanli and their three children live with the family. The family once enjoyed a comfortable standard of living in a large house with servants and had plenty of money to spend on good food and entertainment. However, due to the policies of the Cultural Revolution, their wealth and capital have been confiscated and only enough money remains for the family to survive. Now everything has to be budgeted for and the family is living in poor circumstances.

As the Cultural Revolution continues, the hardships confronted by the family increase. Its younger members are sent to different parts of the country as part of the 'down to the countryside campaign'.[6] The family's fortunes are restored when the Cultural Revolution ends and the father's property is returned to him. With this, the various family members return to their old life-styles.

The novella is written in the third person and Duanli is the protagonist as well as the internal focaliser for major parts of the story. The character of Duanli develops along with the changes that take place in the family. In fact, the other characters are described and introduced to us through the eyes of Duanli and we know only those parts of their personalities that Duanli focuses on. In describing the changes in Duanli's life, the novella also allows us to identify areas that do not change; these are the basic ideas about gender relations, a particular gender identity paradigm through which the character becomes recognisable to us. It is the unchanged traits of her character, the things that remain unarticulated, which allow us to identify her relationship to orthodoxy as a quasi-perfect response to gender relations.

The setting of the character: a traditional family structure It is important to define the setting of the character because this forms the boundaries within which discourse is articulated. The character is objectively located in one identifiable social setting rather than another. This is both a descriptive indicator, in that action is located within its confines, and a determinant indicator, since it determines the actions that the character performs.

Ouyang Duanli is a character situated within the traditional family structure of China. She lives with her husband's family which consists of her father-in-law and mother-in-law, her brother-in-law Wenguang and her sister-in-law Wenying. She is the wife of Wenyao, who is the eldest son. The father-in-law's business has been the main source of income for the whole family. Duanli and Wenyao have three children, two daughters, Duoduo and Mimi, and a son named Lailai.

The first half of the story depicts Duanli in the role of housewife and mother. Her position is also stated by the narrator who tells us that, although Wenyao works, Duanli is left at home to look after the children. She was assigned a job after graduation but chose not to take it because it meant leaving Shanghai. Now that the family can no longer afford to keep a maid, she has to go out early in the morning to shop. We realise that this task is new to Duanli because she is still not used to the cold of early morning Shanghai. We are told: 'She had never risen this early before, let alone gone outside, she had never expected it would be so terrible' (p. 89).

While shopping, Duanli's thoughts are busy with the needs of her family as she tries to decide how best to stretch her budget to cover as many items as possible. We follow her reflections as she remembers how well the family used to eat and how little choice they have nowadays. She decides to spend her 80 fen on buying meat for a change, even though she knows she is overshooting her budget. Great detail is provided about the kind of dishes she will make for the family (pp. 90–1). On her return, she takes care of the family's breakfast and helps the children get ready for school. Thus, we know that Duanli's chief preoccupation is the household. After the children have left for school, we again see Duanli cooking and again there is a long description of the food being prepared, contrasting with what the family used to eat in the past. This contrast is used partly to describe the changes in the family's circumstances and partly to show the nostalgia that Duanli has for the past.

Apart from the circumstances in which the character is depicted, Duanli identifies herself as a housewife in a conversation with her sister-in-law Wenying who wants to do further study. Duanli says: 'What's the point thinking about higher education, even if you make it to school, what then? I graduated from college but I'm still a housewife' (pp. 97–8). Thus, from the opening pages of the story, we are able to see that a large amount of narrative space is devoted to Duanli's preoccupation with household affairs, allowing us to identify her as a housewife. Further, she is a housewife who has had to learn to look after her family, having once been rich enough not to have to worry about the mundane details of daily life such as shopping, cooking and cleaning. This identification of Duanli as a housewife is extremely important in terms of determining the actions and events that she is depicted in, thus acting as an important indicator of the objective limits of the discourse universe of the character.

Her relationship with her husband and children The primary relationships in Duanli's life are with her husband and children. Duanli married Wenyao in her last year of college life. In the opening pages of the narrative, she contrasts her recollections of her husband with what he has become now. When she met him he was a forceful and charming young man 'whose good looks and charming airs had attracted many girls'. He had been popular with his classmates and had always excelled in the university's various extra-curricular activities. Now, however, he is shown as lacking any initiative and completely cowed by circumstances (p. 114). All decisions regarding daily family affairs are falling on Duanli's shoulders. She realises that his confidence was not something internal to him but was based on his father's wealth and the security he derived from it. As she thinks, after having made a decision to sell some old clothes to raise money: 'In the past she always depended on him; no matter what the problem facing her was, once brought to him it would be solved. In fact his ability was based on the endless supply of money provided by his family' (p. 114).

However, even though we see Duanli is becoming critical of her husband in her own discourse, the criticism is based on an orthodox discourse on gender relations within which the man should be the provider for the family. Duanli has lost respect for her husband, because she resents his incapacity and sees him as no longer fulfilling his gender role. She is gradually becoming aware of the fact that she will have to depend on her own resources for the family to survive. This does not give her any pleasure, instead she resents her husband for forcing her into this position. She regrets the fact that she had never taken a job for, if she had, it would have provided her with a tidy sum of money now when the whole family is dependent on Wenyao's salary. The changing nature of Duanli's relationship with her husband is also related to the family's circumstances. Although Duanli realises that her husband is incapable of looking after the family, the power relationship between the couple does not change. He is still the head of the family and has the final say in all decisions that are made.

In her own discourse on her husband, Duanli exhibits a sense of disappointment while at the same time accepting his position in the family. We also notice that Duanli tries to deal diplomatically with her husband rather than confronting him on various issues. For example, when after the sale of old clothes she informs him about the amount of money earned, he insists on giving some to his mother. She manages to dissuade him diplomatically (p. 113). Thus, although we are made aware of Wenyao's short-comings in the eyes of Duanli, she remains within the framework of a traditional relationship where she still accepts her husband's right to make the final decisions. The strategy open to her within her own position is a traditional one, that of diplomacy. Again, she herself is not critical of the balance of this relationship. She accepts it as natural that she should have to persuade and cajole her husband to her way of thinking rather than be the one to make the final decision. Her relationship with her children is good and she is a concerned and loving mother. Her family is the centre of her existence and the reason why she is willing to put up with the various problems that confront her. We know that this is so from Duanli's own discourse. As she says when her daughter Duoduo comes back from the countryside for a visit:

> We are going to stay a family from now on. No one and nothing will ever part us as again. She loved her family now more than at any other time in her life. That love included all of them: the headstrong and unpredictable Duoduo, Lailai, who was always hungry, and honest Mimi. Even her useless but some-how lovable husband. She sensed that she was the protector of the family and this fact made her proud and happy. (pp. 152–3)

Apart from loving her family, Duanli is shown as the one who handles all their problems and stands up for them. When her daughter Duoduo is being sent off to the countryside, it is Duanli who confronts the members of the revolutionary committee who come to the house to recruit Duoduo. After listening to their speech, she says: 'You have come here tonight to persuade us, but the down to the countryside campaign is supposed to be on a voluntary basis, so don't put the pressure of "background" on us. If you think that Duoduo must go because of her bad background then transfer her residence' (p. 158). This outburst shocks her children who are unused to seeing their mother raising her voice or arguing with anyone. As Wenyao, her husband, says in response to her outburst: 'You are certainly full of fire! When did you learn to be like that? You sounded just like one of those women who do the shopping for other people' (p. 158). This little interchange allows us to see the way Duanli is changing and the way the other members of her family, especially her husband, are starting to comment on the change unfavourably.

However, all these events show that Duanli identifies with her family and sees herself as the person who is responsible for their welfare and survival. This is her primary identification. Within this gender identity paradigm no sacrifice by the mother on behalf of the family is too great. Here, her character corresponds to the expectations of an ortho-dox discourse which sees women's loyalty as essentially tied to the family.

Her relationship with her in-laws Duanli has little relationship with her father-in-law. He is the overall head of the family and ultimately his decisions are considered binding. Duanli's main interaction is with her mother-in-law – demonstrating the traditional boundaries within which the character is structured – whom she both resents and yet defers to. These are normal tensions which exist in a joint family structure, and Duanli is always concerned that her mother-in-law does not fully accept her. The traditional pattern of their relationship is clearly seen when Duanli tells her son Lailai to eat a bowl of rice porridge when he complains of hunger. However, on seeing the disapproval on her mother-in-law's face, she gives him some money to go and buy something to eat (p. 99). A little later, Duanli reflects on the fact that her mother-in-law always blames her for being a bad mother whenever the children fight (p. 100). Although the family does not eat together, there is still the usual give and take that exists in a joint family structure, and Duanli has to accept the authority of her mother-in-law regarding family affairs.

Duanli's relations with her brother-in-law and sister-in-law are tolerable and, as she herself admits, better than in the earlier days when they indulged in constant jealousy and petty backbiting. Now that there is nothing left to fight over, they tend to spend more time together and get along better. It is through Duanli that we form an idea of the character of her brother-in-law and sister-in-law. Wenying is a spoilt young girl who is unable to handle the hardships that face her. Duanli's traditional discourse is reinforced by the fact that she is always advising Wenying to get married because she sees it as the best future for a woman. However, when Wenying is assigned to the countryside, it is Duanli who ensures that she has all the things she will need for her stay and it is Duanli who goes to Anhui province to change her residence permit and bring back all her things. And when Wenying begins to have mental problems and her mother is considering marrying her off in the countryside, it is Duanli who stops the match and insists that her sister-in-law receive medical treatment (p. 153).

Duanli's relationship with her brother-in-law is ambiguous. She thinks that Wenguang is spoilt and rather selfish. She recalls how the family has always indulged his every whim; tutors have been hired at every turn to make him pass his exams and he has been pampered and coddled all his life. However, she also feels sorry for him. When Wenguang applies to go to Heilongjiang, his parents are heart-broken and unable to decide how best to change the situation. It is Duanli who finally talks to him and tries to understand why he chooses to act in this way. She finds out that he is bored and depressed and seeking the 'meaning of life'. Here we find Duanli's practical sense identified. When asked by Wenguang what the meaning of life is, Duanli replies, 'to eat, and to work' (p. 183). Thus, although Duanli is not particularly close to her brother-in-law and sister-in-law, she is nevertheless, as the wife of the elder son, willing to take responsibility for helping them out.

Duanli's relationship with her family is one of concern and caring and she is ready to fulfil her role as daughter-in-law. However, from being a meek daughter-in-law, her relationship with the family changes to one of more authority, as we see when her mother-in-law consults her about Wenying's marriage. It is interesting that Duanli's identity is completely bound up with that of her husband's family, which has become her own, and her natal family does not appear at all. Here we see the traditional family structure of China quite intact: after marriage, a woman is expected to identify only with her husband's family and embrace the interests of family members as her own. Finally, however, it is her father-in-law, who does not have much to do with her, who acknowledges the change in Duanli and appreciates her efforts on behalf of the family. As he says towards the end of the narrative, after the family fortune has been restored: 'These past ten years Duanli has suffered a lot. The whole family was dependent on her. What she has done for Wenying and Wenguang cannot be measured in terms of money' (p. 168). In terms of gender discourse, it is also significant that the final approval of Duanli's qualities as a wife, mother and daughter-in-law comes from her father-in-law, the head of the family.

Her relationship with other characters   On the whole, Duanli does not have much to do with people outside her family. The two important 'outsiders' worth mentioning are her downstairs neighbour Auntie A'Mao and another lady called Auntie Golden Flower. They play a small but crucial role in the development of her character, and they can be identi-fied as 'helpers' as we shall see in the next section.

Duanli begins by being suspicious of and disliking her neighbours. The ground floor of the house has been confiscated and allocated to an ordinary worker's family, and, when they first move in, Duanli is aghast and refuses to let her child Mimi even look at them. She describes them as 'rude slum dwellers' and is scared of them as she has never had anything to do with workers before; she has no idea how she is going to deal with them (p. 105).

The other important outsider in this phase of Duanli's life is Auntie Golden Flower. She is very helpful to Duanli and finds her various little jobs from baby-sitting to knitting sweaters. It is she who finally suggests that Duanli take a job in a workshop where she will be able to earn a little extra money for the family. We notice Duanli relating to other people for the first time in the factory where she works. Here, however, she is again an outsider, not having much in common with the other girls who work with her.

Duanli's relationships with other people show us the idea she has of her own social space and of the place of the others who are of the working class. Her reaction to her neighbours and co-workers and, in turn, their reaction to her, show us a glimpse of her class habitus. Her co-workers, for example, sympathise with the fact that, despite coming from a wealthy family, she has to work. Thus, the objective setting of the character and her relations with others help us to identify the way in which her gender identity paradigm is structured by her specific class and social position.

The development of the character Lapse of Time starts with a Duanli who is hesitant and scared of the outside world, a Duanli who has never had to do anything more strenuous than go to the tailor for a dress-fitting. When recalling her earlier life, Duanli remembers herself as a beautiful and cosseted young woman. Long passages describe the time and money she used to spend on her appearance (pp. 95–6). We are told how she could never pass a clothes shop without stopping to buy something, even though she did not need it. We are also told of how particular she was about the style and fit of her clothes; a badly fitting dress completely ruins her mood.

We know that she was considered to be very beautiful by all those who saw her. Wenying tells her: 'As far as I am concerned, you look good in whatever you wear, even in mourning clothes' (p. 97). We are also told of the amount of time that Duanli spent in front of the mirror, looking after her hair and skin. Her hair had been thick, black and luxurious but she was forced to cut it off during the Cultural Revolution (p. 97). Thus, we know that there was a time when all that mattered to Duanli was her appearance. In fact, we are told that she did not even breast-feed her own children because she was scared of losing her figure. She was a typical rich and idle housewife who had nothing more serious to think of than her clothes.

The past, in terms of narrative time, reveals Duanli as a particular type of woman – a woman who corresponds to the way orthodox discourse on women expected them to be. She is concerned with external appearance and with presenting herself as the wife of a rich man. This is the more traditional habitus which still underlies the arbitrarily imposed socialist orthodoxy. This paradigm corresponds more to a classical gender identity paradigm which is represented by the bourgeoisie before 1949. However, when the circumstances of the family change, it is Duanli who emerges as the strongest and most decisive character, albeit still accepting her traditional role as wife and mother. In fact, her identification with this role becomes even stronger now she has neither nannies to look after the children nor servants to do the housework. Duanli begins to take decisions about major issues within the family and attempts to come to terms with the new circumstances. We notice from her relationship with the other members of the family that they are all dependent on her to handle whatever new situation arises. It is Duanli who takes care of the troubles of her sister-in-law and brother-in-law and calms down her mother-in-law. She realises that she will have to depend on her own strength to ensure her family does not starve. Finally, through her neighbour, she gets a job baby-sitting. After that she attempts to take up knitting as a means of earning extra money. The catalyst in this change comes from outside, in the character of Aunty A'Mao who tells Duanli: 'You will not get through life by being soft. You have to be tough ... Like getting on to a crowded bus on your way to work, the more you let people push you the less your chances of getting on. One has to push along with the rest of them' (p. 131).

Listening to Auntie A'Mao talk, Duanli feels that a new element has emerged in her character. She starts to change her attitude to things and we see a tougher Duanli emerging. This changed Duanli is seen reflecting on several incidents. After she has finished knitting a sweater for Aunty Golden Flower, she reflects that, although she feels awkward about earning 4 yuan in such a way, she also feels productive. As the narrative states: 'She had a sense of her own strength; the strength that had been lying dormant for the past thirty-eight years of her life had suddenly come to life' (p. 142). This change is also reflected in the way she deals with other situations. For example, once while she is queuing to buy fish, some hoodlums try to usurp her place. Instead of being scared by them, she flings their shopping bag away. Another time, when her son Lailai is bullied in school, she complains to the school and forces the boy responsible to apologise (p. 142).

Taking a low-paid job in a workshop which makes spare parts for transistors, is an indication of how far Duanli has come from being a rich and pampered housewife. To be on time for her job, she has to get up at dawn. Even though the work is back-breaking and monotonous, and she feels awkward when she overhears her co-workers talking about how bad her family circumstances must be for her to take this job, she continues to work and even feels a sense of pride once she is able to complete the first assignment (p. 146). It is at her new workplace that she begins to realise that other people are suffering in the Cultural Revolution as well. As she reflects: 'It seemed to her they were all in the same boat, that the Cultural Revolution had not brought them any benefits either' (p. 147) .

However, these changes in the life of Duanli last only for the duration of the Cultural Revolution. Once her father-in-law's property is restored, we find Duanli slipping back into her old life-style. But again, this is not an easy transition. When her father-in-law tries to give her a large sum of money, she is filled with a 'strange foreboding' (p. 168). And even when Wenyao nudges her, she still decides to refuse because 'taking the money would make it difficult to be her own person' (p. 169). In the event her apprehension is justified. As soon as they return to their room, her husband starts reasserting his authority: 'Who do you think I am? I am your husband. The head of the household. You have to consult me' (p. 169).

Although she resents his sudden show of authority, after having taken a back seat through the difficult times, she still listens to his suggestion that she take the money and quit her job. She becomes angry at this and points out how her job had been essential to keep the family going. Wenyao recognises this and says: 'You've become so tough now ... In the past you used to be so gentle. Like a little pet, even afraid to cross the road' (p. 169). Duanli says nothing but turns to look in a mirror. She sees an unfamiliar face. Her hair is done up indifferently and there are bags under her eyes and wrinkles around her eyes and nose. Her skin has become coarse and her hands bony and wrinkled. 'I have aged a lot', she thinks (p. 170). From looking at herself, she turns to look at her husband, who seems as youthful as he was ten years ago. She realises she loves him (p. 171). Later in the night they go to deposit the money in the bank. However, though she has accepted the terms of her traditional gender identity again, the critical self-confidence and sense of independence she acquired through working and fending for herself has still not vanished. As the narrator shows her reflecting: 'Shall I leave my job ... although it is not really suitable work it was difficult to get, and who knows when conditions may change again ... one can't depend on anything' (p. 171).

This whole section is of interest in terms of analysing gender discourse. It is after she has come face to face with her age and ugliness in the mirror that she finds herself weak in front of her husband. The mirror gives her gender identity back to her. She realises that from being a beautiful and well-kept woman, she has become like any other woman who has to work and face the daily hardship of crowded city life. During the period of hardship, she had hardly ever had time to look into a mirror or to consider her appearance, and had been content with a kind of inner strength, acquired through working and being able to support the family.

After this incident, Duanli rapidly slips back into her old life-style.

First she takes sick-leave from work and goes shopping for clothes and other fashionable items. The next time she looks in a mirror, when she goes to the beauty parlour for a hairdo, the transition is complete. This time her husband is pleased with what he sees. As he says, examining her hair style from the back, "It looks much better, much better" (p. 173). Duanli also looks in the mirror and feels different: 'She liked what she saw. She felt as good about herself as at any time in the past. There is nothing to keep me from living a life of fulfilment from now on, she was thinking' (p. 173).

Duanli falls back into the pattern of her earlier life. Now that she has a maid to take care of the housework, she has nothing more to worry about. After shopping with her husband for the first time, she becomes a regular shopper, a veritable 'encyclopedia of information on what the different stores contained' (p. 174). She starts by buying her children expensive imported watches. She also starts getting together with other housewives in a similar situation. They spend their time hosting lunches and gossiping. Her life becomes full of these activities and she feels herself to be a young woman again, full of vitality, and she knows she can once again experience fulfilling life (p. 176).

Her husband's attitude also influences her greatly. Wenyao again becomes a charming and forceful personality, encouraging Duanli to start enjoying herself again and to spend money on objects that she fancies, irrespective of the price (p. 175). He too is content to have his wife back in her supportive role, where he is the provider and un-questioned head of the family.

In short, Duanli has come almost full circle. Her sense of her place and her understanding of gender relations, which had been disturbed by the misfortunes of the family, are again confirmed. In fact, this is the advice she gives her son Lailai, who is studying for university entrance exams: 'University? What's the point of going to university? Mama is a graduate from college, during the Cultural Revolution I was a nanny, an apprentice in a workshop. What didn't I do? I've thought a lot about it and come to the conclusion that if you have money then everything is alright' (p. 178).

After this she keeps taking sick-leave and, despite several reminders from the workshop, keeps putting off the decision to return. She is happy buying new things for the house and is once again immersed in family disputes and worries. She even breaks off her daughter's relation-ship with a young man she considers 'not good enough for her' and is happy when her daughter finally marries a boy with prospects of going abroad. Thus, we find that Duanli is once again responding to the demands set by her social status and role as a rich housewife. Matters finally come to a head when a decision has to be made for her to go back to her old job. Although her husband encourages her to give up the job, something in her resists. Even then she is not sure whether she will really be able to go back to work 'to that cold dark, stone basement warehouse' (p. 189).

However, the return to her old life-style does not make Duanli satisfied or happy. The constant round of buying, entertaining and inactivity leave her feeling that she has lost the sense of starting a new life (p. 187). Towards the end of the narrative she is shown reflecting about herself during the period of hardship that the family suffered: 'Those days she was so capable of doing things, had so much strength and energy. Where has that capable woman vanished? But then was that capable woman really her in the first place?' (p. 188).

This twinge of regret is never sufficient for her to return to work or to try again to go against the accepted demands of her gender habitus. The gender identity paradigm that she reveals means that a critical understanding of her habitus is necessary if any change is to come about in her circumstances. The narrative leaves her talking to her brother-in-law Wenguang about the meaning of life. She cries when Wenguang says: 'There is someone who spent his whole life looking for the meaning of life, till one day he suddenly realised that the real meaning of life is very simple; one must be able to stand on one's own feet. ... use your own strength to row this little boat called life to the other side' (p. 194). Although Duanli is moved by these lines, a little doubt flickers in her mind and she thinks, 'It sounds good when you say it but to actually live it in reality is extremely hard' (p. 194).

In the end we are left only with the narrator telling us that time is passing and yet it does not pass in vain. We could take it to mean that Duanli goes back to her job. Yet the way she has been living her life in the past, and the changes that have once again occurred in her self-image, make it seem improbable. Although we see her self-doubt and awareness of the fact that the return of all the money will make her slip back into the old situation, she is still unable to make that final decision to go back to work and retain a degree of independence from the family.

Responses to gender discourse The purpose of this analysis was to understand the character Duanli in relation to the orthodox gender identity paradigm. Two points need to be stressed here to help us classify the story as one which corresponds to a relatively orthodox position on gender discourse. The first is that Duanli's sense of her own identity is based on how orthodox discourse says women should be: beautiful, dependent and idle. Secondly, the discourse of others on her also judges and places her along the same grid. Her family, and particularly her husband, want her to be docile and delicate; a Duanli who was afraid even to cross the street without her husband at her side.

Duanli is presented to us in all the traditional family relationships and her self-image is also governed by her position within these relations. In terms of traditional discourse she is in an ideal position, wife to the eldest son of a wealthy Shanghai family, with no regard for money or any idea of hardship. Thus, her habitus is that of a traditional woman who has married well. This identification creates the wider boundaries within which Duanli's identity is constructed. It largely determines the choices that Duanli makes and influences her response to the objective circumstances that she faces. It is identification with this discourse that allows us to classify the character Duanli as constructed along an ortho-dox gender identity paradigm. Yet the subsequent developments in her life also show the fragile nature of this orthodox discourse, or the superficial nature of her security. The security and strength that she derived from her social position is wiped out in one stroke through government policy and the Cultural Revolution. From being a wealthy family, her in-laws are reduced to being pariahs in society, forced to sell old clothes to make ends meet.

Through the narrative we learn of a different gender identity paradigm which Duanli could have adopted: that of a criticial response to her circumstances and a refusal to return to the old life-style when she had the chance. However, her awareness of her own strength and capacity is once again pushed into the background as soon as the family's wealth is returned. Although the story reveals the possibilities that exist for women to counter the demands of orthodox discourse, it also creates conditions for its constant re-emergence. Duanli's identification with an orthodox gender identity paradigm remains dominant and reasserts itself as soon as the old circumstances of the family are restored. This also shows us that the objective circumstances of her life structure her identity to a large extent.

Even though the context of the Cultural Revolution forces Duanli into different circumstances, and supports the claim that gender relations during this period were disturbed, the result of these circumstances is contradictory. While she sees the shaky ground on which her identity as a 'lucky' Chinese girl was based, she is still nostalgic for the past, when she could be the ideal Chinese woman. It is this sense of nostalgia and the emotional security that she derives from being looked after by Wenyao, her husband, that show the dominant gender paradigm as her main identification.

The end of the Cultural Revolution throws her back into her old position. She leaves her job and drifts back into her old life-style. Although this leaves her feeling empty and bored, and even though she remembers how in the adverse and difficult time of the Cultural Revolution she had been such a strong woman, she is unable to make the concrete decision to go against the wishes of her husband. Duanli comes full circle without actually questioning the reason for her sense of dissatisfaction. In other words, she never acquires a critical understanding of gender relations and of her position in the family. Like the orthodox discourse on gender relations which attempts to mystify the contradictions inherent in the role that women should occupy, Duanli's identification with orthodox expectations also hides and suppresses the inner contradiction that she feels. Although she misses the sense of purpose and confidence that she acquired through working and facing hardships on behalf of the family, she is willing to succumb to her husband's wishes with regard to her life-style and personal appearance.

In the case of Duanli, two discourses can be reconstructed as important for the development of her character: these are the discourses of gender and class. Her capitalist class position determines her objective circumstances and also the events that determine her choices. The other significant discourse is that of gender; this also determines her sense of identity. Both these discourses interact and, at a certain point of the story, even come into conflict with each other. Despite the fact that she realises that taking her father-in-law's money will make it difficult for her to become the person that she wants to be, she gives in to the security and ease which money seems to provide for her. She becomes once again the ideal and useless social butterfly, who finds her sense of identity in a constant round of social engagements and shopping sprees. We see the Duanli who was strong and self-sufficient and had no time for personal vanities disappear without too much trouble, swallowed up by the superficial things that had attracted her earlier. The inner strength that she had gained through being productive is lost. It is here that her gender identity resurfaces and she becomes almost an ideal caricature of what a rich housewife should be.

This situation of Duanli can be seen as close to the kind of ideals that orthodox discourse presents for women. They are supposed to be good housewives and mothers. With Duanli, we see that this is definitely the case. We have no indication that her husband ever takes part in the housework or shoulders any other household responsibility. Even though she becomes aware that her husband's authority is grounded on his father's wealth, she is never critical of her own role as his cosseted wife. She looks down on him because of his failure to provide for her and the family. She never questions her own desire to remain dependent on a traditional and outmoded family structure instead of standing on her own feet. The sense of worth that she had achieved working and being productive during the Cultural Revolution is seen as a kind of hardship that she has managed to come through.

Finally, an analysis of Duanli's character also helps us see that identity is not something that remains constant but changes as different discourses in the character's personality come to the fore. The character becomes a composite of class and gender discourses, both in terms of how she identifies herself and how others in her immediate vicinity identify her. At the level of discourse, it is these two major discourses which interact to make Duanli the character that she is. Her responses in terms of the choices she makes are in fact the stereotyped choices of a woman in her situation. They also reveal how traditional gender identities continue to persist in China because of the way women accept and internalise a dominant gender identity paradigm, despite the fact that today other possibilities are open to them. The conflicts that arise in Duanli's life are a result of the interaction between a traditional and socialist gender identity paradigm.

A socialist gender identity paradigm: Lu Wenting in *At Middle Age*

Shen Rong published her novella *At Middle Age* (*Rendao Zhongnian*) in 1980. It won the author wide-scale recognition and various literary prizes, such as the award for the best story of the year. In 1983 it was made into a feature film, which also won acclaim and popularity. This publicity is interesting because this was a period of excitement and innovation in the literary world of China as a whole, with many young and new writers experimenting with both form and content. Earlier I noted how, in China, both critical acclaim and censure are politically motivated. No literary work acquires the legitimacy that Shen Rong's did in the early 1980s unless it has been approved of by the highest echelons of Party power (Link 1985). The praise that this story has attracted is all the more interesting because it features as its protagonist a female character, Lu Wenting. This in itself made it a rather obvious choice for me to select for analysis in terms of assessing 'orthodox responses' to gender discourse. The position of the character, or the discourse universe inhabited by it, correspond closely to the way an orthodox socialist discourse sees the position of women. In that sense, we are not seeing a real woman or reflections of a real woman but the construction of a woman who represents the 'ideal' form that women should aim for in relation to socialist orthodoxy in China. As argued earlier, orthodox discourse on gender relations in China exhibits a curious mixture of socialist rhetoric on the equal rights of women while continuing to support and mobilise women in their more traditional familial roles.

The context of the story Shen Rong locates *At Middle Age*[7] in the aftermath of the Cultural Revolution. As its background, the story tells the plight of middle-aged intellectuals and other scientific people in China, showing the difficult conditions under which they work and live, in cramped living spaces and with low salaries. The story attempts a criticism of the Cultural Revolution by holding the policies of this period responsible for the conditions of the intellectuals and for the lack of respect with which they are treated.[8]

The story also attempts to show the projected role of intellectuals in China's new modernisation programme. As already pointed out, the literary works of this period were focusing on the psychological and emotional damage caused to people because of the political emphasis attached to the 'class' question. The term was used in an extremely dogmatic fashion and anyone who did not belong to the official working class or peasantry was automatically suspect. Intellectuals were often the main victims and they were even classified as the 'ninth stinking category'. Shen Rong's story stands out because she chose to focus on middle-aged scientific intellectuals, a category of intellectuals who are politically acceptable and whose importance has been stressed by the current leadership if China is to achieve the goals of its modernisation programme. In fact, the characters in the narrative also constantly voice their support for the modernisation programme and complain about those things which are identified as hindering it. Within the tradition of modern Chinese fiction, the story could be classified as one which attempts to create a 'positive character' who can be held up as an example.

The protagonist of the story is, thus, located in the context of the post-Cultural Revolution period and is used to illustrate several of the problems that continue to persist in China. In the broader perspective, the story highlights the new role of Chinese intellectuals and attempts to point out their selfless dedication to China's modernisation.

The story centres around the life of a middle-aged lady doctor named Lu Wenting, who works as an ophthalmologist in a big city hospital. The story starts when she suffers a heart-attack. The main narrative technique employed is that of the flashback, her own memories and recollections of her life by other characters. The story represents an excellent example of discourse on the character and the character's discourse about herself.

The setting of the character The character Lu Wenting is set against the background of a large city hospital where she works and against her family life. Lu Wenting is an ophthalmologist. Although she is already middle-aged, and has been working in the hospital for eighteen years, she is still a junior doctor. This is because during the Cultural Revolution promotions as such were stopped. Regarding her personal background, we are very briefly told that she is the daughter of a poor seamstress whose husband abandonded her. She remembers her mother as prematurely old and working long hours to make ends meet. In effect, her childhood is painted as one of deprivation and hardship. It is only after the Communist Party comes to power that she gets a chance to go to medical college. In the story, she is married and has two children. Her husband is a physicist and works in a research institute. I shall discuss these two backgrounds – work and family – separately.

The professional setting: Lu Wenting the doctor The character Lu Wenting is shown to be a dedicated doctor in three ways: in the actions she is depicted in; in her total absorption in her job, brought out in her own discourse; and in the comments of patients and colleagues. Her daily routine at the hospital is shown to consist of long hours of work as she covers various duties from surgery to out-patient examination. As the narrator points out: 'One operation after another. How come they arranged for three operations in one morning? She had removed vice-minister Jiao's cataract, transplanted a cornea on Uncle Zhang's eye and corrected Wang Xiaoman's squint. Starting at eight in the morning, she had sat on the high operating stool for four and a half hours under the bright lamp concentrating on her work' (p. 53). We are further told that this is not an exceptional day for her but a fairly regular occurrence. Lu Wenting still works at the hospital where she was a student. As a student she is described as hard-working and diligent and she is also shown to have been a conscientious pupil. The head of her department, Dr Sun, remembers her as a promising oculist in her student days. He remembers how she impressed him during her interview by her ability to answer all his questions. He chose her 'for her simplicity, seriousness and keenness' (p. 57). Since then, her dedication to her work is further demonstrated to Dr Sun by an incident in which she asks him to examine a patient whose problem she thinks has been wrongly diagnosed. Dr Sun agrees with her diagnosis, going on to say 'Dr Lu has not been in our department for very long. Her careful research and responsible attitude are to be admired and are very praiseworthy' (p. 58).

We know that the other staff at the hospital also regard her highly.

Dr Zhao, the head of the hospital, chooses her to perform an eye operation on a senior Party cadre who happens to be a vice-minister. We are told of her complete indifference to the rank and title of her patient. She is introduced to the vice-minister and interviewed by his wife about her background and health. Throughout the polite conversation that follows, she is concerned not with trying to impress the vice-minister and his wife but with those of her patients who are still waiting. When the wife of the vice-minister asks her questions about her personal health because she feels that no ordinary doctor is good enough to operate on her husband, Lu is shown thinking: 'What does she [the vice-minister's wife] mean by asking such questions? Lu spent all day caring for others so that she had never even had time to think about her own health. The hospital did not even have her case history. And none of the leaders had ever inquired after her health before' (p. 61).

Her selfless dedication is further highlighted by the memories of vice-minister Jiao. During his operation, he remembers that once, during the Cultural Revolution, when he had come to the clinic as an ordinary patient, Red Guards had chased him into the operating theatre, demanding that the doctors refuse to deal with him since he had been dubbed a rightist and a reactionary. Instead of giving in to their threats, Lu Wenting had calmly ordered them out and proceeded with the operation, creating a deep impression on the vice-minister (p. 79).

The nurses and other medical staff admire her, and her surgery days are regularly attended by younger doctors who want to learn from her. As we are told: 'The theatre nurses all respected Dr Lu, while at the same time being afraid of her. They admired her surgical skill and feared her strictness. A doctor's authority was established through the scalpel ... Lu had no position, no power, but through her scalpel she wielded authority' (p. 79).

Her dedication to work is also brought out in the way she looks after her patients. She works long hours without complaint and is willing to spend time with her patients not just as an impersonal doctor but also as someone who listens to their fears and anxieties. This is clearly demonstrated in her attitude to Wang Xiaoman, a young girl afraid of having an eye operation. Lu Wenting spends time with her, allaying her fears and making her feel at home (p. 81). She does the same for the old man, Uncle Zhang, who has travelled all the way from the countryside for his eye operation. She is concerned about his money problem and tries to help him out (p. 65). Lu Wenting's patients also think highly of her, as is brought out in the case of Lao Zhang who comes to visit her when she is sick and tells Dr Sun how important doctors like Lu are to the hospital (p. 87). Wang Xiaoman is also shown to trust her completely and feels at home in the operating theatre because of Lu's kindness and concern.

Thus, Lu Wenting is shown as a dedicated professional in every respect. She shows equal concern for all her patients, irrespective of rank or position. This in turn earns her the respect of all her colleagues and patients. Their discussions about her character show that Lu Wenting represents a socialist heroine, an example to be emulated. Her main identification is shown to be with her work, for which she considers no sacrifice too large. She further lives up to this image of being a socialist heroine by also being a wife and a mother.

The personal setting: Lu Wenting the wife and mother Lu Wenting is presented to us not only as a dedicated professional but also as a wife and mother. As Jin Zhiyu, a Chinese literary critic, puts it: 'She is not just a good doctor, she is also a good wife and a good mother' (1986: 27). It is this emphasis on both her role as a modern professional woman and on the more traditional role of wife and mother that makes Lu stand out as an ideal character.

She meets her husband while she is working as an intern in the hospital to which he is admitted as a patient. They fall in love and, again, this love is shown as an ideal: they complement each other professionally and are both serious-minded individuals interested in the greater good of their nation. They get married and have a son and a daughter. Again the narrator presents us with an ideal couple and family. Her husband Fu Jiajie is a scientist working on problems of metal fatigue. We are told: 'Every time the neighbors naughty children peeped into their small room to spy on the newly married couple, they always found them at work: In the evenings, Lu occupied their only desk to study foreign medical books ... while Fu read reference books on a stack of chests' (p. 67).

At home she puts the needs of her husband before her own. This is brought out in the way in which she blames herself because her husband does not have enough time to study. Because of cramped living space, their bedroom is also their study. She says to her husband one evening: 'I have been too selfish. I only think of my work ... I have a family but my heart is not with them. Doesn't matter what housework I am doing, my mind remains preoccupied by my patients ... Really, I have failed in my responsibility as a mother and a wife' (p. 72).

The same sentiment is repeated in her dialogue with her husband one night when she can't sleep and her husband is sitting up late in order to finish an article. She suddenly decides that he should go and live in the university hostel in order to have more time to work. She says: 'Do you know what I am thinking? I think you should move into your institute. Then you will have more time ... I am serious, you have things to do. You are a scientist. I know the children and I have been tiring you and that influences your work' (p. 77). When Fu Jiajie objects because all the household chores and child-care will fall on her shoulders, she says: 'Haven't you often remarked that I am a tough woman? I can cope. Your son won't go hungry, your daughter won't be ill-treated' (p. 77).

Thus, we see that she is not for a moment thinking of her own needs. In fact, she seems to have no needs or weaknesses. Throughout the conversation there is no question of her missing her husband or of being emotionally dependent on him. She is again an ideal communist heroine with her single-minded dedication to work, not only on her own behalf but also on behalf of her husband. Further, the dialogue between the husband and wife reads like a Communist Party propaganda bulletin, with its rhetoric of modernisation and progress.

The couple's dedication to their country is further highlighted by a description of their material circumstances, which are not very good. They live in a crowded two-room apartment with their two children. Despite such little return for their work, they do not complain. As Dr Zhang, the administrative head of the hospital, notes: 'What? Four in a room? And what is her salary? Only 56.60 yuan. That is why people say it is better to be a barber than a surgeon with a scalpel' (p. 62).

We know that her husband considers her a strong woman from his thoughts about her. While sitting beside her sick-bed, he thinks: 'She was not weak, he knew that well. Slim in build, she was in fact fit and strong. Though her shoulders were slight, she silently endured all hardships and sudden misfortunes. She never complained, feared, or became disheartened. You are a tough woman, he had often said to her' (p. 76).

On the other hand, her dedication to her profession has meant that her husband is forced to take part in housework, a task which is not seen as normal practice. In a dialogue with his friend, he says: 'I wish your hospital understood how hard it is to be a doctor's husband. As soon as the order comes to go out on medical tours or relief work, she's up and off, leaving the family' (p. 70). Although the interchange takes place in a joking fashion, the narrator presents it as a bitter joke, another thing to be blamed on the Cultural Revolution – a scientist forced to become a house-husband.

In this above description of her husband Fu Jiajie we see the two discourses on femininity. One concerns Lu Wenting's role as a wife: as such she should put the interests of her family before that of her work.

The second is the discourse of socialism which demands that her first duty is to the goals of the state. In both cases, we see her as someone who is uncomplaining and always puts the interests of others before her own.

Lu Wenting's relationship with her son Yuanyuan and her daughter Xiaojia is one of care and guilt. During the period of her sickness, Lu Wenting often reflects on the fact that she has neglected her children for the sake of her patients. This is demonstrated in one incident when Lu is busy at work and is informed by Xiaojia's kindergarten nurse that the child is sick. Instead of rushing off to be with her child, like most mothers would be expected to do, she forgets about her daughter until she has finished examining her patients. As she reflects while continuing with her work: "'I'll go to the kindergarten when I am through with the patients", she thought returning to her desk. At first she imagined her daughter crying and calling her. Later she saw only the patients' eyes' (p. 66). Even after she finally gets to her daughter, she has no time to stay with her, leaving her in the care of a neighbour and rushing back to her patients.

Lu Wenting is aware of the problem, and, as in every other case, she blames herself. When her friends praise her as a hard-working doctor, she says:'You ask him [her husband] if I'm not selfish, driving my husband into the kitchen and turning my children into vagabonds. I've messed up the whole family. The fact is, I'm neither a good wife nor a good mother' (p. 70). This sense of failure is again what points out the ideal construction of the character. She would like to be perfect but is unable to be so because of her work. This dual responsibility to work and family leaves Lu Wenting feeling guilty during her illness because she has always put her work before her family. She remembers how she never had time to plait her daughter's hair, despite being repeatedly asked to do so, and how she did not have time to go and buy her son a pair of shoes (p. 85). Here we also see how tired she really is, trying to combine different roles. In her state of semi-consciousness, she wants to die and put an end to all the hardship. As the narrator tells us: 'For years, she had simply had no time to pause, to reflect on the hardships she had experienced or the difficulties lying ahead. Now her mind was blank, there were no memories, no hope nothing' (p. 84).

Thus, we see that Lu Wenting is not only a dedicated ophthalmologist but also a woman who is striving to care for her children and family in the best way possible. In fact, it is the guilt that she feels about having neglected her family that helps us speak of the operation of gender discourse. This is a specifically female problem in China, since orthodox discourse expects a woman's main identification to be with her family.

She is in fact trying to achieve the impossible task of shouldering the double burden faced by Chinese women today.

Relationships with other characters Apart from her immediate family, Lu Wenting's relationships with other people are through her workplace. The most important of these relationships is with her closest friend and colleague, Yafen. Yafen and Wenting studied together and started their specialisation in ophthalmology at the same time.

The narrator sketches Wenting's character in contrast to Yafen's. Although they are very close friends, Yafen is shown as being less serious and single-minded about her profession and she is emigrating to Canada in search of a better life for her children. Yafen compares herself with Lu Wenting in the last letter she writes to her. Explaining her reasons for leaving China, she says: 'Compared with you I am a weaker character. Though I had less trouble than you in the last ten years, I could not bear it as you did ... No one could shake your faith. I knew that you had a strong will which enabled you to resist all kinds of attacks and go your own way' (p. 91).

The opinion of Yafen's husband Liu is similar to his wife's. He is also shown to have enormous respect and admiration for Lu Wenting. His opinion is brought out in the following statement during their farewell party: 'Who are you? ... You live in cramped quarters and slave away regardless of criticism, not seeking fame or money. A hard-working doctor like you is like an ox serving the children, as Lu Xun said, eating grass and providing milk' (p. 70).

From the different impressions gathered, we see that the narrator creates a character who is described by all who know her as a strong woman and an excellent doctor. She is also shown as being principled and ethical, never currying favours from her superior and never rude to her subordinates. She is someone who is shown to inspire respect and admiration from all those with whom she comes into contact. Her family friends and colleagues all consider her exemplary. The attention and love that she receives during her illness are testimony to that fact. She is a woman who seems able to combine the extraordinary demands placed on her with superhuman intensity.

Thus, based on what other characters think of Lu Wenting, we can come to the conclusion that she is indeed a paragon of all virtues. She is incapable of doing wrong; she represents the high standards and moral virtue demanded of good socialist citizens; and she seems able to suppress the contradictions inherent in seeking to occupy the various positions of wife, mother and professional woman dedicated to her career.

The development of the character The beginning of the narrative shows us Lu Wenting lying sick in the hospital, and the end of the narrative has her walking out of the hospital. In terms of chronological time only a month and a half passes. However, we learn about the character through what she represents to other people.

In terms of character development, she is rather static. In general, both personal and political events do not seem to have had much influence on her. However, two major changes have determined the course of her life. The first is the victory and consolidation of communism in China. From being the daughter of a poor seamstress with little or no future, the policies instituted by the Party provide her with the opportunity to gain an education and enter medical college. (Interestingly enough, this event is stressed as important by several Chinese critics, being in line with Party propaganda that constantly stresses the improvements which communist rule has made to the lives of the Chinese people.) We know that from her university days onwards, she has been earnest and hard-working. When her classmates are going out with boys and engaging in harmless fun, she spends all her time studying. She continues to work hard during the years of her internship. Lu Wenting's life follows an even course of development until the second major change occurs: she meets and falls in love with Fu Jiajie. This event is shown to be of enormous importance since it is the first time that she falls in love in all her twenty-eight years. As in all things, she falls in love with single-minded intensity. Here again it is Fu Jiajie who takes the initiative and she remembers how he read her the poems of Petöfi. As the narrator says: 'Never having imagined love could be so intoxicating, she almost regretted not having found it earlier' (p. 54).

Lu Wenting and Fu Jiajie marry as soon as her four years of internship are over. Her love seems to change her life to the extent that instead of being lonely and serious, we are told that the intensity of her feelings allowed her to experience the beauty and joys of life with a fresh insight. In fact, it is her husband's reading of Petöfi at her bedside which brings her back from the brink of death.

Although her marriage can be seen as a major change and development in her character, it does not seem to alter her single-minded dedication to her profession. In fact, her family and her children have to put up with her frequent absences as the needs of her patients and the demands of her heavy work schedule take precedence. This is reflected in the amount of narrative time devoted to her relationship with her family, for the narrative throughout is dominated by her dedication to her profession and to serving the masses, in this case her patients. The only time we see her questioning her single-minded concentration on her work is during her illness when she recollects how she has neglected her children.

It is these passages of guilt and regret that show us the operation of gender discourse. They also show us Lu Wenting as an ideal character who sets high standards for herself. There is no question in her mind that society may be demanding too much of her. She thinks nothing of sacrificing her interests and finally her health in order to fulfil to the best of her ability the double set of expectations that gender discourse in China has of women.

Responses to gender discourse: the socialist way The character Lu Wenting in *At Middle Age* is quite different from the character Duanli in *Lapse of Time*, yet both characters can be analysed as expressing an 'ideal' response to gender discourse. In China, orthodox discourse on gender reflects a combination of traditional attitudes regarding the social role and duties of women, while at the same time attempting to impose certain new ideological demands on women. These have to do with changed attitudes to women working outside the house.

Although socialist orthodoxy stresses the importance of women's economic independence and espouses equal opportunities, women in China continue to play their traditional roles, especially within the family. The result of this ambiguity is the gruelling double burden faced by women, especially in urban China, where more than 60 per cent of women aged between eighteen and fifty-five hold jobs outside the house.

The irony in this is that most women themselves do not question this double burden, trying instead to respond to the demands of orthodoxy by being good workers and good mothers. In effect, socialist orthodoxy demands the impossible from women. The ideal communist heroine is one who can juggle the demands of her family life and yet perform miracles in her workplace.

The character Lu Wenting can be analysed as responding ideally to the demands of this new socialist orthodoxy. She is not only a dedicated professional, she also has a family. Her work is excellent and so is her relationship with her co-workers; she is also shown to have an ideal relationship with her husband and family. Even within the family, she is the one who is willing to take on a double burden while encouraging her scientist husband to shift to a dormitory so that he can concentrate on his work. In fact, one wonders how her husband Fu Jiajie could have accepted moving out of the house to concentrate on his work, if space did not already exist for a man to be able to do so. It is an accepted fact of gender discourse in China that men have the right to concentrate on their careers without having their families interfere.

Women, however, have no such discursive space available to them. They are expected to be able to combine their commitment to the family and to their careers. It would, for example, be impossible to imagine Lu Wenting moving out of the house and leaving her husband to look after the family while she devoted herself to her work. Lu Wenting can be analysed as attempting an ideal response also because she is an unrealistic character. She is too good to be true and seems to suffer from none of the self-doubts and recriminations that affect her friend Yafen.

She is, in fact, the ideal socialist heroine.

Critical praise and ideality

In terms of an analysis of gender discourse, one more aspect concerning the novellas becomes extremely important. This is the way literary critics in China have analysed the two stories discussed above. As already pointed out in Chapter 3, literary criticism in China is a political weapon which is used to propagate the ideological position of the Party. While literary criticism concerned with women's literature may not seem to address political questions directly, it reveals the way gender issues are spoken about in society. Literary criticism, especially in the influential dailies and official literary journals, represents the voice of the establishment and is linked to the wider discourse on gender relations. Here, the ways in which critics analyse issues of both style and content become important indicators of acceptability. The acceptability of the kind of stories created attests to the way these stories match the expectations of orthodox discourse.

Among literary critics in China, Wang Anyi's other stories are better received than *Lapse of Time*. However, even criticism of her other stories has certain specific features. Most critics consider her to be a versatile and promising young author. This is certainly true. Apart from being prolific, she also writes well; her narrative style 'represents objective reality artistically and beautifully' (Xu Qihua 1985: 43). Her earlier stories contain female characters who are young, gentle, ethereal and idealistic . Bing Xin, in a foreword written for Wang Anyi's collection of stories, describes her as someone capable of combining traditional roles with modern times. She quotes from an interview Wang Anyi gave in which she said: 'I hope that with the coming of prosperity the Chinese people keep the good aspects of traditional values; not become like the West today, where people are so separated from each other' (Bing Xin 1985: 94).

This desire of Wang Anyi's to preserve the status quo or the doxic aspect of social relations, which are natural and traditional, can also be seen reflected in *Lapse of Time*. Gender relations, as we have seen, form the basis of tradition. Continuity is established and maintained because everyone fulfils their ordained roles. Women's maternal and nurturance roles are part of Wang Anyi's traditional ideality.

Those who have commented on this story see it as part of Wang Anyi's rich narrative style which paints a realistic picture of life in China. Nan Fan, a Chinese critic who has commented upon Wang Anyi's work, sees her as a young writer with enormous talent, a writer whose work gives people a 'strong feeling of continuity which excludes the limits of reality' (Nan Fan 1984: 107). He sees Duanli as a character who has always been a housewife and even though her experiences during the Cultural Revolution take her out to work, afterwards she again choses the same role (1984: 111). Nan Fan sees this choice as leading to `boredom and emptiness'. Although official socialist discourse does not see Duanli as an ideal character, we can see that the gender identity paradigm adopted by the character represents the limits and options available to a woman in pre-communist Chinese society. The conflicts that arise are a result of the interaction between a traditional and a socialist gender identity paradigm.

An extremely interesting reading of Wang Anyi's work is given by Liu Min (1989). Heavily influenced by feminist psychoanalytic theory, the main points of Liu Min's article are worth quoting here for two reasons. First, because they show that the understanding of the field of Chinese studies is not without complexity and, second, because they show the use of comparative literary theory by Chinese critics. Liu Min points out that Wang Anyi's female characters are all located in a traditional space. As she says: 'In her recent stories, we find Wang Anyi has changed the role of her female characters. Instead of being daughters, they are mothers and wives. Her conception of female nature locates them within the atmosphere of family life' (Liu Min 1989: 137).

Liu Min further goes on to explain that Wang Anyi's use of language and narrative technique, especially her narrator, seems to represent a male viewpoint. To quote Liu Min: 'Wang Anyi wants her female protagonists to voluntarily leave the world of work and production. She wants them to voluntarily return to the bosom of the family. She feels that it is natural for a woman to do so – a viewpoint which is not considered strange in China' (1989: 139).

The impressions of Liu Min, I feel, are corroborated by my reading of the character Duanli in *Lapse of Time*. Here too we notice that the family is a sort of refuge from the rest of the world. In fact, it is the only place where Duanli feels a sense of identity, a sense of belonging. Wang Anyi's female protagonists can thus justifiably be seen to represent the voice of traditional ideality regarding male–female relations. Her desire to preserve the continuity of traditional values makes her a writer who appeals to the literary establishment. This of course does not detract from her enormous talent as a writer and her feel for language and literary creation.

The excessive praise that Shen Rong's *At Middle Age* attracted in China in 1980 implied that the ideological perspective presented in it was acceptable. Chinese critics have highlighted those aspects of it which address the question of the position of intellectuals in China. The novella often reads like a piece of propaganda intended to highlight the suffering of intellectuals as a whole. Lu Wenting is seen to represent an ideal and selfless intellectual whose chief concern is to work for the good of the nation. As one Chinese critic puts it: 'The success of *At Middle Age* is due to several reasons. The most important of these being that Shen Rong creates a typical representative of the new socialist personality [*shehui zhuiyi xinren de dianxing*] which moves people' (Wang Chunyun 1986: 50).

Later in the same article, Wang Chunyun says: 'In the character Lu Wenting we can see the heroic and romantic spirit of Chinese intellectuals from the May Fourth Movement till today' (1986: 51). Thus, Lu Wenting is considered a typical representative of all the good qualities of socialist ethics and life-style. Other literary critics have also highlighted these aspects of the novella. Lu Wenting has been held up as a model to be emulated not just by women but by individuals in China as a whole. Wang Chunyun points out: 'Her [Lu Wenting's] spirit reflects the heroism of an ordinary worker. This heroism is her capacity for self-sacrifice. She loves her work and her patients and can be compared to certain characters during the liberation struggle' (1986: 10–11).

Lu Wenting is thus considered to epitomise everything an individual should be under socialism. She is a successful example of a typical new socialist personality, dedicated to the four modernisations. Like most critics, and the editorials in newspapers such as *Literary Gazette* (*Wenhui Bao*), he sees the story as reflecting the problems faced by middle-aged intellectuals in China.

Again, the problem of Lu Wenting isn't seen as a problem specific to women, but of both sexes. For us it is more important to note that these characteristics of self-sacrifice and dedication are also closely related to gender roles. Orthodoxy, both of the traditional and the socialist variety, tends to emphasise values of self-sacrifice above all else. These values are also those which have traditionally been identified as essentially female, as pointed out in my discussion of Confucian orthodoxy in China in Chapter 2. Those critics who do talk about the character as a woman see her as representing the best advances made by women under socialism. As Wu Jianluo says: 'The quality of her character and her views represent a combination of eastern female beauty and the individuality that has developed in the West' (1989: 44).

In the case of Lu Wenting, we see the demands of the traditional supportive role being combined with those of socialist orthodoxy; women have to be good workers whose dedication lies with the two units, the traditional family and the state. Chinese critics see Lu Wenting as fulfilling this demand. As Jin Zhiyu says:

> The character Lu Wenting gives us the aesthetic impression of a clear mountain stream, which although it is small keeps flowing steadily on ... She is quiet but dignified. She is indifferent to fame and gain but has a great deal of self-confidence, she is tender but still strong. She is not only a good doctor but also a good mother and wife. It is really an illuminating depiction of the depths of female qualities. (Jin Zhiyu 1986: 27)

Her ability to combine the roles of wife, mother and doctor is seen as an example to be emulated. Yet the novella, and the fate of the character Lu Wenting who collapses unexpectedly, can be read as the failure of attempting such a combination. This conclusion, however, has to be read on to the text, for the text itself suppresses this contradiction. Lu Wenting and the other characters in the story never acknowledge that her collapse is in any way related to her situation. In other words, the gender-specific nature of the problem is never highlighted. Instead, both the criticism directed at the story and the fate of Lu Wenting tend to emphasise the fact that she is an intellectual, rather than the fact that she is a female intellectual.

A feminist reading could, for example, argue that Lu Wenting's collapse is inevitable, since the conflict created by gender orthodoxy does not allow for any other solution. Thus, although Lu Wenting does ultimately recover, her near death is shown as the result of over-work and the shabby way intellectuals are treated in China as a whole, not as a problem which is gender-specific. Although a critical reader can spot this fact, the text as a whole represses the contradiction in much the same way that socialist orthodoxy on gender relations hides the conflict inherent in the double role that women are expected to play.

It is this aspect that allows us to analyse the character Lu Wenting as attempting an ideal response to gender orthodoxy in China. Instead of questioning or examining her life and the various relationships she is in, she tries to suppress all tensions by attempting to live up to the ideal expectations of her cultural context. She is both feminine, gentle and emotionally caring, and at the same time is a good citizen and doctor.

This characterisation fulfils the criterion set by literary criticism when it analyses women characters in fiction by women. Here Lu Wenting's 'nature' remains essentially feminine; she is not one of the *nüxing xionghua* or female viragoes. The discourse which she represents is linked to the social discourse in her being held up as a model and typical character by the establishment. This is in direct contrast to the two female characters who will be discussed in the next chapter.

The character Lu Wenting is thus shown as constructed within the framework of orthodox positions on gender discourse. In terms of a response to gender discourse, Lu Wenting can be read as a character who attempts an ideal response. Yet the fact of her collapse shows the impossibility of realising an ideal response. The novella, while attempting to suppress this fact, also allows us to see the way women in China are expected to fulfil the demands of socialist orthodoxy on gender relations. Above all, it shows us the way women writers in their participation in the field of literary discourse bring into the open the ways in which female identity is constructed and deployed.

In the next chapter two more stories will be studied. These, however, will be shown to represent a critical or heterodox gender paradigm; a paradigm which is different from and critical of the dominant ways of viewing male–female relations and questions the role of marriage and the family. They illustrate the different discourses that exist on gender relations in China alongside orthodox discourse.

Notes

1. The link between institutions and an orthodoxy of discourse is clearly visible in the case of China. The previous chapters show how a particular type of gender discourse is deployed by institutions linked to the state.

2. The idea that we are all participants in discourse and accept the limits imposed by particular discourses is important for understanding the popularity of orthodox discourse.

3. Women writers, in their own work, make use of social discourse in the way they construct characters. In this sense, they are participants in discourse. In terms of an orthodox discourse, they create the possibility of identifying the salient features of an orthodox discourse by deploying it in the construction of narrative characters.

4. Wang Anyi's novella *Lapse of Time* (*Liushi*) was first published in the magazine *Shou Hou*. Later, it was used as the title of her collection of short stories published by the Sichuan People's Publishing House.

5. For details of the Cultural Revolution, see Robinson (1971).

6. The down to the countryside campaign (*Xiafang*) was an important part of the Cultural Revolution. Intellectuals were expected to go to the countryside to re-educate themselves and learn from the masses.

7. Shen Rong's *At Middle Age* (*Rendao Zhongnian*) was first published in the magazine *Shou Hou.*

8. For an understanding of the fate of intellectuals during the Cultural Revolution, see Thurston (1988).

6
Heterodox responses to gender discourse

The female protagonists of the two novellas analysed in Chapter 5, *Lapse of Time* and *At Middle Age*, both reflect orthodox patterns of behaviour and choices of gender roles. However, this is by no means the only form of response to gender discourse within the arena of fictive characterisation. Women characters can also represent positions which situate them at a distance from the gender identity paradigm provided by orthodoxy.

Bourdieu stresses the existence of orthodox *and* heterodox discourses. The choices one makes between different identity paradigms, the acceptance or rejection of the demands placed on them by those in a position to define norms, show our agency and reveal the sense we make of our social and cultural space. As Bourdieu points out:

> The process that gives works momentum is produced by the struggle between the 'orthodox' and the 'heretic,' between on the one hand actors who tend towards conservatism, to defend routine and routinization, in a word, the established symbolic order ... and those who incline to heretical breaks and the criticism of established forms and the subversion of the current model. (Bourdieu 1977: 545)

Thus, those discourses which are institutionalised do not exist in a totally authoritarian fashion. In practice, their hegemony is being constantly challenged. It is often the case that orthodoxy also possesses the institutional means to suppress, deny and marginalise other discourses. However, it is precisely this denial which, paradoxically, works to legitimate counter-discourse as heterodoxy. In China's case, this fact is perhaps too obvious since the regime has the right to confine its citizens for articulating or organising around positions contrary to those of the Party. Gender discourse, as we shall see, has not been left out of this struggle between orthodoxy and heterodoxy.

As pointed out earlier, orthodox discourse on gender in China today consists of a socialist state rhetoric which builds upon specific features of the more traditional discourse on femininity and womanhood. Women down the ages have questioned the boundaries of orthodoxy. Margery

Wolf points out that women in China found different ways of expressing resistance to the very strict Confucian code of conduct demanded of them (Wolf 1978). In China, literature has often been a medium through which the limits of orthodox discourse have been challenged. As far as women are concerned, we have the example of the generation of May Fourth writers such as Ding Ling, who in their writings explored the problems and alternatives faced by women in China in the 1920s and 1930s. Literature became a major field where alternative life-styles for women were discussed.

My purpose in this chapter is to analyse two novellas in which the development of the female characters and the choices made by them reflect positions which are different from that of orthodoxy. The characters in these novellas provide an alternative gender identity paradigm to the demands placed on women by orthodoxy, both of the traditional options available to women as wives and mothers, and the double role offered to women by a state-sponsored ideology of protectionism. As in the previous two novellas, those chosen for analysis in this section feature women characters as the protagonists.

Zhang Xinxin's *On the Same Horizon* (*Zai Tongyi de pingxianshang*)

The early 1980s saw the emergence of several new writers, Zhang Xinxin among them. She started writing in 1978 and her stories have attracted attention and controversy. According to herself: 'She is one of the lucky ones whom notoriety has made famous' (Zhang Xinxin 1982: 431). A diverse and stylistically sophisticated writer, she has in several of her novellas sensitively portrayed the emotional dilemmas faced by women in their personal relationships and at work. She is particularly well known for the frank psychological exploration of the inner thoughts of her female protagonists (Kinkley 1990). Major themes in her work include the misunderstandings that arise between couples, and the way women who go against the traditional image of femininity are often left to face the world alone. The novella chosen for analysis here is a good example of her work.

The context of the story Zhang Xinxin wrote *On the Same Horizon* in 1981–82 and it was first published in the magazine *Shou Hou*.[1] The story attracted attention both for its content and for its style. In it, Zhang Xinxin describes the alienation that springs up between a young married couple. By Chinese standards it is a modern story, as it is one of the first to experiment with stream of consciousness or *yishi liu*.[2]

Zhang Xinxin uses a simultaneous exploration of the feelings of both her characters, switching from the female voice to the male voice and vice versa. Both characters are nameless, designated only by *ta*, which means he and she. Each character is also the focaliser at different times.

The story follows the changes that the female protagonist is making in her life. She falls in love and marries an artist, sacrificing her own last chance to enter university. In the beginning, she dedicates herself to caring for her husband's needs and to creating a home for them. A few years of marriage, however, leave her feeling frustrated and empty. Gradually they begin to grow apart and finally divorce. She enters a film institute and goes on to specialise in directing.

The main context of the story, however, is the conflict that arises in the relationship between the male and the female protagonists. Although the couple end up divorcing, the story focuses on the complex psychological and emotional traumas that the female protagonist must overcome before she can take the ultimate decision to go her own way. It is this type of psychological narrative, dealing with issues not directly related to China's political and ideological aims, that makes Zhang Xinxin a controversial writer. Her stories all reflect her view of the changing reality of China, especially the way relationships between people are changing.

Zhang Xinxin depicts the increasing competitiveness and individualism that has marked post-Mao urban China. It is this attitude of the survival of the fittest (*shengcun jingzheng*) that determines the choices finally made by her protagonists. The following lines from the story sum up this sentiment: 'In reality, whether people accept it or not, and whether people live by it to varying degrees, society like nature is arranged in an hierarchy, where the fittest survive' (p. 213).

In the following analysis, I have chosen to see the female character as exemplifying a critical and heterodox response to the demands of orthodox gender discourse in China. Due to the style of the narrative, its use of stream of consciousness and other stylistic techniques, chronological order is imposed on the narrative by the reader. Although the complexity of the text is lost in this way, it makes the task of analysing the female protagonist much simpler.

The setting of the character The character in the story occupies different settings during different periods. However, despite changes in her personal circumstances, she can be identified as an intellectual and artistic woman living in urban China. This is evident both from her life-style, the friends she has and her interests. Her husband is a painter, her other good friend Yaping is a writer. Her own ambition is also to be an artist, a film director. She, like other young high school students of the late 1960s, goes to rural China during the period of the Cultural Revolution. While there, she falls in love and marries a painter. On their return from the countryside at the end of the Cultural Revolution, she finds herself in the role of a housewife. During this period, she cooks for her husband, cleans for him and generally fulfils the traditional role of a wife (p. 128). This is brought out in the recollection of both parties. As she recalls, once she has left her husband and has started living in a hostel: 'Speaking for myself, if I compare this student life with my married life, I feel a sense of relief ... I no longer have to worry about what time he is coming home ... whether he has eaten ... what he would like to eat ... worry about the grease and mud stains on his trousers' (p. 164).

Thus, we know that at a certain stage of her life she has identified with being a housewife, not working outside the home and only looking after the interests of her husband. The narrative, however, provides numerous statements which prove that even during this period her primary identification remains that of someone keen on her own pursuits. In fact, her desire to pursue her own intellectual ambitions is shown as the start of the problems which arise between them. This conflict is the main feature of the relationship between the couple and will be dealt with in detail later.

After she enters the film institute, she becomes a student and lives in a hostel, attending classes and even participating in sporting events. The contrast with her earlier setting is brought out in the way her daily routine changes. Her participation in the life of the institute is further made evident in the long narrative space given to a sporting event where she competes in a 10,000m run. The incident is used both to create an atmosphere of university life and to introduce several minor characters into the narrative (p. 164). Her participation in a long-distance run is also used as an allegory which describes life, especially the life she has chosen, as a long-distance race, where only those with stamina succeed.

The female protagonist is also shown to be very involved with her course work. As she discusses with a friend: 'I now realise how complicated directing a film is. It is really like a production process. A lot of objective factors matter like the complex relations between different people ... one needs a great deal of organisational skill' (p. 161).

Towards the end of the narrative we find her established as a film director, having successfully completed her ten-minute graduation movie. At the end of the process she says: 'Ten minutes, two months' work, a small thing. All the hard work and struggle over, like a matchstick. The only good thing is that it excited controversy. Not just about the film technique but about the characters' (p. 228).

The female protagonist of the story is thus set against the background of the changing intellectual conditions and possibilities that emerged in China during the immediate post-1978 years. She herself becomes a professional artist by joining and graduating from the film institute. In terms of her setting within the story, she can definitely be classified as an intellectual.

Her relationship with her husband The character's relationship with her husband is the primary relationship in the story. In fact, the story is constructed around the problematic aspects of this relationship, and we are shown it from both sides. The male character's views about the relationship are also made known to us. In the following section, however, the focus of my presentation will be the views of the female protagonist, since the analysis is primarily concerned with her responses. I will focus on the male character only when his discourse is specifically about her.

Our protagonist meets her husband for the first time in the house of a friend who is a writer. There she finds and is very impressed by some of his paintings. In marrying him, however, she gives up her own last chance to enter university. As she says in a letter that she writes to him: 'At that time we wanted to get married immediately ... I took the train that you asked me to without hesitation. The origin of this decision lay in the feeling I had of being unable to go on alone for too long ... I wanted to depend on you ... I felt you were stronger and more capable than me' (pp. 178–9).

At the beginning of her marriage, she finds herself very vulnerable, crying easily and feeling increasingly insecure. She feels that he does not have enough time for her. As she says: 'Those days I used to love to cry, fight with him unnecessarily, what did I want really? Just for him to love me. But his career occupies all his time' (p. 200). In the same passage she describes how she feels that she has become old before her time, that she has been travelling a long road (p. 200). This feeling of being alone in the relationship is also brought out in the following recollection: 'In our life together, he never gave me anything. He only counted on me loving him without having to love me in return. He wanted to experience the happiness and comfort of having a family life and he wanted me to make it possible' (p. 128).

However, the character's relationship with her husband is not one of simple dependence. She is also aware of the reasons for her dependence and the fact that, while he is becoming progressively more famous and has the time to pursue his career and ambitions, she has nothing to look forward to, except having children and deriving some emotional comfort from him.

This is a difficult prospect for her to face, since before her marriage she was an ambitious young woman who wanted to put her creative talent to good use. She realises that to be his equal she has to have something of her own. As she says: 'How much further can I go? Shall I let the last of my aspirations go ... have a baby. No! If I don't have anything of my own, I will never be his equal in spirit or in work ... I would not be able to be sure of equality in this relationship' (p. 128).

It is this rejection of her rather idealistic dream that forces her to chose a different path for herself. She is quite clear about the reasons for her decision. She does not want simply to be a shadow of her husband and it is this feeling that leads her to have an abortion. She does not inform her husband that she is expecting a child, although she tells the doctors that she has discussed everything with him. However, her decision is not shown as a cynical and heartless one, but as something that leaves her feeling empty and very aware of her loneliness. Although it is a painful and difficult thing to do, she goes ahead (p. 126).

In terms of narrative time, this is the beginning of the story; the female protagonist is introduced to us after she has already had her abortion. In order to fulfil her desire to become a film director, she applies for admission to the film institute. While filling in the forms, she realises that married candidates are not accepted. She deliberately leaves the column blank and passes all the tests. However, in the end she is forced to confess that she is married. This makes her ineligible for admission (p. 124).

The only way for her to gain admission into the school is to divorce. This makes her choice clear: the only way to pursue her own dream is to apply for divorce. She approaches her husband with this, telling him about the institute's policy and asking for a divorce. The dialogue that follows, shows the distance that has grown up between them:

He: Why bother to ask me since you have already made up your mind?
She: Since we both want the relationship to end, why not just go ahead and do it?
He: It's not so easy. All this while I've been running around for us, now you only think of yourself.
She: You ran around for yourself, never for me. (p. 137)

Her desire to be equal to him in every sense of the word is the chief source of tension between them. His failure to understand the reasons for her obstinate wish to pursue a career is brought out in the following dialogue, where he tells her, 'You want to be too independent ... but you are not a bad woman ... think about it. All that has happened between us is because of this' (p. 176).

However, we are told that the decision to be independent and strong is something that she feels has been forced on to her by her husband. As she lets us know when she goes to invite him to attend her graduation ceremony: 'I never wanted to be totally independent ... now that we have reached the stage of separating, I want to say that it is not at all what I wanted but you left me with no other choice but to go alone' (p. 238).

Although she does leave him and starts a new life, the decision does not bring her peace of mind. In fact, she finds that having to come to terms with her feelings for him is not easy. She finds herself thinking of him, and every time they meet she finds herself still emotionally vulnerable. She is shown thinking: 'I hate him. But I still miss him very much. I would like so much to let him look after me ... but I know I will never tell him this ... It is strange, even though I know the contradictions between us are insurmountable, I still think of him' (p. 222).

Throughout this period, we also find her regretting her decision not to have children. When she is playing with the child of a friend she asks herself: 'Why do my eyes always rest on children ... How much I would like to hold and nurture this child, only it's somebody else's baby ... She has given birth to a child, a real person, while I am just beginning to work on directing my first film' (p. 220).

The female protagonist of the story is thus constantly caught in the ambiguity of her feelings for her husband. The reason for her separation is his selfish nature and his desire for a placid and calm wife. He recognises the problem of their relationship and puts it down to the fact that neither one of them wants to make any sacrifice for the other, as each is bent only on pursuing his or her own path. As he says: 'When I came home, I wanted her to be there for me, gentle and silent ... but she wanted her own things ... I still don't understand why she was so difficult ' (p. 155).

Thus, the relationship between the two protagonists is depicted with great sensitivity. It is shown to consist of misunderstanding and confusion on both parts. These complications arise mainly because he has a traditional idea of what a relationship should be, and she refuses to play this traditional role. Although the female protagonist remains emotionally attached to her husband, she is eventually able to see the inevitability of their separation. For her, the decision symbolises a victory. Although she is dependent on him and wants him to love her, she is able to move out of her state of weakness and to take concrete steps towards fulfilling her own aspirations. In the end they part on amicable terms, going out for dinner together. They propose a toast to each other, wishing each other better luck with any future spouses. And they say to each other: 'We are alike you know, very difficult to satisfy. We both wanted to change but now it's too late' (p. 244).

Her relationship with other characters The female character in the story is also shown to have strong friendships with other male characters, the chief of whom is Yaguang. He is a writer who has been her friend since high school days. They were sent to the countryside together. Her relationship with Yaguang is platonic and intellectual and they often discuss each other's work. In fact, we learn the female character's personal philosophy of life from her discussions with her friend. One particular incident best describes their relationship. When discussing the latest story that Yaguang has had published, she says: 'Who says female characters have been best portrayed by male writers ... "Woman" is an abstract concept. Each one is different, has different emotional and intellectual needs' (p. 194).

It is Yaguang who advises her on her relationship with her husband, urging her to leave him because he is not worth loving. Thus we see that her friendship with Yaguang is good, if unusual. We know that others think it strange for her to have a platonic friendship, because Yaguang's wife is jealous of their relationship. In this respect, the female protagonist is different from the kind of characters that we find in other stories, because she has friendships of equality with both men and women.

The other young man with whom she has a friendship is Deng Xiaoda, a senior student at the film institute. He is responsible for guiding her initially and helps her to find a cast and a crew for her film. They become friends when they find that they have had similar experiences in life and have several ideas in common. He is impressed by her determination to succeed as a woman director and points out how much more difficult it is for a woman to enter the movie world than for a man. He considers her a 'strong person' (*qiangzhi*) (p. 165).

Yaguang and Deng Xiaoda can best be described as men who present a contrast to her husband and serve as helpers in her development. Further, both Yaguang and Deng Xiaoda consider her to be an intelligent and strong woman, in contrast to the way her husband treats her. Her relationships with her friends help us to see the other aspects of her character which are more in keeping with the objective choices that she makes about her life, but these relationships are not significant in the development of her character. The primary relationship in her life has been with her husband.

The development of the character The development of the character occurs in terms of her search for self-identity; she wants to be a person in her own right. By following the character through the narrative, we can trace the way a specific discourse helps construct her identity. We begin the narrative with a woman who is emotionally and psychologically dependent on her husband, and end the narrative with a woman who is able to come to terms with life as an individual.

The development of the female character can be traced in two ways. One is her development in terms of changing objective circumstances, the other is in terms of her self-identity. These two aspects do not occur simultaneously. The change in her objective circumstances occurs before she has emerged as a woman with a definite idea of her aims and aspirations and a consciousness of her own identity.

We can identify three temporal stages in her development. These are, the time before her marriage, her life as a married woman and her life as a single woman who is a student and aspiring film director. Little information is available about her life before her marriage. All we are told is that she, like most others of her age group, was sent to the countryside. We know that she would have pursued a university education had it not been for her marriage.

Her decision to get married is the first major change in her life. During this period we know that she is dependent on her husband not only financially but also in terms of her identity. At the time that she gets married, she is seeking security and hopes that her husband will provide it for her. In the beginning of their marriage, she constantly needs his attention and is plagued by insecurity because she thinks he does not care enough for her. Her life centres around him and she is desperate to have his undivided attention. She admits that she would throw scenes simply to get his attention, and she blames him for her feelings of lack of fulfilment and unhappiness.

In the beginning, her decision to make something of her life is also seen as a way for her to gain some security for herself. She is dissatisfied because she has this ideal image of a husband in her mind and feels betrayed when he does not live up to her ideal. Her personal development lies precisely in seeing that, although she has blamed him, the problem lies with herself and with the choices that society offers women. At the same time, the choice between a career or marriage is much harder for her because of his failure to understand and encourage her. He is a 'macho man' (*nanzi han*) who seeks to dominate her.

It takes her a long time to realise that she will have to decide to fight for herself and that she will have to do it alone. The most important part of her self-analysis made available to the reader is contained in a letter that she writes to her husband but never posts:

What I felt for you was sincere, but I know finally that it wasn't for you that I gave up a chance for education. You were only a pretext ... every time that you won a fight between us, I let you win ... of course, I can justify my behaviour because of my education as a woman which teaches me to be obedient ... But I rebelled in my youth and that made me perverse. (p. 177)

A major development in her character occurs once she has reached this decision. In a way, her marriage serves as an interim period before she picks up with the life that she had envisioned as a student. Although she marries him and gives up her ambitions, she is nevertheless aware of what she has given up. The desire to have her own career and life is not quashed with her marriage; instead, it is temporarily pushed aside. However, it does not take long to resurface. She soon realises that her marriage cannot offer her the security that she seeks. That security has to come from within. Thus she is able to see that, even though she initially reacts to her husband's authority by accepting it as a woman in China should, the seeds of rebellion which finally lead her to take choices which counter the image of traditional femininity in China already exist. It is the completion of this psychological development which allows the story to end.

However, this achievement of a sense of her own personality does not occur before she has separated from her husband. Even during her period as a student she is still emotionally attached to him. We see her regretting her decision not to have a child and settle down. She still hopes that he will change and accept her desire for equality. This, as we know, does not happen. Even after she finally graduates and has made her film, she wants him to see it more than anyone else. This is prompted by her desire for him to see her as an equal, someone who has managed to achieve something in her own right, not just as his wife.

The development of the character is a long process of coming to terms with her own weaknesses and resolving her conflict, not by slipping back into a relationship of dependence but by emerging from it as a woman who has a future of her own. We are provided with an excellent glimpse of the psychology of the character and the ups and downs that plague her. In the end she emerges as someone who has achieved her aspirations. This success, however, is not easy but requires great strength on her part. It shows us also how difficult it is for women to make choices which counter dominant expectations of their roles in society.

On the Same Horizon, in the final analysis, it is not the individuals who oppress each other, but society which forces individuals to make difficult choices. She is 'on the same horizon' as her husband because, even though she is not able to live with him, she is able to understand

and sympathise with him. She sees society as a jungle and refers to the doctrine of the survival of the fittest as the best way to describe its laws. There can be no generalisation of what is right or wrong, since human beings are complex characters with both good and bad in them. In the opening paragraph of the story: 'No great scientific work, nor the experience of any one person can prepare one for knowing whether the numerous choices one makes in life are right or wrong, moral or immoral. There is no proven theorem' (p. 119).

Responses to gender discourse The above analysis helps us to understand the female protagonist in relation to the demands made by orthodoxy regarding the role of women. In the 'ideal' responses analysed in Chapter 5, we saw how the two women accepted and remained within the limits of prescribed gender roles. Their main identification was with their familial and traditional roles as mothers and wives and, in Lu Wenting's case, as a doctor as well. Although their lives are not easy, psychologically and materially they remain within the traditional roles associated with women.

In contrast, the character discussed above represents a critical response to gender discourse. This reading is substantiated when we compare the choices that the female protagonist makes and compare these with the expectations that orthodox discourse has of women. The character in this story constantly breaks down the established order on gender roles. None of the choices that she makes is premised on what women in China are traditionally expected to do. She leaves her husband and chooses to have an abortion instead of settling down to motherhood. The fact that she is not willing to be a source of comfort for her husband but has her own demands from life which she takes concrete steps towards achieving, shows how the attitude of women in China has changed.

The choices made by the character place her at a distance from other women and show us the consequences faced by women who chose to counter traditional gender roles. The woman loses her husband and suffers emotionally because she insists on leading a life of her own. Although she wants his understanding and sympathy, she does not want this at the expense of her individuality and aspirations. She has the same demands and expectations about what life can bring her as her husband. She wants her own success and career and wants to be treated equally in the relationship. To achieve these goals she is willing to sacrifice the things which have traditionally provided women with security, and which she herself wanted when she decided to get married. These are a 'normal' family life, where the female partner is willing to look after the needs of the family and play a supportive role for her husband. The story shows that in China it is still difficult for a woman to have both a career and a family.

The contrast between her marriage and other more 'normal' marriages is also an indication of the difference between her and the social expectations about women. The other women in the story are shown in traditional roles; they are married and have families. Although she does regret her choice on occasions and wonders what she has really gained, ultimately she realises that her choices are also meaningful. For her the self-respect she has gained as an independent woman makes the pain of divorce ultimately bearable.

She can no longer accept the limited role accorded to women in China by a traditional sexual division of labour. The story also shows that unchanged ideas of gender roles persist because men continue to demand and accept certain roles from their partners. The male character in the story is unable to understand his partner's need and desire to have a life and career of her own. Legally she is able to gain admission to the school only if she divorces, but his constant failure to understand her, and his attempts to make a more docile woman of her, are also reasons why she is forced to make a choice between marriage and career rather than being able to combine the two. In this respect, the attitudes of the husband represent for us the expectations of orthodoxy. He feels justified in his attitude because he sees others in society living by these rules. His wife is an exception, a woman who wants too much, and is too strong.

Although she tries to fulfil his expectations at the beginning, the consciousness of her own capabilities and the seeds of rebellion that already exist make for an unstable and unhappy marriage. She demonstrates the contradiction between wanting a man to take care of all her needs on the one hand, and, on the other hand, wanting equality and individuality. Ultimately, the desire for the latter wins out.

The character also represents a critical response to gender discourse because it shows us the oppressive nature of gender discourse which is premised on stereotypes of women's roles. The decision to escape the limits of tradition is not an easy one. It entails sacrifice. The result is the kind of psychological ordeal that the female character in the story undergoes, showing us the way women internalise and accept the limits imposed on them by gender discourse. The process of overcoming the personal sense of failure she feels as a woman because her marriage has failed is one aspect of this phenomenon. As a woman, she finds herself caught in the classic situation of blaming herself. Her development lies precisely in being able to overcome both her own guilt and her sense of injury at the hands of her husband. She realises that he is not to blame either. What is to be blamed is a society which structures the expectations that the sexes have of each other by promoting a particular form of gender relations. It is this orthodoxy of gender relations that the character seeks to question and, indeed, succeeds in subverting.

In the end, we leave the character facing the unknown. She has succeeded in achieving a certain peace with herself and she has finally overcome her lingering sense of regret over the decision to leave her marriage and all the traditional forms of emotional and social security that marriage as an institution provides. Whether she will have a life of happiness or of misery will depend to a large extent on factors outside herself. Her inner development as an individual with a sense of social purpose is complete. Whatever the consequences of her choice, she has entered a different stage in her life. Her decisions are not those of a selfish and aggressive woman, as some Chinese critics have called her, but the demands of a woman who has been educated in urban China and sees herself as equal to her male contemporaries. She not only represents the struggle of women to achieve equality but also the process of the development of a self-identity. Ultimately, the story is a critical response because it attempts to widen the limits of orthodox discourse. It forces orthodox discourse to confront the problems faced by women in China in terms of achieving what she identifies as her aim in life. She emerges as a character with great strength and dignity; a strength which allows her to face the future with confidence and hope.

Zhang Jie's *The Ark*

Over the past decade, Zhang Jie has emerged as a major writer in China. She is the author of a number of short stories, novellas and novels and first came to fame with her novella, *Love Should Not be Forgotten* (*'Aishi puneng wangji de'*) (1978).[3] It was the first story to focus directly on male–female relationships and examine the expectations that people in China have of love and marriage. She criticised the lack of love and emotional fulfilment that characterises the majority of Chinese marriages. Since then, Zhang Jie has written several stories which explore the position of women. She is famous for her unflinching criticism of the way women's lives are structured by oppressive and outmoded social mores. *The Ark* is an excellent example of Zhang Jie's work and reveals a glimpse of the position of women in China today.

The context of the story *The Ark* (*Fangzhou*) was first published in the magazine *Shou Hou* in 1978. The novella is located in urban China and deals with the lives of three women friends who find themselves in similar circumstances. They are intellectual, middle-aged and, most important, divorced or separated from their husbands. Like *On the Same Horizon*, this story examines the social and emotional consequences of divorce. However, it focuses more on the social and economic problems faced by the three friends, and the impact these problems have on their self-perception and self-worth, than on the contradictions which arise in their relationships with their husbands. By focusing on divorced women, Zhang Jie has highlighted a growing problem in urban areas. From figures released by the government, we know that the rate of divorce in urban China has been increasing over the last decade, with a greater number of cases being initiated by women.[4] In Zhang Jie's story, the reason for each divorce is different, but all three face similar social attitudes.

In the following analysis, I will endeavour to show how each woman's circumstances differ while they are all confronted by the same social attitudes. What ties the narrative of these three different characters together is, in fact, the response of orthodox discourse to their circumstances. Although their fate represents the continuation of traditional dominant values, it also represents the possibility of counter-discourse and counter-positions that are emerging for women in China. To a certain extent, it shows us the changes that have occurred in women's own consciousness and the new opportunities that are emerging for them.

The author calls the women's house the 'widows' club' (*guafu julebu*). As Cao Jinghua, one of the three women thinks to herself: 'Their apartment was like a "widows' club" [*guafu julebu*]. She found it curious over time that she met more and more women like them. Someone might do some serious research on why the divorce rate among women of their age was so high – not just dismiss the phenomenon as a result of bourgeois ideology' (p. 128).

The story traces the changes that occur both in the internal development of the characters and in terms of their objective and material circumstances. Although the development of the characters occurs on the basis of their individual experiences, the narrative shows the three women, former school friends, sharing a house and providing a means of support for each other.

In the analysis that follows, each character will be dealt with separately. *The Ark*, unlike the other stories analysed, does not have its characters develop within the space of the narrative; the three women friends are already developed or finished characters. My emphasis will be on analysing the characters rather than on showing the different stages through which the character develops, as in the previous stories. The analysis of gender discourse will be carried out by placing the characters in terms of the deployment of gender discourse in China.

The setting of the character: Cao Jinghua Cao Jinghua is the first character we meet. She is a philosopher working on problems of Marxism, and is set against the background of a research department in some kind of unnamed institute. We learn that she takes her work seriously and is considered a capable and even brilliant and independent-minded researcher. We infer that she has suffered privations and hardships in the past from the state of her health. She is said to have a bad back which at certain times immobilises her. She is also unused to luxuries, as we see when a colleague brings her a modern diathermy machine from Shanghai and she thinks: 'The convenience and style of this machine served only to emphasise that she had had few luxuries' (p. 4).

From her other recollections we know that Cao Jinghua was branded as a rightist during the Cultural Revolution, had insults and abuse hurled at her and was later sent down to a remote forest area where she lived for some time in extremely difficult conditions. We are told: 'Having to live in those forests had been a cruel fate for any woman as frail as Jinghua. The temperature in that small wooden hut would fall to minus 20 degrees in the winter, cold enough for her to feel frozen stiff as an iron rod' (pp. 5–6).

In the past she has not only been mistreated for her political beliefs but has also been mistreated by her husband. She can remember every time he hit her or shouted abuse at her. Ultimately he divorced her because she looked after her father and her sister (p. 6).

Although she has suffered in the past for her intellectual convictions and work, she still identifies with her work as a philosopher. Comparing it to the carpentry that she did in the forest, she says: 'Carpentry work was much easier and more beneficial than writing those articles which were always receiving criticism' (p. 162).

We know that she is well thought of as a philosopher from the people's reaction to one of her articles: it is highly praised and reprinted several times. Even people she does not get along with praise her article, such as a man whom she calls Knife-face who says to her, 'Comrade Cao Jinghua, your elaboration of Marxism is a superb contribution to our overall understanding' (p. 162).

We are told, however, that Jinghua herself is not interested in personal fame or making a name for herself. She does not want to be swallowed up by fame and become like people 'who found themselves trapped, lost their objectivity and integrity and were eventually swallowed up piece by piece, like a mulberry leaf being devoured by a silk worm' (p. 163).

Thus, in terms of the character's setting, we can argue that Cao Jinghua is set against the backdrop of China's Party intellectuals. She is an earnest and serious scholar, committed to philosophy which she feels she has a moral responsibility to pursue. In many ways, her setting allows her the possibility of a radical critique and her objective circumstances lend credence and legitimacy to the way she analyses society and the situation of women within it. In the development of her character, her past hardship and suffering as an intellectual and a woman play a major role.

Her relationship with other characters The primary relationships in the story are between the three women and I shall analyse these only after each character has been individually sketched out. In this section, therefore, I shall deal only with each character's relationships with other characters in the narrative.

Cao Jinghua is a divorced woman. Her father, an intellectual, was branded a reactionary in the Cultural Revolution and lost his job, so the burden of supporting her sister and her father fell on her shoulders. Apart from this detail, we are told little else about her family. In the past her primary relationship was with her husband. Once again, little narrative space is devoted to the details of this relationship. We are told of the major incidents leading up to the divorce in Jinghua's recollections. At the beginning of their marriage, when she discovers she is pregnant, she has an abortion. This leads her husband to abuse her. She clearly recollects her husband abusing her and saying: 'Why did you have to go and have an abortion? Just so you can make money to send to that father and sister of yours? You killed my child! Why in hell did I marry you in the first place? Well, now I am going to get a divorce' (p. 128).

We are further told that she married in the first place because she thought her husband would help her to support her family. Instead, he is one of the main people to accuse her of being a reactionary intellectual and it his testimony which is responsible for Jinghua being sent to the forest. He puts up a wall poster on the wall of the school where she is teaching, accusing her of being unfaithful (p. 129). Recalling her relationship with him, she reflects:

> Uncanny, how she remembered distinctly every blow he had landed on her face, every insult he had shouted at her ... She could never forget the powerful odor of garlic which he always carried around him. But odd to say, she could not recall how he had looked, though she had slept on his heated brick kang

and eaten at his table for six or seven years. If she was to come face to face with him now, Jinghua doubted whether she would recognise him. Everything, the suffering, the humiliation had all turned into memory, but his face had grown cloudy and obscure. (pp. 128-9)

Thus, the scars inflicted upon her have begun to heal and, after her rehabilitation following the end of the Cultural Revolution, she is able to begin life again as a single woman.

The other important relationship in her life is her friendship with An Tai (referred to as Lao An), her Party branch secretary, who has great respect for her courage and integrity. He openly defends her at a public meeting after her article on Marxism has excited controversy. As he says: 'Why do I support Comrade Cao Jinghua? Because she speaks the truth' (p. 166). For Cao Jinghua, Lao An, in his behaviour and character, demonstrates all the qualities that a good Communist Party member and leader should have.

It is Lao An who constantly tells her to be more tactful. He is the one who brings her a diathermy machine from Shanghai and sees to it that her colleagues do not malign her. They are good and trusting friends. She is the only one with whom Lao An discusses his personal life; he is in love with an Overseas Chinese woman. Of course, rumours abound about their relationship and Zhang Jie uses this to show the narrow confines of male-female relationships in China, where ordinary friendships between the sexes are constantly misconstrued.

Apart from Lao An and the two other women, Liang Qing and Liu Quan, Cao Jinghua has few other relationships. She is shown as a fair woman who has no time for polite conversation and is, in fact, quite difficult to get along with. This is clearly illustrated in her treatment of her neighbour Mrs Jia, who is depicted as a caricature of the neighbourhood gossip. She is suspicious of these three women living on their own. Once she visits early in the morning to see who has been in their apartment, using as an excuse the fact that her tomcat has jumped over the wall after their cat. Jinghua, while pretending to be scrupulously polite, tells Mrs Jia that she was overheard saying something politically dangerous in her sleep. This she does only to scare Mrs Jia, as she later admits to Liu Quan (p. 136).

Jinghua is similarly dismissive of the character 'Knife-face', a colleague who represents the drawbacks of certain Communist Party people. He is always out to get Jinghua but is scared to deal with her face to face. Once, during an important seminar, Jinghua has a headache. 'Knife-face' offers her a tablet which is actually a sleeping pill. When she finds out about it, she warns him: 'The drug you gave me could only put me to sleep for a matter of hours, I'm afraid. Why didn't you have the guts to give me arsenic? ... If you don't have the guts to give me arsenic, I am sure somebody will give you some sooner or later' (p. 165).

Thus, Jinghua is a tough and forthright woman who has suffered in the past and is not willing to do so any longer. She does not suffer fools gladly, but is sincere and supportive of the few genuine friends that she has. She is impatient by nature and rather brusque. She has strong opinions and is not afraid to air them. This does not always make her the most likeable of people.

Characterisation We first meet Jinghua as a mature woman in her mid-forties. In a sense, she is presented to us as a character who is set in her ways, not a character in the making. Although past events have shaped her character, such changes do not occur in the space of the narrative. She has very definite characteristics and knows what she wants from life and how to get it. In this analysis, therefore, I shall focus more on the character Jinghua as we find her at forty.

We learn of her childhood from the recollections of Liu Quan. Even as a child she was strong and independent and did not take kindly to bullying. Before becoming good friends with Liang Qian, she had often stood up to her. She had an intellectual upbringing, going through university and, before the Cultural Revolution, teaching in a high school. During the Cultural Revolution, like a large number of intellectuals, she is sent to the countryside. Here she survives severe weather conditions and little food. Although this breaks her health, it does not break her spirit. She teaches herself carpentry; this not only helps her make the dilapidated hut which is allotted to her habitable, it also gives her something to do. As she remembers: 'She had learnt this skill while she had been living in the forests, in order to drive away the feelings of hopelessness and loneliness during those bitter days. Sometimes she would do a carpentry task for that reason alone, not to make anything in particular' (p. 161).

This resilience is also visible in the way she reacts to criticism about the article that she has written. She is not afraid of the criticism and defends her viewpoint, even though she has suffered in the past.

We know that she has no time for self-pity and does not seek sympathy from others. She has a painful back problem but she fights against being dependent on anyone. When Lao An presents her with a diathermy machine, he takes care to point out that it is not a gesture of pity. This stubbornness in her character is demonstrated by the 'coal' incident. She is alone at home when the coal supply on which they are dependent for cooking and heating arrives. She not only helps the harassed worker unload the truck, she also helps her neighbour Mrs Jia carry her share up to her flat. Only the timely arrival of Liang Qian saves her from seriously damaging her back.

In both her character traits and her ideas, Jinghua differs from the 'ideal' woman. She is stubborn, forthright, cynical and strong, a far cry from the traditional image of gentle, supporting wives and mothers whom we meet in the stories of Shen Rong and Wang Anyi.

The setting of the character: Liu Quan Like Cao Jinghua, Liu Quan comes from an intellectual family background. Her father was a scholar and had at one time studied in England. Liu Quan remembers him as a 'great encyclopedia, full of dignity in its place on the bookshelf, with a sober brown cover and gold lettering down the spine. Precise and comprehensive, it contained all the knowledge that an ordinary person needed to know' (p. 156). She herself is a graduate of an English department and, when we meet her, she is working as a translator with an export company. Her job is uninspiring. She takes care of all the office work which requires English. This includes drawing up charts of the company's liaison work, handling company reports and so on. Her job also requires her to travel occasionally. We know that Liu Quan is good at her work and is a talented translator. However, the job is beneath her qualifications and she is using Liang Qian's help to get herself transferred to the Foreign Affairs department.

Although she comes from an intellectual background, and has received a university education, she has become 'proletarianised' in her appearance and mannerisms (p. 150). This is because of the way she is forced to live as a divorced women. Not having a house of her own, she has been forced to live with one friend or relative after another. Her company refuses to help her find a place to live.

In terms of her situation as a character, we are presented with a complicated picture. She has been brought up in an intellectual milieu, but the roughness of her appearance and behaviour is stressed. It is also reflected in the way she has lost confidence in herself and in her ability to handle people. She is reduced to asking for help and favours. This situation, as we know, is the result of her humiliation at the hands of her husband and the situation she has to face after her divorce.

Her relationship with other characters Of the three characters, Liu Quan's relationships with others are the most complex. Cao Jinghua and Liang Qian have a confidence and strength of personality which make their relationships with people easier for them. Liu Quan, on the other hand, finds herself in a weak and insecure position regarding other characters in the narrative.

Her father is an intellectual and obviously well educated. He has been exposed to outside influences and is supposed to be liberal in attitude. Yet we find that his attitudes towards the position of women in society and towards his own daughter's unhappy marriage are conventional and represent traditional Chinese morality. After her marriage, her relations with her father are strained since he does not like her commercially minded husband. However, even though she is not happy after her marriage, she is supposed to make the best of a bad situation. Her father, though educated in the West, still retains traditional attitudes towards marriage and divorce (p. 156). He considers divorce immoral and worries that her behaviour will bring disgrace to the family. As Liu Quan recollects: 'Ultimately it seemed as though the ancient customs, handed down over thousands of years, dictated that she should stick to her husband, for better or for worse. Although her father had studied in England, returning with all the harpings of his Western education, his thinking was bound up by these traditions' (p. 156).

Liu Quan's relationship with her husband is an unhappy one. When we meet her, she has already come to terms with this and is able to think of her ex-husband without anger or resentment. Nevertheless, she does tell us that it was a demeaning relationship. Her husband treated her like a sex object, never once providing her with emotional or financial support. As she recollects:

> He would come home drunk and foul tempered, and force her to make love. He was rude and loud and treated her as if he had bought her merely for her body and was determined to get his money's worth ... Every night of their marriage had been a terrifying, inescapable trial, and as the dusk began to thicken a cold shudder passed through her body, as if she were suffering from a fever. (p. 183)

After her divorce, she loses custody of her son Mengmeng. Her relationship with Mengmeng is emotional and fraught with tension. She is very fond of him and yet, at the same time, she has problems trying to achieve a balanced relationship with him because she is allowed to see him only once a week. She is often upset with him for not taking enough pains with his school-work. Although on the surface she seems an unreasonable mother, we are told that she has been fighting for the custody of her son for the past five years and is still the one taking care of his material needs. Her husband is shown as an out-and-out materialist who has no time for his son and even tries to poison his mind against his mother. The problems of a divorced mother are clearly brought out in this relationship. We are told how children suffer in the middle of the conflict between parents.

Liu Quan's relationships at work are also complicated by the way her boss, Manager Wei, treats her. He harasses her sexually and is constantly forcing her into awkward situations. Her biggest fear is being sent off on another business trip with him; on a previous occasion, he had made himself extremely obnoxious while they were travelling together (p. 155). Manager Wei not only sexually harasses her but also finds other means to humiliate her and make her feel insecure, such as allowing his driver to give her orders and calling her into his office on the slightest pretext. The only person she receives support from in her workplace is Lao Dong, her immediate superior. He tries to find ways for her to avoid being alone with Manager Wei. He also supports her in other ways, such as sympathising with her plight and even speaking up for her to get a raise in salary (p. 155).

Liu Quan's relationships with other people are also governed by her lack of self-confidence, although she is a very capable woman, able to handle complicated situations well. This is shown in the way she handles her temporary job with the Ministry of Foreign Affairs as an interpreter to a delegation. She is efficient and good at this job and earns the praise of all the delegates. However, she does not have sufficient confidence to approach Mr Xie, who is supposed to confirm her appointment in the ministry. The impression she conveys is best summed up in the reaction of Zhu Zhenxiang, the department head, when he sees her in Xie's office, waiting to speak to him about her job transfer:

> Liu Quan's smile made Zhu Zhenxiang feel a little ill at ease; he would have felt better if she had not smiled so eagerly. He could feel she was worried and needed help. She seemed quite nervous, like a young girl whose family's ill-fortune had forced her to go out and fend for herself. He knew little about Liu Quan's circumstances, but during his contact with her over the past twenty days, when the American delegation had been making its visit, he had been impressed by her dignity, endurance and efficiency. (p. 177)

Thus, although Liu Quan has enormous capabilities, she is also uncertain and insecure because of her past experiences. This is reflected in her relationships with other people and is also the strongest indicator of the difficulties faced by women in the workplace; single women have no support behind them and often have to put up with sexual harassment.

Characterisation We know from several incidents that among the three friends Liu Quan's personality has undergone the most changes. In school, she was clever and bright, a class monitor and a conscientious pupil. At university, she was also a good and hard-working student. She has, however, lost all the confidence she had as a beautiful and intelligent woman and allowed herself to become careless about her appearance and personal well-being.

These changes are the direct result of what she has suffered at the hands of her husband, and at the hands of society in general. From being a young girl with great promise, she finds herself at the age of forty living as a divorcee, fighting for the custody of her only son, having to fight sexual harassment at work and constantly having to plead with people to get even a small measure of comfort and security for herself. Life has not been easy for Liu Quan.

However, she has not lost all her spirit and sense of achievement. After Liang Qian helps her with a temporary transfer to the Ministry of Foreign Affairs as an interpreter, she does a good job and is seen as capable both by the American delegates whom she accompanies and by the people of her own staff. We also see glimpses of the younger and stronger Liu Quan in the scene in the marketplace when she threatens a bullying stall manager with exposure by pretending to be a journalist.

Like the other two main characters, in a sense Liu Quan is presented to us as a 'complete' character. She does not evolve throughout the story but confronts certain incidents within a short space of time as a mature woman of forty. Again, the factors that have forced her to become the way she is in the present are a result of social pressures and misfortune. She was treated badly by her husband, and received no support from him after their divorce. She is forced to turn to anybody who is willing to help her. This she does without losing her dignity or using her femininity. In fact, one of her biggest problems is the fact that men tend to treat her like a sex object because she is a beautiful woman. We often find her thinking what a curse her beauty is because it seems to bring out the worst in men.

On the whole, Liu Quan is a woman who has lost her zest for living and become a frail and rather pathetic woman who allows people to upset and bully her. She has lost confidence in herself.

The setting of the character: Liang Qian Liang Qian is the third friend in the trio. She is also forty and has separated from her husband, who is a musician. They have one son. In terms of social background, she is the best placed of the three. Her father is a senior Party member and minister. We are never told exactly what he does, but we are given numerous examples of his power and influence. He is also the reason why she cannot get a divorce, as her father's daughter, she cannot give rise to scandal.

Her own profession is that of a film director, a field which she chooses because of her love for the cinema. We are told that she never uses her father's influence to further her own career, only using it when her friends are in trouble and need a flat and when she is able to help with Liu Quan's transfer to the Ministry of Foreign Affairs.

When we first meet Liang Qian, she is busy trying to finish a film that she has been directing. The descriptions of her workplace give us an idea of her as a professional woman. Here again we see the kind of male chauvinism that operates in Chinese society. Liang Qian is confronted with authority problems: the crew do not respect her and resents her attempts at perfectionism. This is clearly brought out in her confrontation with the music director, who technically should be taking orders from her but who disregards them: 'He clearly thought little of Liang Qian's instructions and paid her no more attention than he would some young bassoonist in his orchestra' (p. 138).

Her decision to become a director had been made on impulse.

Although she had never really found anything which exactly suited her, Liang Qian had finally chosen a career. Maybe it had all been a mistake. She had always imagined that her love for directing would automatically transform itself into an ability to direct. Now she knew that even though she might have produced a few films, none of them would ever be remembered. (p. 139)

Liang Qian, thus, can be described as a socially well-connected urban intellectual. Her father's position, which she does not really exploit, serves as a security net for her. She is involved in the art world of post-Mao urban China. Her main work-related contacts are with people from this background. In a certain sense, her relationships to people are also influenced by her social setting in society.

Her relationships with other characters The strength of Liang Qian's character and her difference from the accepted social responses of women in China are made visible in the way she approaches life. Like Cao Jinghua, she is a direct and forthright woman, not scared of having opinions of her own or of expressing them candidly. This fact alone is enough to make her lack traditional feminine virtue. Says Xie Kunsheng, a subordinate of her father's: 'You can't trust her not to insult you ... what would men do if all women were like her?' (p. 142).

Liang Qian's primary relationships are with her husband and father. Her father is never directly introduced in the story, but he plays an important part in her life, forcing her to continue her marriage. We know that she has a great regard for her father and thinks of him as a lonely old man. As she says to Bai Fushan, her husband:

'You can't imagine how my father has suffered because of his position. Everyone has tried to squeeze something out of him ... everyone thought that someone in his position must enjoy boundless privilege.' But how lonely he must have been, and how much he has suffered. He had no one with whom he could give vent to his true feelings as she could do with Liu Quan and Jinghua. (pp. 145–6)

In a way she idealises her father and is willing to sacrifice her own freedom from Bai Fushan for his sake. On the other hand, she is also oppressed by his high status: 'If her father had not had such a high status, no one would ever have been able to say that all her achievements were purely due to him. When would she be allowed to be herself? When would society begin to recognise her own struggles?' (p. 146). Although she loves her father and does not blame him for having to live a lie, she finds the effects of it rather deadening to her soul. Her attitude towards her father reflects her acceptance of his role in her life and is a significant determinant of her own actions and choices.

Her relationship with her husband Bai Fushan is quite the reverse. She despises him and sees him for what he has become: a superficial string-puller and social climber. When she married him, he was a young and upcoming violinist. She was in love with him and had seen him as a romantic figure. However, she soon found out that he was not the idealist that she had imagined. On the contrary, he had soon started drinking and using his father-in-law to gain whatever advantage he could. His own plan was to settle abroad.

Just as Liang Qian has lost interest in him, he has lost interest in her. However, unlike her, he has no problem with living a lie regarding their relationship.

He [Bai Fushan] could never understand why Liang Qian always kept him at such a distance. Even if there were no love left in their relationship, couldn't they at least be like good business partners, continuing to help one another in various way? If only she could get her father to do a few favours for him, then she need no longer go on struggling in this way and he would see to it that life was made more comfortable for her. (p. 143)

Liang Qian, on the other hand, sees him only as a selfish schemer and tries to avoid him as much as possible. She has no illusions about him and does not blame him for the past.

We are not told of any other major relationships. Her father's position puts her at a distance from people. In fact, most people tend to be extra-polite and nice to her because of her father's position. This is demonstrated in the way Xie Kunsheng and his secretary Qian Xiuying flatter her and promise to do what she requests. She, in her turn, has no respect for such people, seeing them as shallow and superficial (p. 147). On the whole, Liang Qian can be described as a character who is strong and rather arrogant. She does not suffer fools gladly and is not averse to be being rude to people, such as her husband, when she thinks that their actions are morally reprehensible. She is a rather principled woman, refusing to use her father's influence to promote her own career.

Characterisation Liang Qian is presented to us as a mature and thoughtful woman. She has always been rather domineering as we know from several incidents in her childhood. She retains her strong personality, and although her marriage to Bai Fushan only serves to disillusion her, its failure does not make her lose confidence in herself, as happens with Liu Quan. Her sufferings during the Cultural Revolution, like those of Jinghua, only serve to make her stronger and more determined than ever not to give in. In the scene before the three friends finally move into their flat, Liang Qian has just been released from prison. 'Damn the bastards', she says, rolling up her sleeves as if getting ready for a fight. When Jinghua expresses her astonishment at her swearing, Liang Qian answers, 'I've not only learned to swear, but I've learnt a lot more about the world besides. Don't worry, I will find some way to get us an apartment' (p. 159).

Although like the rest of them she has changed drastically physically, she is still a tough character who takes no nonsense. She is no longer trying to change her personality or her life-style. The narrative shows her struggle against society as she experiences it in the present. We see her struggling to achieve something in her profession and to be free of her father's influence so that she can live with the openness she desires.

We see her as a woman of forty, confronting the social pressures that women face as professionals. She knows that her problems with managing her film crew have to do with her being a woman. She also knows that this fact influences her own ability and confidence. In many ways she, like the other two, longs to give up and rest and be looked after. Yet she knows that it is not possible for her. She is thus a mature character who knows herself and has learned to live with her strengths and weaknesses. She is by no means perfect. She has her faults like the others. She is impatient, short-tempered and often rude to people, but she is also kind and just, never hurting anybody deliberately. On the whole, this is a portrait of a woman who, like her other two friends, has broken out of the circle of accepted life-styles for women in China. It is not only her personal experiences which determine her life-style; more importantly, it is the critical consciousness that she has of her circumstanes which makes her relationship to gender discourse one of difference and distance.

The inter-relationship of the characters as a response to gender discourse *The Ark* features three women who are childhood friends and who, for different reasons, all find themselves in the same situation. They are women who are past their youth and have experienced both the hardships and the joys of life. They have been married, have pursued careers, have certain opinions about life and understand themselves. Their friendship and mutual support is the main prop in their lives.

This picture of female solidarity is based on the awareness of the subordination and double standards that women have to put up with, and it is this underlying theme which makes it a critical response to gender discourse. The story is a direct confrontation with dominant values and orthodoxy on gender relations in China. It attempts to show how all three women differ from those women who simply accept their fate or deliberately try to use their femininity to gain advantages. The critical consciousness of the characters is beautifully brought out in the toast that Liang Qian suddenly proposes towards the end of the story, and which Jinghua silently fills in: 'I want to make a toast to women ... to all the rights that women have gained and will gain, to all their sacrifices and their contributions, to all their known and unknown sufferings, to all the aspirations that they have achieved and will achieve. Let every woman consider this as a greeting – to us' (p. 222).

The theme of the story is the contradiction between the way the three women aspire to live their lives and the way dominant discourse perceives women's roles. The ensuing conflict is lived out separately by each of the women.

In the case of Liang Qian, her forthrightness distinguishes her from the accepted norm, as does her attitude to her son. She has a problematic relationship with him because she entertains wider expectations of life. Motherhood is not shown as the ultimate fulfilment for women, but as a source of conflict. Although she acknowledges that people who do not care for children should not have them, she is unable to give her son the time that he needs. Rather than presenting this in a negative light and as a judgement on her as a bad mother, we are shown the real conflict and pain that an aspiring career woman in China has to face. Her words in reply to the final criticism of her film clearly reveal her critical consciousness: 'Women have to fight for women's liberation, not merely a political and economic liberation but for a belief in women's own strength and worth, and in trying to realise this worth' (p. 218)

Jinghua, the Marxist philosopher, is shown as a fearless and strong woman. She is criticised for her point of view but refuses to back down. Her case is also used as an illustration of the narrow confines of male–female relationships in China, where ordinary friendship between the sexes is viewed with suspicion. Her friendship with Lao An is often gossiped about.

Her critical consciousness about the need to defend women's rights is brought out in her appreciation of the Western film *A Strange Woman* (*Yige qiguai de Nüren*), which deals with male–female relationships and shows the expectations of a modern woman in the West. The film excited a lot of controversy in China, and many critics claimed they were unable to understand it. Jinghua, on the other hand, finds it easy to understand and she realises that the gender gap is universal.

Liu Quan, who is the most emotional of the three women, is shown confronting sexism at work. She fears being reduced to a sex object. Although she is not such a strong character as the other two, this is partly because she has lost confidence in herself and is now struggling to earn a living while coming to terms with the disappointments she has suffered in the past. Her refusal to exploit her femininity sets her apart from other women in the narrative who use stereotyped female characteristics such as flattery and coy behaviour to obtain favours.

Although the story sharply illustrates how women in China are beginning to look critically at male–female relations, it does not paint an optimistic or Utopian picture. On the analytical level, the story emphasises the debilitating side of the struggle of women with orthodox culture in China; but at the same time it presents strategies of female resistance against dominant culture and its institutions. In a sense, the story exemplifies a period of transition. It exposes the discourse of oppression but does not provide easy solutions.

In the final analysis, *The Ark* can be seen as a work which depicts female solidarity and bonding. Their very living together sets the women apart as a 'widows' club'. Rather than accepting the social image of themselves, these three friends provide a source of comfort and care for each other. Their house is a place where each of them can live a dignified and independent existence. They are living together because they have each been through the hardships of life and realise that what binds them together is their experiences as women. The story looks behind the myth of family harmony and female equality and brings to the fore the discrimination women continue to face in terms of being considered equal in discourse.

Critical discourse

While examining the criticism directed against the two stories discussed in this chapter, three things need to be kept in mind: (1) what is said about narrative style, bearing in mind the stereotypes about women's writings; (2) what is said about the content of the stories; and (3) the relationship of critical discourse with the social discourse on femininity as such. All three elements can be seen as interrelated when we speak of the deployment of gender discourse within literary criticism.

Zhang Jie is usually described as writing in a subjective style (*zhuguan shiren*) (Zhang Fa 1984: 133). Zhang Fa, a well-known critic of her work, sees her as an emotional writer, whose sentiments are rich, honest and yet restrained, and this affects the characters that she creates. Zhang Fa says: 'Zhang Jie's characters are created from personal experience and seem a depiction of her ideas – the depiction of what the writer knows about herself [*zuojia de ziwo biaoxian*] (1984: 135). He sees her stories as largely concerned with love and the inner thoughts or psychology of her characters. He cites *The Ark* and *Love Should not be Forgotten* as excellent examples of her emotionalism and subjective style (1984: 136).

A similar analysis of Zhang Jie's style is made by Zhao Fusheng who sees Zhang Jie's stream of consciousness style as 'a subjective style which reflects a subjective world-view' (1989: 11). This highlighting of Zhang Jie's emotionalism and subjectivity is in keeping with the way literary criticism analyses women's writing as a whole. As pointed out earlier, a female style of writing is seen as the inevitable outcome of female natures. Thus, women writers, like women in general, are credited with an emotionalism which colours their understanding of society. An emphasis on the emotional and subjective nature of Zhang Jie's stories also allows for them to be read as the individual voice of an author rather than as a serious and objective assessment of social problems.

While stylistic criticism directed at the work of Zhang Jie seems to reflect a general idea of female writing, the criticism of the content of Zhang Jie's stories reveals the way orthodox discourse on gender relations places women like her characters: it highlights the negative aspects of their lives. For example, one point which is often stressed is their loneliness (*gudu xing*) and avant-gardism. Zhao Fusheng's article (1989) is a case in point. His article compares the female characters of Ding Ling, who wrote in the 1920 and '30s, with those of Zhang Jie. He says: 'These women characters are women of different generations but facing them is a similar loneliness, a similar road. Loneliness, in a sense, becomes the basis of their existence and life style and this feeling of loneliness also becomes their basic emotional state' (Zhao Fusheng 1989: 4). However, he also sees a difference in the way the two writers' characters are drawn and can be understood. According to him, Ding Ling's character Sophie in her novella *The Diary of Miss Sophie* ('*Shafei nüshi de riji*'), and Zhang Jie's characters express a different type of loneliness. Ding Ling's story is located in pre-revolutionary China (1928). Thus, the social criticism and loneliness expressed by Sophie are seen to reflect a social problem caused by the corrupt capitalist government then in power. Zhang Jie's women characters, because they are located in post-Mao or contemporary communist China, are not seen as reflecting the reality of their period. Instead, they are seen as reflecting an individual point of view. He says: 'If one says that Shafei [Sophie] represents the voice of the youth of her generation, those who bore the spiritual hurt and lonleiness of that period, then Zhong Yu etc. [characters in Zhang Jie's stories] represent a group who spin a web around themselves, cocoon themselves off from the world and are unhappy idealists' (Zhao Fusheng 1989: 5).

Zhao Fusheng also sees them as women who accept their fate and do not really struggle; he believes they are lonely because they feel nobody can understand their sentiments (1989: 5). Such criticism is representative of the trend of criticism addressing Zhang Jie's work. By reading her stories as being concerned with an individual problem, the problem is marginalised. It is seen as an existential problem of few intellectual women rather than as a comment on society. Here the context of Zhang Jie's stories becomes important. Similar sentiments expressed by Ding Ling's character are considered critical fiction because they criticise the conditions of society prior to the communist takeover. Zhang Jie's characters' criticism is directed against the attitudes towards women which persist under communist rule, thus they are identified as negative characters. Zhao clearly states this perspective when he says: 'In the contemporary period, the majority of women are economically, politically and socially liberated. Further, in the sphere of love, marriage and family affairs they have gained a greater voice – intellectual women have gained the respect and admiration of society' (Zhao Fusheng 1989: 7).

Statements such as the above clearly show that it is the gains of the revolution that women writers are expected to extoll rather than expressing an alternative or critical perspective on the lives of women. As Zhao Fusheng further clarifies: 'Although this first really conscious group of women represents progress in some ways, this progressive element also resides apart from the whole. A great divide exists between the advanced element and the backward. If the backward element is out of line, the advanced element can also fail' (1989: 8). Thus the article cautions against avant-garde feminism and women's desire to break out of the conventional life-styles and patterns under which the majority of women live. The argument that the ideas expressed by Zhang Jie are divorced from the lives of normal women tries to curtail the message which the story carries.

Other critics acknowledge that Zhang Jie depicts the darker side of marriage in her stories. But Yang Guixin (1984) sees her characters as also reflecting a resilience of spirit. As he puts it: 'In the novella *The Ark*, Zhang Jie shows the darker side of marriage and human relationships. But more importantly she shows that their [the three female characters] suffering is compounded by the fact that their career aspirations are not understood and their contribution to socialism denied' (Yang Guixin 1984: 30).

Although the critic is being sympathetic to Zhang Jie, the sympathy lies with what he sees as the women's contribution to socialism. No attempt is made to recognise the fact that their career aspirations are denied precisely because social discourse on women does not really create a space for divorced women and finds it difficult to see women in positions of effective power. Yang Guixin further goes on to blame the kinds of problems faced by women which Zhang Jie describes on the mistakes of the Cultural Revolution – another pet excuse for all the ills prevailing in communist China. To quote him:

> The question we need to ask is does the modern intellectual woman who has grown up in socialist China still feel unhappy? We cannot answer this question in terms of yes and no. Of course, in comparison to the old society with its arranged marriages etc, their lot is greatly improved. The problems that exist now are the result of the leftist mistakes of the past ten years. (Yang Guixin 1984: 30)

The above article, more sympathetic than that of Zhao Fusheng, nevertheless reveals the limited extent to which critics can highlight the problems exposed by Zhang Jie. Her characters are under no circumstances either to be seen as representative of women in China nor are they to be held up as role models. Every attempt is made to emphasise how much the position of women in China has improved since the founding of the communist government.

Turning to criticism of the work of Zhang Xinxin, we find a similar attempt to discredit her women characters. We also note a similarity in the remarks made about her style. Like Zhang Jie and other women writers, Zhang Xinxin is seen as writing in a subjective style characterised by the stream of consciousness (*yishi liu*) and a focus on the inner psychology of her characters (Zeng Zhennan 1985: 121). As another critic puts it: 'The subjectivism in her stories [*chuangzuo de zhuguan zhuyi pinxiang*] is clearly pronounced. However, the relationship of these subjective things to reality is not very obvious' (Yang Guixin 1984: 19).

The consequences of this emphasis on the subjectivity of the writer has already been discussed in the case of Zhang Jie. In terms of the content of Zhang Xinxin's stories, she has been heavily criticised for the kind of character and vision of society she exhibits. An article by Tu Lin in the influential *Wenyi Bao* (6 December 1983) makes the following criticism:

> The works of Zhang Xinxin reveal several wrong and negative trends such as nihilism [*xuwu zhuyi*], pessimism [*beiguan zhuyi*] and individualism [*geren zhuyi*]. In her works characters who have a happy and satisfied life are missing. All the characters seem to believe in the philosophy of the survival of the fittest and their relationships to each other lack purity or feeling till in the end only impersonal and cold exchanges exist between them with the attitude that if you win I lose. (Tu Lin 1983: 3)

The article further criticises her for depicting the 'alienation of the individual' (*geren de yihua*). Zhang Xixin's focus on the commercialisation of society and individual relations is also severely criticised. As Tu Lin puts it:

> In her descriptions, the author seems to be painting a picture of society as it exists. In reality this is far from true. Since the 11th Party Congress the attitude of correctly depicting reality has been strengthened and the relations between people under socialism have improved. Zhang Xinxin's stories cannot incite people's hatred. Only a few youth who lack social and life experience still express a sense of hopelessness about socialism. (Tu Lin 1983: 3)

In making these criticisms, the writer of the article is clearly reflecting an official perspective. Individualism and competition are alien to the kind of ideology propagated by socialism. Further, lack of faith in socialism is considered to be a fundamental flaw of Zhang Xinxin's characters. Their selfishness and desire to realise individual aims and happiness are considered contrary to socialist ideals which stress family harmony and community, and encourage people to work for the good of the nation-state. Her strong individuals (*qiangzhi*) are seen as reflecting the spirit of capitalism. The article goes on to say: 'In this period of socialist construction there is no place for the kind of characters being described by Zhang Xinxin. In the works of literature we must attempt to depict characters who are playing a positive role in the reforms of this period not man-eating Bengal tigers' (Tu Lin 1983: 6).

These aspects of Zhang Jie's stories have been almost universally criticised. However, less attention has been paid to the specific manner in which her female protagonist in *On the Same Horizon* attempts to contravene the stereotypes about women in society. While all her characters are considered to be lacking in the spirit of socialism, her women characters are criticised for their individualism. On the whole, however, her women characters are also concerned with love and marriage and represent a search for the ideal in both. Again, this concern and focus are seen as common to all women writers. By reading Zhang Xinxin's women characters as concerned only with love and marriage implies that these are specifically women's problems rather than social problems.

While critics may vary in their approach, the majority of them agree that the 'she' of Zhang Xinxin's story is not like most other women. As Wang Fuxiang puts it: 'Most of her women characters seem to go against their nature' (1984: 16). Other critics see her female characters as unfamiliar women with whom it is difficult to identify, especially in the kind of ideas they have about love and marriage (Zeng Zhennan 1985). The female protagonist in *On the Same Horizon* is also criticised for being a virago or *nüxing xionghua*, a type which is considered negative by the establishment, as discussed earlier. As Wang Fuxiang puts it: 'Given the increased levels of female liberation, a new trend of women's liberation can be discerned in women's writings. They want even greater independence and in certain aspects they are even opposed to men. In the face of a conflict between work and family, they are willing to sacrifice their husbands and children' (1984: 21).

The criticism within China of the two stories analysed above shows that the women characters are not typical of urban China and represent a life-style which is not strictly welcomed by the government. Most articles attack the female protagonists for being viragos, who go against nature, and for advocating feminism. From a general reading it becomes obvious that women who are *nüxing xionghua* are strong individuals, like the characters in the above stories, and are criticised for appropriating what dominant discourse assumes to be male characteristics, for example, intelligence and independence. Like men, they have successful careers which come before domestic bliss. It is here that the presumed existence of a female nature is employed to discredit the women characters.

The parameters within which this criticism is located show that an individualistic challenge to orthodoxy on gender relations is not acceptable to official literary criticism. Although women are expected to have careers and contribute to the 'four modernisations', they must not lose their capacity to be wives and mothers, roles that remain dominant for women within orthodox discourse. Women writers who try to expose the dark side of male–female relationships and the persistence of patriarchal ideology are seen by critics and by society as creating characters who are unnatural and who end up unhappy losers.

It is these aspects of *The Ark* and *On the Same Horizon* which make it possible to classify them as critical responses to gender discourse in

China. The reception of the stories, and the criticism of the lives and choices of Zhang Jie's three women Cao Jinghua, Liu Quan and Liang Qian, and the 'She' of Zhang Xinxin's story show the unchanging aspects of gender discourse. Women who choose to opt out of a family ideology sponsored by the state are treated to the same degree of scorn and social censure as women in pre-1949 China. Moral attitudes towards women provide a thread which binds a more classical traditional discourse on the position of women to socialist rhetoric under the Communist Party.

Conclusion

An analysis of the characters in the above two stories shows us an example of the way a heterodox discourse on gender works. A heterodox discourse can be identified by showing the manner in which the popular or accepted aspects of gender discourse are contravened. In the case of China, I have identified an orthodox discourse as one in which traditional institutions of the family, the sexual division of labour within the family, the self-identity and aspirations of the characters remain within the frame of dominant or unquestioned ideas about gender relations. In contrast, I have identified those ways of being which project a different life-style as heterodoxy. Heterodox discourse questions the norm on gender relations and articulates a possible alternative. At the same time, it comes from within orthodox discourse. In a sense, it is created by orthodoxy as its other.

The characters discussed above make difficult choices and adopt life-styles which set them apart from the 'norm' regarding femininity and gender discourse. These choices invite the censure of institutional discourse. it is interesting to note here that orthodox or, in this case, institutional discourse, precisely by identifying a certain discourse as dissident, by making it the target of censure, confers upon it a certain legitimacy. This is what is meant by heterodoxy forcing orthodoxy to reveal itself. These characters are constantly aware of their marginality. At the same time they also show us the opening which now exists at the level of discourse and allows women to express a critical relationship to the expectations of orthodoxy.

The women in these two stories have attempted to break out of their social and cultural habitus by consciously attempting different life-styles. This also shows us that while an ideal response to orthodoxy appears to correspond to the structure of habitus, a heterodox response attempts to break down the taken-for-granted, thereby leading to both orthodox and heterodox discourses on gender relations. This difference between the two discourses shows us the limitations of the universe of discourse as such, and shows us how gender discourse, whenever it makes an appearance, points to the changes that are taking place in society.

While orthodox discourse may enjoy institutional power, heterodox discourse also possesses a definite power: the power of naming, of bringing things into the open. Literary works which deal with issues other than those allowed reveal the authoritarian nature of orthodox discourse. Heterodoxy, in turn, can provide the focal point for articulating resistance and bringing together a change in the way social relations are spoken about. In these two stories, one already sees a certain similarity. They deal with a common theme: the problems faced by women in China. They are, in a certain sense, the forerunners of other works by women exploring the theme of women and society from a gender-specific and alternative position. Today, young women writers such as Yu Suola, Ge Fei and others are exploring similar themes and are addressing the problems being faced by young intellectual women. The stories and novellas of Zhang Jie and Zhang Xinxin can be said to have opened up a space which presents the alternative discourse of women that exists in society. This discourse may always have existed, albeit hidden or unarticulated, but today it has found a niche which allows it to play the role of a heterodoxy, and therefore challenge the hegemony of a state-sponsored orthodoxy on gender relations.

Notes

1. All translations are mine, unless otherwise noted. In this analysis, the version available in Zhang Xinxin's book, *Zai Tongyi de Pingxian Shang* has been used.

2. The style of *yishi liu*, the stream of consciousness or 'free indirect discourse' as it has also been called, became popular in China after 1977. It represented an alternative to the official and popular style of Socialist Realism. Wang Meng, Zhang Jie and several other writers have also written in this style.

3. Zhang Jie's 'Love Should not be Forgotten', published in 1976, caused a stir in China because it dealt with an unconsummated love affair between a senior Party leader and the mother of the main protagonist. The story was one of the first of its kind which criticised the unnecessary emotional sacrifices made in the name of loyalty to the Party and the revolution.

4. Divorce in China has been on the increase in recent years and more and more cases are being initiated by women. It is, however, still not encouraged by the state, which always attempts to mediate between couples in the name of family harmony. See Lan Chengdong (1985) who examines the reasons for the increased divorce rate in China.

7
Cultural specificity and comparative theory

Discourse, gender and the literary field

In this book I set out to demonstrate how a study of the mode of characterisation of female protagonists in the works of women writers can help us analyse existing discourses on gender in society. A study of women writers, if placed within the wider framework provided by a sociology of literature approach, deepens our understanding of the relationship women have to gender discourse and to forms of cultural representation such as literature.

I have employed an interdisciplinary theoretical approach in my research, drawing on the example of feminist scholarship in different fields and subjects. I hoped to prove that theoretical models developed outside the culture being studied can provide a means for understanding the problems of cultural representation without losing sight of the specificity of the culture under study. In other words, we can use a comparative theory framework for the understanding of gender discourse in a culturally specific setting.

The concept of discourse, as put forward by Michel Foucault, sees discourses – the vehicle of knowledge – as linked to power. Foucault points out that a discourse on a particular subject is not a measure of objective truth. It is the production of a particular way of apprehending and knowing that subject which shows the power of those who have the right, first, to produce certain discourses, and, second, the power to deploy these discourses, to ensure their truth by putting them into practice. Further, the concept of discourse provides a link with the way universal categories particularise themselves. That is, the way the same object of knowledge, in this case woman, is spoken about across disciplines and in different contexts.

This notion of discourse has been used to understand gender relations in China. In this book we see that gender discourse becomes apparent in the way the sign 'woman' gets spoken of and deployed in different places and different circumstances. Every time the word 'woman' or, here, the term 'woman writer' is invoked, it implies certain ways of identifying, classifying and particularising the term 'woman'.

The emergence of women writers in China has given rise to a particular discursive paradigm within which discussion of women writers is located.

Discourse, understood in the above manner, can be used to explain literature. Like other discourses, literary discourse also sets up its subject by creating rules for what qualifies as literature and by setting up norms and criteria of judgement. These norms and criteria are not objective standards only; they are also what determines the composition of the field. In classifying its subject and domain, the rules of discourse formation also set up the limits of the field, and the qualifications necessary to participate in the field.

Literary discourse and its content are determined to a large extent by the nature of the 'literary field' as such. Here, I have made use of the work of Pierre Bourdieu. He points out that the study of any discourse – literary, scientific, historical etc. – must be located within its own field. A field has its own specific rules of organisation and production. One field of discourse differs from another because it has different rules of formation. The concept of 'field' helps us identify both the rules of discourse formation as well as the qualifications required from those who participate in discourse production. By examining literary discourse and identifying its rules of formation, we can link literature to its context.

In reading literature in this particular fashion, we stop seeing it as sacrosanct. It becomes a field of diverse power relations; power relations which can be assessed in the production of literary discourse. In a sense, the very nature of literature, dealing as it does with discourse and its various subterfuges, allows it to become a medium for the production of different discursive paradigms, a terrain where we can examine the construction, deployment and effects of discourses.

In this book I have concentrated on examining how literary discourse sets up rules for assessing the literary content and style of women writers. I found this approach a useful supplement to feminist literary theory because it shifts the debate about the specificity of women writers from one based on nature to the context under which they produce as creative artists. Within the literary field, we need to focus on seeing how the work of women writers sets in motion a specific discourse on womanhood and femininity when it comes to reading women writers and assessing their place within the field of literary production. Finally, I have argued that the concept of discourse can also help us understand how women writers themselves make use of specific discourses on gender in their portrayal of female characters. The characters created by women writers and the type of femininity described by them can be important indicators of how they perceive and deploy gender discourse.

Thus, by reading the works of women writers, I was in effect examining two different but related aspects. First, how the literary field assesses, evaluates and creates rules for the way women can participate in literary discourse. I have argued that women's place in the literary field is directly influenced by the way social discourse on gender describes and deploys the sign 'woman'. Second, by reading women writers I examined how women relate to gender discourse and how they themselves participate in the production of discourses. In doing so, I also discovered gaps and problems in using only the model of discourse analysis provided by Foucault. In a sense, the field of literature illustrated the limitations in Foucault's framework. It showed that, despite allowing us to speak of discourse in relation to the social context of power, it lacks a way through which we can distinguish between discourses of power and discourses of resistance.

As pointed out, Bourdieu provides us with an excellent method of differentiating between discourses. Bourdieu's framework has been used to distinguish between different strands of gender discourse, namely orthodox and heterodox gender discourse. Certain discourses can be classified as orthodox discourses because they describe their objects in a particular way and because they enjoy both institutional power and social legitimacy. Moreover, orthodox discourse attempts constantly to set itself up as the only legitimate way of speaking about a subject.

However, orthodox discourse comes into existence only in order to oppose or discredit other ways of understanding our complex reality. These other ways, ways that question orthodoxy, Bourdieu describes as heterodoxy. Thus, discourse on gender relations, for example, is not simply one set of descriptive indicators of social life; it is also a contested discourse and an expression of the unequal power relations that exist in society between men and women. In other words, different discourses can also articulate resistance to orthodoxy.

Shifts in different discursive positions represent the very real struggle over the right to determine what constitutes the basis of truth, reality and social interaction. Representation is a constant attempt to know and thereby control the object represented. These struggles, the constitution of new orthodoxies and heterodoxies, also represent change. A new orthodoxy is not necessarily more progressive than an older one. It is different. It constitutes its understanding of the social on the basis of different discursive paradigms. It is this which allows us, if at all, to speak of different epochs and different historical periods such as modernism and post-modernism.

In conclusion, one can argue that discourse is above all a way of classifying, defining, characterising things and describing their nature in one way rather than another. It is this process of selecting definitions which reveals the principles of exclusion and inclusion which underpin all discourse production. Discourse, as this book tries to show, is a vehicle of both power and resistance. While orthodoxy attempts to hide the tensions that exist within the social fabric, heterodoxy exercises the power of naming the unnameable and the unarticulated, and represents the voice of resistance.

The above model certainly holds true for China. In the specific cultural context of China, it was found that the role played by institutions of the state, which were in turn subordinate to the Party, in the production of an orthodox discourse was extremely important. Secondly, those discourses which fell outside the terms of institutional discourse were criticised, suppressed and banned. Thus, in the case of China, it was easy to identify a discourse of the state as an orthodoxy and the discourse which stood in opposition or against it as a form of heterodoxy.

The role of the Party becomes that of the legitimiser of what must be included in a discourse on gender and what must be excluded. This process of exclusion and inclusion works in a rather unsubtle fashion in China. The Party, in effect, has the right to create a collective idea of women. The Party is quite direct in its message – a message which it conveys through official and institutional channels of communication. Further, the Party, as it has often demonstrated, is not averse to the use of actual coercion in containing counter-discourses which seek to challenge its authority. However, in doing so it also provides heterodoxy with a certain legitimacy and recognition.

This shows that specifying the link between orthodoxy and institutions of the state can provide a way for us to distinguish between discourses of power and discourses of resistance. This distinction becomes extremely important when our concern is with the study of the social relations of gender, for gender discourse is not merely a discourse of power. Its terrain and content shift as participants in the production of gender discourse contest and contravene the legitimacy of any one discourse to speak on behalf of the universal.

This focus on the cultural and organisational specificity of the field of literature is important within a feminist methodology. While we may accept certain basic principles of feminism, such as its concern with eradicating female subordination, our reading of what is feminist writing should be based on what can be identified as feminist within a specific cultural context rather than the use of categories of feminism developed universally. For example, what may appear as feminist in the case of China, may seem unimportant in the West. Similarly, our ideas of resistance are also culturally specific. While a particular act may have little significance to someone from another culture, the same act within its own cultural context may epitomise resistance to cultural values and norms. Reading discourses in relation to each other, and identifying a discourse of power and discourses of resistance within a particular field, can help us to understand how a culture builds its ideas of power and resistance.

Orthodox gender discourse in China

It is this methodological and theoretical framework that I hoped both to illustrate and to hold a dialogue with in my specific focus on women writers and gender discourse in China. In examining the changes that occur at the level of discourse on women, one notices that while the economic and political roles of women have expanded under the rule of the Communist Party, the fundamental and traditionally accepted place of women in relation to the family, marriage and sexuality has hardly changed. My thesis shows that the supposed nature of women remains the dominant discursive myth of gender in China.

The Communist Party in China questions traditional patterns of gender relations, which were based on Confucian ethics, and attacks the blatant and sanctified subordination of women as an heterodoxy. However, its own critique is limited by the cultural habitus to which its members belong. Ideas about women's role as providers of the nurturance needs of the family are wedded to the very structure of gender relations in China and are seen as a corollary of female nature. This discourse on female nature continues to find expression in the various policies and statements that the Party makes on the issue of gender relations.

We see a clear shift in the Party's discourse once it has achieved state power and set about constructing its own discourse as orthodoxy. Here again, a clear link is visible between orthodox discourse and institutional and state power. The wide variety of discourses which exist on gender relations during the period of the May Fourth Movement (1919) are systematically suppressed by the Party which attempts to create the only true discourse on all subjects.

The Party, in its attempt to create a collective socialist identity for women, premises its own discourse on the natural difference between men and women and its own belief in the rationality of its project. The Party's position on women is supposed to be the correct and logical understanding of gender relations. Once again, this understanding is based on Marxist theory which links the subordination of women to the rule of private property and capitalist relations of production. This in turn allows the Party to explain away the continuing discrimination faced by women as an effect of feudal custom. Female liberation can occur only if social and economic progress occur. It is this reductionist thesis which constantly subordinates the issue of women's liberation and leads to the postponement of any real change in gender relations. Instead, the Party attempts to create an ideal gender identity paradigm for women which corresponds to what it sees as China's reality.

The orthodox gender identity paradigm in China can be said to consist of two major aspects. The first aspect clearly locates women within the family. This is an aspect of traditional or pre-communist discourse on women, which is unconditionally taken over by the Party and even built upon. A clear sexual division of labour is legalised by the Party through protective legislation. We notice that women's supposed nature qualifies them for the kind of sexual division of labour that exists in other areas, such as in the labour market, in legal legislation and in social life in general. In short, this particular discourse on gender works in a discursive fashion and can be classified as orthodoxy because it enjoys institutional legitimacy.

In the case of China we also see the limits of protectionist strategies towards women. Women are constantly identified as those whose interests must be protected, the weaker sex so to speak. Those women who do speak in a voice different from that of the Party are marginalised and cast as divisive. Although the Party has broken traditional patterns by allowing women to enter public space, it is in the very areas that fall out of traditional patterns of gender relations, in those areas which are seen as non-traditional, as lying outside the domain of gender, that we witness the insidious and unquestioned deployment of a discourse on female nature.

It is this underlying discourse which determines the place of women within the social and economic life of China. This discourse not only places women in a particular position but it also affects the way they perceive their own roles in society. For example, over the past ten years, women have been losing out in the domains of education and employment, the very areas which are used as examples to illustrate the gains made by Chinese women. The majority may accept the definitions of orthodox discourse with regard to their own roles in society. A discourse on female nature and its deployment continues to exist in doxa, forming, as it were, the underpinnings of gender discourse in China. It is this discourse on a female nature which is at work whenever women are spoken of in different fields. In this book I have focused on the deployment of this gender discourse within the field of literature.

The literary field in China

The specific organisation of the literary field in China forms the background against which my study of women writers was carried out. In the case of China, the notion of the literary field is particularly interesting. Literature, and what qualifies as literature, in China is based on Marxism and Mao Zedong Thought. Literature is a medium which can promote social change in the direction outlined by the Party, and it was expected to serve the interests of the peasants and the working classes.

This broad expectation has meant that the content and style of literature have been strictly determined. While in terms of style we see an emphasis on Socialist Realism, in terms of content, writers have been forced to create plots and characters which fulfil the ideological demands of the Party. The emphasis has been on creating characters who could serve as model communist heroes and heroines to be emulated by the masses.

The creation of a literary organisation at the national and provincial levels, the necessity for writers to belong to some official organisation and the control of publishing outlets ensure that the Party's ideological demands from writers are put into practice. Thus, the very organisation of the literary field determines the boundaries of literary discourse in China. Further, the role of the Party and the institutions created by it becomes an extremely important factor in putting an orthodox discourse into practice.

From the death of Mao in 1976 until the suppression of the democracy movement led by students in 1989, there was a certain expansion of the limits of literary discourse in China. Writers of all ages used this period to explore a diverse range of themes. Above all, they soon started questioning the right of the Party to constitute a collective identity for its people. It is within this relatively relaxed atmosphere that women started writing in large numbers, leading to the appearance of a women's literature (*nüxing wenxue*) in China. This in itself is interesting because it shows that women writers take advantage of the space available to them to expand the discourse on gender. Further, we notice that the terms of gender discourse in China expand and contract depending on the degree of freedom allowed by the Party. This also testifies to the successful control that the Party has exercised over the literary field since 1949.

The loosening of Party control in post-Mao China gave rise to a variety of discourses on gender relations which can be identified within the literary field. I feel three such discourses can be clearly distinguished.

The first is the re-emergence of a discourse which draws its legitimacy from feudal tradition and culture. This has once again provided women with a traditional ideal of femininity, female beauty and women's roles as mothers and wives. The second is the discourse of the Party, which attempts to combine certain aspects of tradition with its own emphasis on the participation of women in the labour market. The third clearly articulated discourse is a critical discourse within which women as writers and intellectuals are examining the social and psychological problems faced by women. The questioning of the boundaries of discourse by women who themselves produce discourse on gender, sets in motion a response from orthodoxy and its agents.

'Women's Literature' and the deployment of Gender Discourse

The reaction of critical literary discourse to the works of women writers illustrates quite clearly the discursive nature of gender discourse. The critical establishment makes use of a discourse which is less original than it imagines. What we find taking place is not only a discussion on women writers but a whole discourse on the nature of the sign woman, on femininity and femaleness. Women, in writing as elsewhere, are expected to fulfil their natures. The organisation of the literary field in China implies that this orthodox literary discourse enjoys the power to propagate its ideas in the different literary forums that exist. In this manner it helps to maintain a dominant value system.

Women are supposed to write in emotional, gentle, flowery language. Their writings are expected to bring peace and harmony. Above all, they are expected to portray and represent the lives of women; a representation which shows their concern with family life, love and dedication to the nation. These classificatory criteria, which define the content and style of women's writing, serve two purposes. They set forth the rules of exclusion and inclusion and tell us what is acceptable as writing by women and what contravenes this writing. Once again, the ground rule for this lies in the discursive practice of gender discourse and it is here that we again see the deployment of a discourse on female nature. It becomes the thread that binds together the discussion of women writers with the sign woman. Here, we see parallels with what feminist literary theory has pointed out in the West, and, more recently, with work by Indian scholars on the way shifts in the social fabric of gender discourse reveal themselves discursively in fields such as literature.

In the case of China, we notice that the terrain of literary criticism, in so far as it addresses the question of types of female characters, also serves a political message. Influential dailies and journals have commented upon the kind of female characters that should be created. Critical discourse on female characters can serve as an important indicator of the way the Party would like to constitute gender relations in society. Women characters in fiction are expected to be good socialists and fulfil the expectations that the Party has of them. At the same time, when actually reading women writers from China we can spot differences among them in both theme and content. It is this difference in their responses to dominant gender discourse which tells us that the effects of gender discourse are not uniform. Women are participants in discourse; they construct themselves through gender discourse as much as in relation to it.

Agency and gender identity paradigms

Agency, or the actions of individuals which show us their response and understanding of the social world in which they are situated, is at once difficult to specify and at the same time identifiable in various ways. We can, for example, choose to study people's daily lives, interview them regarding their views on different issues, or assess their critical consciousness by examining social and political movements.

In this book I have argued that literary discourse is also a site where orthodox and heterodox opinion articulate themselves. In other words, literary discourse is also an arena of struggle. The different identifiable discourses represent contesting ways of understanding the social. Cultural representations are a major source of knowledge about people's ideas of the social world and society. The different values encoded in different systems of representation are a clue to the values that exist in society. I have argued that literature is also an important system of cultural representation – one which takes its meaning by selecting, identifying and articulating different discursive perspectives that exist in society. Here different discursive arrangements can be identified, such as those pertaining to class, religion, morality and gender.

In the case of China, I chose to exemplify agency on the part of women by focusing on the role played by women writers. Women writers can choose, as we have seen, to articulate a particular gender identity paradigm in the type of characters they construct. A gender identity paradigm reveals the pattern on which identity is based. The selection of things, issues or, in other words, the discursive pattern of life that people represent, is what forms identity.

Identities are as much constructed for us as by us. Agency lies precisely in the selection and creation of discursive patterns of identification. The various options available from which we select can be determined by cultural, geographical, class, educational and other factors. Above all, identities are structured within a habitus, a way of relating to and apprehending the world which forms our very dispositions so that we begin to embody it. Habitus is not something that stands outside us. It is not something we are conscious of being part of. Instead, habitus lies precisely in the very things that we take for granted, starting with the ways through which we place ourselves and others.

In the case of women, it is not so much that women occupy overlapping multiple identities but that multiple discursive options are available to them. Often, as is the case in China, one grid or pattern of identification and consequent action may be considered more acceptable than another. In China's case, the ideal woman retains her feminine qualities while still being a dedicated professional who places the interests of the state and socialism above all else. A particular habitus of gender relations is maintained where women's primary identifications are seen as lying with the family.

Thus, being a woman first of all means acquiring the disposition of a woman. Women's identities continue to be constructed within the more traditional habitus of gender relations, a habitus which is accepted by both sexes. China's case proves that the efficiency of orthodox discourse is not based on coercion alone. It is effective because, in large measure, it is close to the patterns of gender relations that have always existed. In other words, orthodoxy succeeds partially because it appeals to the habitus of gender relations within which we construct our identities.

Orthodoxy and heterodoxy: participatory positions by women writers

My purpose in this book was partly to assess women's relationship and understanding of the very clearly articulated orthodoxy that exists in China. I chose to do this by focusing on female protagonists or female characters and analysing them in relation to gender discourse.

In focusing on characters, an interdisciplinary framework has been used. Narratological tools have been used to assemble the character, while sociological methods help us to understand the construction of characters in relation to the discursive practice of gender discourse. By assembling the character in terms of the different elements through which gender identity is constructed, I hope to have highlighted the existence of a specific pattern of identity construction in fiction. The characters in fiction articulate or bring into existence the different discourses that exist in the social world. They give shape to the different discursive identity paradigms possible.

The construction of particular types of female protagonists, the selection of a particular gender identity paradigm for the construction of female characters, show us the participatory agency exhibited by women. The difference that exists among women writers, a difference that specifies the role played by agents in the articulation and selection of different discursive paradigms, also becomes apparent. From reading the works of women writers we learn that while an orthodox gender identity paradigm is selected by some writers, other writers create an alternative gender identity paradigm, based on a different discursive arrangement, showing the existence of discourses on gender relations which are other than orthodoxy.

The orthodox gender identity paradigm reconstructed in the analysis of Duanli and Lu Wenting shows us one vision of the position of women in society and represents a particular discourse on gender relations. The female protagonists of both these stories correspond closely with positions that orthodoxy offers women: marriage, the family and dedication to the nation are their main forms of identification. Further, the reproduction of this particular gender identity paradigm is appreciated and praised by critical literary and political discourse. The characters are held up as examples to be emulated and as role models.

The construction of this collective gender identity paradigm on the part of a woman writer does not necessarily show her own individual acceptance of this discursive relation. Instead, it shows that female identity constructed along this particular discursive arrangement is immediately recognisable as natural and normal. This aspect became apparent to me when I interviewed Shen Rong, the author of *At Middle Age*. Shen Rong pointed out that the character in the story did not reflect her own views; rather, she had hoped to create a typical woman character and reflect the situation of women as it exists. However, for our purpose, the character corresponds with an orthodox gender identity paradigm. The female protagonists in the story are never shown as questioning their place in the social fabric. Instead, their attempt is to live up to the expectations that society has of them. While Duanli represents the idealised life-style of a rich urban woman whose identity is clearly premised on being the wife of a rich man and mother of children, Lu Wenting is the ideal communist heroine, who in her dedication to her work and service to the community as a doctor and at home to the needs of her family ignores the dangers to her own health. Here, the forms of violence experienced by the women are never recognised as such. Instead, the characters make every attempt to become an even greater part of the roles expected of them. They attempt to reproduce their habitus.

In contrast to the above two characters, the 'She' of Zhang Xinxin's story and the three characters in Zhang Jie's story represent what I have qualified as a heterodox gender identity paradigm. These two stories bring to light the questions and dissatisfaction that women have with the narrow identity paradigm offered by orthodoxy. The characters in *On the Same Horizon* and *The Ark* do not comply with the demands of orthodoxy. They present an alternative gender identity paradigm which questions their sense of habitus. This alternative paradigm consists of rejecting the options and choices which are considered normal for women. The choices that these women make are not without pain and hardship. They show how difficult it is to resist the norm, the accepted and expected. In a certain sense, the characters in these stories are outsiders. Within the context of China, the lives of these characters represent the voice of resistance.

Although the stories illustrate the possibility of women existing outside the norm of family and marriage, they also show how deeply ingrained these structures are. Yet in breaking the doxa of gender relations, these women writers exercise a power of naming the unnameable about gender relations. This is the psychological and material subordination still faced by women in China. The stories question the myth of gender equality sponsored by the state. They also question the logic of Marxist analysis on the women's question, thereby questioning the very discourse on which the Party bases the legitimacy of its social vision.

The stories provide a new gender identity paradigm for women in China. The characters not only show a critical understanding of gender relations, they also provide the possibility for women to create a space and life-style in opposition to the collective ideal set by the Party. The negative criticism of the stories in China also confers the status of heterodoxy on this particular gender identity paradigm. It shows quite clearly that an individual challenge to orthodoxy, as posed by these characters, is not something the Party would like to see popularised.

In the final analysis, however, the existence of this alternative gender identity paradigm shows the opening that has occurred in gender discourse on the whole. In that sense, what we witness through the examination of gender discourse in China is not the existence of one single dominant discourse, but in effect the coexistence of multiple discourses, of which two can be clearly identified because they exist within the domain of discourse. We can know only that which is articulated. Perhaps many other positions exist, thousands of different strategies employed by women to deal with their daily lives. We can never know them all, unless they first enter the domain of discourse and allow us to know them.

Cultural specificity and theory as the outsider

This book represents a conscious attempt at theorising. An attempt which is by definition suspect since it says more about my position than about something which is called 'Chinese women'. Using a particular model to understand a complex reality does not mean that we can arrive at the truth of that reality or even claim that the understanding we arrive at is in any way 'objective'. Knowledge is partial and situates the knower as much as the known. My attempt to understand the lives of Chinese women cannot be an attempt to represent their reality or to speak for them. Instead, my aim has been to examine the discourse that exists within China and constantly describes, constructs and attempts to control the position of women and the nature of the sign 'woman'. In other words, my focus has been on discourse – the vehicle through which we apprehend reality.

More questions have arisen out of this research than I have had space to delve into. Often they have been piecemeal reflections, tangents of thought that lead to totally different ways of looking at old problems. At the theoretical level, the question which remains unanswered, and therefore can be identified as an area of further research, is *why* do women, from similar cultural, class and academic backgrounds, respond differently to the demands of orthodox discourse? While my research clearly shows the existence of this difference, I hesitate to elaborate reasons for it. Perhaps we need an entirely different approach to answer this question, one which implies a close relationship with each individual subject and, through that interaction, examines the points at which an individual takes divergent viewpoints and social stands.

Another question which interests me is what today we call the problem of identifying oneself and thereby one's culture and, at that very same moment, identifying the other and the culture of others. It has become almost a truism to say we can know another world only through our own limitations. In fact, what we choose to comment on is often what we do not understand of the other. By learning about another culture, about another language, we attempt to reach and understand the way that culture locates itself in relation to the world and in relation to itself. Yet this is precisely where the problem lies. In the end, we can never understand the reality of another culture, we can only come close to attempting an understanding of what it says about itself. This is where a study of discourses becomes important. Discourses open up a culture to others. They create patterns which can be identified, different discursive arrangements which provide a clue to the specificity of different cultures.

The context which we seek to apprehend always remains specific. A researcher as an outsider cannot expect to experience that context, can never know its reality except through her paradigm of knowing. Nor can we attempt to theorise the experience of others. We bring to a reading of specificity certain methods and tools which have been developed in different contexts and in different fields.

In the case of China, we cannot say what it means to be Chinese. We can, however, say this is what the Chinese say about themselves by reading how they describe, categorise and apprehend themselves. In other words, we read a discourse through which a dominant collective identity is constructed. It is really the construction of collective identities of gender, race, religion and class which reveal the broad outlines within which we exist. The collective experience of women, for example, or that of the working classes can be read as a discursive paradigm which says this is what it means to belong to one particular group, culture or sex instead of to another.

Collective identities are dangerous precisely because they force particular experience into a universal generalised mode of identification. They begin to act as imperatives. 'One can only be a woman if one is this or that', depending on cultural specificity. Anybody who departs from this pattern of identification faces the constant danger of being identity-less, of being unable to qualify into a category. Being rootless and identity-less becomes a dangerous condition, one of loss and marginality. Having the right to create collective identities is, thus, a form of absolute power. It is this power that we need to expose and counter. Not by creating alternatively tight grids of identification but by questioning the reasoning which highlights identity and identification as the main basis for knowing ourselves or another.

The need to question the space provided for various forms of expression within one culture does not mean the denial of them; just as the use of terms and methods that belong to another culture does not entail an absolute belief in the objectivity of those terms. There are always different ways of knowing. It is only the link between certain ways of knowing and power that turn one way of knowing into the dominant or true way. Contesting the dominant modes of identity construction and knowledge thus means questioning domination at its very root.

In the final instance, I argue that the use of categories developed elsewhere can enrich our understanding of other cultures because using outside categories, other ways of seeing the world, can help break the doxic, the taken-for-granted that makes up our own worlds. A comparative framework can help us question the terms of inequalities which exist within the discourse that we employ to make sense of our own world. In fact, the use of outside categories shows us the manner in which we have recourse to cultural identity and its various metaphors. At the risk of being both pedantic and perhaps lapsing into relativism, I would say no discourse can ever be the absolute standard of judgement on feminist, ethnic, religious or nationalistic grounds. Identities are not constituted indefinitely. They emerge and merge within the complex social milieu that surrounds them. They take new shape when given discursive arrangements around them change.

An examination of the different discursive paradigms which exist at a specific historical point can help us to see the arbitrariness of the patterns through which we constitute our identities. Rather than making a fetish of some pure and original identity, either of ethnicity, class or gender, we must see what identity is today: a widely dispersed network of discursive identity paradigms that correspond to the influence of cultures upon each other, to the influences of colonialism and the diaspora created by it, to the technological revolution which has made it possible to know and reach the remotest corners of our world, making it impossible for us to lay claim to an original identity of any sort. We are a composite and it is this mixture, this *masalla* as Mira Nair[1] so aptly calls it, that we need to revalidate.

Notes

1. Mira Nair's film 'Mississippi Massala' (1991) examines the problem of identity faced by a young Indian woman born in Africa and brought up in America, but still influenced by her Indian culture. It shows the effects of colonialism in the creation of mixed and multiple identities for a large number of cultures. It demonstrates the problem of seeing identity as being constructed only on the basis of one form of cultural habitus for a large number of people in the world today.

Bibliography

Andors, P. (1988) 'Women and work in Shenzhen', *Bulletin of Concerned Asian Scholars* 20 (3), 22–42.

— (1985) 'The Incomplete Liberation of Chinese Women', *China Now* 113 (Summer), 8–12.

— (1981) *The Unfinished Liberation of Chinese Women 1949–1981*. Bloomington: Indiana University Press.

— (1976) 'Politics of Chinese Development, the Case of Women, 1960–66', *Signs* 2 (1), 89–91.

— (1975) 'Socialist Revolution and Women's Emancipation: China during the Great Leap Forward', *Bulletin of Concerned Asian Scholars* 8 (1), 33–43.

Anhui Provincial Women's Federation, Office of Investigation and Study (1985) 'How Women Can Become Achievers', *United Newsletter of Social Science* 12 32–91.

Ashcroft, B., Griffiths, G. and Tiffin, H. (1989) *The Empire Writes Back: Theory and Practice in Post-Colonial Literatures*. London: Routledge.

Atwood, M. (1986) 'Paradoxes and Dilemmas: The Woman as Writer: Women in the Canadian Mosaic', in M. Eagleton (ed.), *Feminist Literary Theory: A Reader* Oxford: Blackwell, pp. 74–9.

Aziz, R. (1989) 'Mothering Face', *China Now*, 130, 26–7.

Bady, P. (1981) 'The Modern Chinese Writer: Literary Incomes and Best Sellers', *China Quarterly* 88, 645–57.

Bakhtin, M. (1981) 'Discourse in the Novel' (1934–35), in M. Holquist (ed.), *The Dialogic Imagination: Four Essays*. Austin: University of Texas Press, pp. 259–422.

Barrett, M. (1982) 'Feminism and the Definition of Cultural Politics', in R. Brunt and C. Rowan (eds), *Feminism, Culture and Politics*. London: Lawrence and Wishart, pp. 37–59.

— (1987) 'The Concept of Difference', *Feminist Review* 26 (July), 29–41.

— (1979) *Ideology and Cultural Production*. London: Pluto.

Bal, M. (1985) *Narratology: Introduction to the Theory of Narrative*. Toronto: University of Toronto Press.

Balbus, I. D. (1982) 'Disciplining Women: Michel Foucault and the Power of Feminist Discourse', *Praxis International* 5 (4), 466–85.

Barnet, A. D. (1967) *Cadres, Bureaucracy, and Political Power in China*. New York: Columbia University Press.

Behean, C. L. (1975) 'Feminism and Nationalism in the Chinese Women's Press, 1902–1911', *Modern China* 1 (4), 379–416.

Beijing Review (1986) 'Is Women's Lib out of Date?', *Beijing Review* 50 (15 December), 7.

Benton, G. (1982) *Wild Lilies, Poisonous Weeds: Dissident Voices from People's China*. London: Pluto.

Berger, P. L. and Luckmann, G. (1966) *The Social Construction of Reality: A Treatise in the Sociology of Knowledge*. New York: Doubleday.

Bianco, L. (1971) *The Origins of the Chinese Revolution*. Stanford, CA: Stanford University Press.

Bidet, J. (1979) 'Questions to Pierre Bourdieu', *Critique of Anthropology* 13/14, 203–9.

Bing Xin (1985) 'Wo zhuyi xunkan (Wang) Anyi de zuopin', *Wenhuibao* (5 October), 2.

Birch, C. (ed.) (1963) *Chinese Communist Literature*. New York: Praeger.

Boorman, H. (1963) 'The Literary World of Mao Tse-Tung', in Birch (ed.), *Chinese Communist Literature*, pp. 15–38.

Bourdieu, P. (1990a) 'Reading, Readers, the Literate, Literature', in P. Bourdieu, *In Other Words*, pp. 94–105.

— (1990b) 'Social Space and Symbolic Power', in P. Bourdieu, *In Other Words*, pp. 123–39.

— (1990c) *In Other Words: Essays Towards a Reflexive Sociology*. Trans. M. Adamson, Cambridge: Polity Press.

— (1990d) 'The Intellectual Field: A World Apart', in P. Bourdieu, *In Other Words*, pp. 140–9.

— (1988) 'Flaubert's Point of View', *Critical Enquiry* 14 (Spring), 539–62.

— (1987) 'What Makes a Social Class', *Berkeley Journal of Sociology* XXXII, 1–16.

— (1985) 'The Social Space and the Genesis of Groups', *Theory and Society* 14, 723–45.

— (1979) 'Symbolic Power', *Critique of Anthropology* 13/14, 77–87.

— (1977) *Outline of a Theory of Practice*. Trans R. Nice. Cambridge: Cambridge University Press.

— (1974) 'Cultural Reproduction and Social Reproduction', in R. Brown (ed.), *Knowledge, Education and Cultural Change*. London: Tavistock, pp. 71–108.

Braidotti, R. (1989) 'The Politics of Ontological Difference', in T. Brennan (ed.), *Between Feminism and Psychoanalysis*. Cambridge: Methuen, pp. 89–105.

Brubaker, R. (1985) 'Rethinking Classical Theory – The Sociological Vision of Pierre Bourdieu', *Theory and Society* 14 (6), 745–75.

Brugger, B. (1981) *China: Radicalism to Revisionism 1962–1979*. London: Croom Helm.

Burns, J. P. (1987) 'China's Nomenklatura System', *Problems of Communism* 36 (5), 36–51.

Caplan, C. (1986) *Sea Changes: Culture and Feminism*. London: Verso.

— (1982) 'Radical Feminism and Literature: Rethinking Millet's Sexual Politics, in M. Evans (ed.), *The Woman Question: Readings on the Subordination of Women*. London: Fontana.

Chachchi, A. (1991) 'Forced Identities', in D. Kandiyoti (ed.), *Women, Islam and the State*. London: Macmillan, pp. 119–34.

Chan, A. (1974) 'Rural Chinese Women and the Socialist Revolution: An Enquiry in the Economics of Sexism', *Journal of Contemporary Asia* 4 (2), 197–209.

Chan Yanyi (1986) *Lu Xun Qu Qiupai*. Tianjin: Tianjin Renmin Chubanshe.

Chang Jiaqin (1988) 'Funü jiefang yu xiandaihua', *Shehui Kexue Jikan* 1, 33–7.

Chao Zhong (1988) 'Miandui dangjin wentan de lengyue chensi Wenxue pianji tan dangqian chuangzuo zuotan huijiyao', *Wenxue Pinglun* 3, 5–10.

Chatman, S. (1978) *Story and Discourse: Narrative Structure in a Fiction and Film*. Ithaca: Cornell University Press.

Chen Huangmei (ed.) (1981) *Zhongguo Dangdai Wenxueshi*. Beijing: Renmin Wenxue Chubanshe.

Chen Huifen (1987) 'Zhaohui shiluo de neibanr: "Renshi ni ziji" – guanyu nüxing wenxue de sikao jiqi renlei yishi de tigao dengdeng', *Dangdai Wenyi Sichao* 2, 8–15.

Cheneaux, J. (1968) *The Chinese Labor Movement, 1919–1927*. Stanford, CA: Stanford University Press.

Cheng Wenzhao (1987) 'Xinshiqi nüzuojia chuangzuo de qinggan licheng yu shidai yishi', *Zhongguo Xiandai Dangdai Wenxue Yanjiu* (Fuyin Baokan Ciliao) 9, 119–25.

Chin, A. L. S. (1970) 'Family Relations in Modern Chinese Fiction', in M. Freedman (ed.), *Family and Kinship in Chinese Society*. Stanford, CA: Stanford University Press, pp. 87–121.

China Handbook for Literature and Art (1983). Beijing: Foreign Language Press.

China New Analysis (1989) 'The Plague of Bureaucratism', *China New Analysis* 1351, 2–10.

Chow Tse-tung (1960) *The May Fourth Movement: Intellectual Revolution in Modern China*. Cambridge, MA: Harvard University Press.

Christianssen, F. (1989) 'The Justification and Legalization of Private Enterprises in China 1983–1988', *China Information* 4 (2), 78–91.

Cixous, H. (1976) 'The Laugh of the Medusa', *Signs* 1 (4), 875–93.

Cocks, J. (1989) *The Oppositional Imagination: Feminism, Critique and Political Theory*. London: Routledge.

Connell, R. W. (1987) *Gender, Power and Society: The Person and Sexual Politics*. London: Polity Press.

Coster, E. Postel (1977) 'The Indonesian Novel as a Source of Anthropological Data', in *Text and Context: The Social Anthropolology of Tradition*. Philadelphia: Institute for the Study of Human Issues, pp. 135–49.

Cousins, M. and Hussain, A. (1984) *Michel Foucault*. London: Macmillan.

Coward, R. (1983) *Patriarchal Precedents: Sexuality and Social Relations*. London: Routledge and Kegan Paul.

Craig, D. (ed.) (1977) *Marxists on Literature: An Anthology*. Harmondsworth: Penguin.

Crane, G. T. (1990) *The Political Economy of China's Special Economic Zones*. Armonk, NY: M. E. Sharpe.

Croll, E. (1984a) 'Women's Rights and New Political Campaigns in China Today', Working Paper: Sub-series on Women's History and Development, 1 (October). The Hague: Institute of Social Studies.

— (1984b) 'Marriage Choice and Status Groups in Contemporary China', in J. L. Watson (ed.), *Class and Social Stratification in post-Revolutionary China*. Cambridge: Cambridge University Press, pp. 175–97.

— (1983) *Chinese Women Since Mao*. London: Zed.

— 1981) 'Women in Rural Production and Reproduction in the Soviet Union, China, Cuba and Tanzania', *Signs* 7 (2), 361–99.

— (1978) *Feminism and Socialism in China*. London: Routledge and Kegan Paul.

— (1977) 'The Movement to Criticize Confucius and Lin Piao: A Comment on the Women of China', *Signs* 2 (3), 721–6.

— (ed.) (1974) *The Women's Movement in China: A Selection of Readings*. London: ACEI.

Culler, J. (1982) *On Deconstruction*. Ithaca, NY: Cornell University Press.

Dai Jianping (1987) 'Yizhong daode guannian yizhong wenxue moshi dui xian, dangdai wenxue zhong lianglei nüxing xingxiang xilie de kaocha', *Dangdai Wenyi Sichao* 1, 41–8.

Dai Qing and Luo Ge (1988) 'Nüchong Hunfan', *Zhongshan* 2, 33–49.

Dalsimer, M. and Nisnoff, L. (1987) 'The Implications of the New Agricultural and One-Child Family Policies for Rural Chinese Women', *Feminist Studies* 13 (3), 583–607.

— (1984) 'New Economic Readjustment Policies: Implications for Chinese Working Women', *Review of Radical Political Economics* 16, 17–43.

Dan Zhen (1985) 'Lun Zhang Xinxin de xinli xiaosuo xilie', *Zhongguo Xiandai Dangdai Wenxue Yanjiu* 9, pp. 119–28.

Davin, D. (1988) 'The Implications of Contract Agriculture for the Employment and Status of Chinese Women', in S. Feuchtwang et al. (eds), *Transforming China's Economy in the Eighties*.

— (1976) *Women, Work: Women and the Party in Revolutionary China*. Oxford: Clarendon.

Davin, D. (1975) 'Women in the Chinese Countryside', in M. Wolf and R. Witke (eds), *Women in Chinese Society*, pp. 234–61.

Deng Xiaoping (1981) 'Zai zhongguo wenxue yishu gongzuozhi de sici daibiao dahuishang de zhuci', in *Zhongguo Chuban Nianjian*, pp. 488–91.

Dews, P. (1984) 'Power and Subjectivity in Foucault', *New Left Review* 144 (March–April), 72–95.

Diamond, I. and Quinby, L. (eds) (1988) *Feminism and Foucault: Reflections on Resistance*. Boston: Northeastern University Press.

Diamond, N. (1975a) 'Collectivization, Kinship and the Status of Women in Rural China', *Bulletin of Concerned Asian Scholars* 7 (1), 25–32.

Diamond, N. (1975b) 'Women under the Kuomintang Rule – Variations on the Feminine Mystique', *Modern China* 1 (1), 3–45.

DiMaggio, P. (1979) 'Review Essay: On Pierre Bourdieu', *American Journal of Sociology* 84 (6), 1460–73.

Ding Ling (1950) *The Sun Shines on the Sanggan River*. Beijing: Foreign Language Press.

— (1941) 'When I was in Xia Village' ('Wozai xiacun de shihour'), in *Dingling*

Duanpian Xiaoshuo Xuan (2 vols). Beijing: Renmin Wenxue Chubanshe, 1981, pp. 541–60.

— (1928) 'The Diary of Miss Sophie', in *Dingling Duanpian Xiaoshuo Xuan* (2 vols). Beijing: Renmin Wenxue Chubanshe.

Dreyfus, H. and Rabinow, P. (1983) *Michel Foucault: Beyond Structuralism and Hermeneutics*. Chicago: University of Chicago Press.

Duke, M. (1985) *Blooming and Contending: Chinese Literature in the Post-Mao Era*. Bloomington: Indiana University Press.

— (1984) 'Chinese Literature in the Post-Mao Era: The Return of Critical Realism', *Bulletin of Concerned Asian Scholars* 16 (4), 2–4.

Eagleton, M. (1986) *Feminist Literary Theory: A Reader*. Oxford: Blackwell.

Eagleton, T. (1988) 'Two Approaches to the Sociology of Literature', *Critical Inquiry* 14 (Spring), 469–76.

— (1983) *Literary Theory: An Introduction*. Oxford: Blackwell.

Eber, I. (1989) 'Social Harmony, Family and Women in Chinese Novels, 1948–58', *China Quarterly* 117 (March), 71–95.

— (1976) 'Images of Women in Recent Chinese Fiction: Do Women Hold Up Half the Sky', *Signs* 2 (1), 25–34.

Eide, E. (1987) *China's Ibsen: Ibsen to Ibsenism*. Monograph no. 55. Copenhagen: Scandinavian Institute of Asian Studies.

— (1985) 'Optimistic and Disillusioned Noras on the Chinese Literary Scene', A. Gerstlacher et al. (eds), *Woman and Literature in China*, pp. 193–222.

Eisentein, J. R. (ed.) (1979) *Capitalist Patriarchy and the Case for Socialist Feminism*. New York: Monthly Review Press.

Engels, F. (1978) *The Origin of the Family, Private Property and the State*. Beijing: Foreign Language Press.

Evans, H. (1989) 'Chinese Women: The Public and Private Face', *China Now* 130, 36–8.

Fang Zhenwang, (1988) 'Marxist Literary Criticism in China', in L. Grossberg and M. Nelson (eds), *Marxism and the Interpretation of Culture*. New York: University of Illinois Press, pp. 715–22.

Feng Mu (1982) 'Make a Fresh Study of and Conduct Serious Research into Mao Zedong's Thinking on Literature and Art', *Renmin Ribao*. Reprinted and trans, *SWB* (28 May), FE/7038/BII/10–11.

Ferguson, P. P., Desan, P. and Griswold, W. (1988) 'Editors' Introduction: Mirrors, Frames, and Demons: Reflections on the Sociology of Literature', *Critical Enquiry* 14 (Spring), 421–30.

Feuchtwang, S., Hussain, A. and Pairault, T. (eds) (1988) *Transforming China's Economy in the Eighties: The Rural Sector, Welfare and Employment*. London: Zed.

Feuerwerker, Y. (1982) *Ding Ling's Fiction: Ideology and Narrative in Modern Chinese Literature*. Cambridge, MA: Harvard University Press.

— (1975) 'Women as Writers in the 1920s and 30s', in M. Wolf and R. Witke (eds), *Women in Chinese Society*.

Flax, J. (1990) 'Postmodernism and Gender Relations in Feminist Theory', in L. Nicholson (ed.), *Feminism and Postmodernism*. London, New York: Routledge, pp. 39–62.

Fokkema, A. (1991) *Postmodern Characters: A study of Characterization in British and American Postmodern Fiction.* Amsterdam: Atlanta.

Fokkema, D. W. (1991) 'Creativity and Politics', in R. MacFarquhar and J. K. Fairbank (eds), *The Cambridge History of China: Vol. 15 Revolutions within the Chinese Revolution,* Part II. Cambridge: Cambridge University Press, pp. 594–611.

— (1980) 'Strengths and Weakness of the Marxist Theory of Literature with Reference to Marxist Criticism in The People's Republic of China', in J. J. Deeney (ed.), *Chinese Western Comparative Literature: Theory and Strategy,* Hong Kong: Chinese University Press.

— (1965) *Literary Doctrine in China and Soviet Influence, 1956–1960.* The Hague: Mouton.

Forster, E. M. (1927) *Aspects of the Novel.* London: Edward Arnold.

Foucault, M. (1984a) 'Truth and Power', interview by Pasquino and Fonatana, in Rabinow (ed.), *The Foucault Reader.* pp. 51–75.

— (1984b) 'What is an Author?', in D. F. Bouchard (ed.), *Language, Counter-Memory, Practice.* Oxford: Blackwell, pp. 113–38.

— (1982) 'The Subject and Power', *Critical Inquiry* 8 (Summer), 776–95.

— (1980) *Power/Knowledge: Selected Interviews and Other Writings, 1972–1977.* New York: Pantheon.

— (1972) *The Archeology of Knowledge and the Discourse on Language.* New York: Pantheon.

— (1970) *The Order of Things.* London: Tavistock.

Freedman, M. (ed.) (1970) *Family and Kinship in Chinese Society.* Stanford, CA: Stanford University Press.

Gallick, M. (1982) 'Some Remarks on the Literature of the Scars in the PRC 1977–79', *Asian and African Studies* VIII, 53–74.

Gerstlacher, A., Keen, R., Kubin, W., Miosga, M. and Schon, J. (eds) (1985) *Women and Literature in China.* Bochum: Brockmeyer.

Gilbert, S. M. and Gubar, S. (1979) *The Madwoman in the Attic.* New Haven: Yale University Press.

Goldblatt, H. (1985) 'Life as Art: Xiao Hong and Autobiography', in A. Gerstlacher et al. (eds), *Women and Literature in China,* pp. 345–64.

Goldblatt, H. (ed.) (1982) *Chinese Literature for the 1980s: The Fourth Congress of Writers and Artists.* Armonk, NY: M. E. Sharpe.

Goldman, M. (ed.) (1977) *Modern Chinese Literature in the May Fourth Era.* Cambridge: Harvard University Press.

Goldman, M. (1971) *Literary Dissent in Communist China.* New York: Atheneum.

Gramsci, A. (1985) *Selection from Cultural Writings* ed. D. Forgacs and G. Nowell Smith, London: Lawrence and Wishart.

— (1971) *Selections from the Prison Notebooks of Antonio Gramsci* ed. Q. Hoare and G. Nowell Smith, London: Lawrence and Wishart.

Guangming Ribao (1983) 'Alienation Theory in Literature and Art'. Reprinted and trans., *SWB* (16 December), FE/7518/BII/5–11.

Guo Xiaodong (1988) 'Nüxing zai pianxie de shejieli lun wenxue de yizhong nüxing xinli xianxiang', *Piping Jia* 6, 15–19.

Gutting, G. (1989) *Michel Foucault's Archeology of Scientific Reason*. Cambridge: Cambridge University Press.

Hai Ronghua (1989) 'Feminism shi shenma, neng shi shenma, jiang shi shenma?', *Shanghai Wenlun* 2, 4–8.

Handlin, J. F. (1975) 'Lu Kun's New Audience: The Influence of Women's Literacy on Sixteenth Century Thought', in M Wolf and R. Witke (eds), *Women in Chinese Society*, pp. 13–38.

Haraway, D. (1990) '"Gender" for a Marxist Dictionary: The Sexual Politics of a Word', in *Simians, Cyborgs and Women – The Reinvention of Nature*. London: Free Association Books, pp. 127–48.

Haraway, D. (1990a) 'A Manifesto for Cyborgs: Science, Technology and Socialist Feminism in 1980s', in L. Nicholson (ed.), *Feminism and Postmodernism*. London: Routledge, pp. 190–267.

— (1988) 'Situated Knowledge: The Science Question in Feminism and the Privilege of Partial Perspective', *Feminist Studies* 14 (3), 401–575.

Harding, S. (ed.) (1987) *Feminism and Methodology*. Bloomington: Indiana University Press.

Hartman, H. and Markusen, A. R. (1980) 'Contemporary Marxist Theory and Practice: A Feminist Critique', *Review of Radical Political Economics* 12 (2), 87–94.

Hartstock, N. (1987) 'Foucault on Power: A Theory for Women?', in M. Leijenaar et al. (eds), *The Gender of Power – A Symposium*. Leiden: Leiden University Press, pp. 98–121.

He Zhiyun (1988) 'Ping Dangdai zhongguo nüxing xilie – jiantan jishi wenxue de xinwen jiazhi', *Guangming Ribao* (7 October), 3.

Held, D. (ed.) (1987) *Theories of the State. An Introductory Reader*. Milton Keynes and London: Open University Press.

Hemmel, B. and Sindjberg, P. (1984) *Women in Rural China: Policy towards Women before and after the Cultural Revolution*. Atlantic Highlands, NJ: Humanities Press.

Hendrischke, B. (1985) 'Feminism in Contemporary Chinese Women's Literature', in A. Gerstlacher et al. (eds), *Women and Literature in China*, pp. 397–728.

Hindess, B. (1977) 'The Concept of Class in Marxist Theory and Marxist Politics', in J. Bloomfield (ed.), *Class Hegemony and the Party*. London: Lawrence and Wishart, pp. 88–101.

Hinton, W. (1983) *Shenfan: The Continuing Revolution in a Chinese Village*. New York, Random House.

— (1966) *Fanshen: A Documentary of Revolution in a Chinese Village*. New York: Vintage.

Holm, D. (1984) 'Folk Art as Propaganda: The Yannge Movement in Yenan', in B. McDougall (ed.), *Popular Chinese Literature and Performing Arts in the People's Republic of China 1949–1979*. Berkeley: University of California Press, pp. 3–35.

Honing, E. (1986) *Sisters and Strangers: Women in the Shanghai Cotton Mills, 1919–1949*. Stanford, CA: Stanford University Press.

Hooper, B. (1989) 'China's Modernization – Are Young Women Going to Lose Out', *Modern China* 10 (3), 317–43.

Hoy, D. Couzens (ed.) (1986) *Foucault – A Critical Reader*. Oxford: Blackwell.

Hsia, C. T. (1963) 'Residual Femininity: Women in Chinese Communist Fiction', in C. Birch (ed.), *Chinese Communist Literature*. New York: Praeger, pp. 158–80.

—— (1961) *A History of Modern Chinese Fiction: 1917–1957*. New Haven: Yale University Press.

Hsu, V. L. (1981) *Born of the Same Roots: Stories of Modern Chinese Women*. Bloomington: Indiana University Press.

Hu Heqing (1986) 'Zhang Jie aiqing guannian de bianhua', *Dangdai Wenyi Sichao* 6, 40–6.

Hu Qiaomu (1983) 'Guanyu rendao zhuyi he yihua wenti', in Chen Taihui, Chen Quanrong and Yang Zhixu (eds), *Wenyi lun Zhengji 1979–1983*. Henan: Hunaghe Wenyi Chubanshe.

Hu Qili (1986) quoted in 'Chuangzuo ziyou he wenyi gongzuozhi de shehui zirengan', *Dangdai Wenyi Sichao* 2, pp. 4–8.

Huang, J. C. (1973) *Heroes and Villains in Communist China: The Contemporary Chinese Novel as a Reflection of Life*. London: Hurst.

Huang Mei (1989) 'Guanyu nüxing wenxue de sikao', *Piping Jia* 4, 23–35.

Huang Ziping, Chen Pingyuan and Qin Liqun (1985) 'Lun ershiji zhonguo wenxue', *Wenxue Pinglun* 5, 3–10.

Idema, W. (1991) *Spiegel van de Klassike Chineze Poëzie van het Boek der Oden tot de Qing Dynastie*. Amsterdam: Meulenhoff.

Irigaray, L. (1985) *This Sex which is not One*, New York: Cornell University Press.

—— (1980) 'When Our Lips Speak Together', *Signs* 6 (1), 69–80.

Jacobus, M. (ed.) (1979) *Women Writing and Writing About Women*. London: Croom Helm.

Jagger, A. (1983) *Feminist Politics and Human Nature*. Brighton: Harvester.

James Hughes, K. (1986) *Signs of Literature Language, Ideology and the Literary Text*. Vancouver: Talon Books.

Jardine, A. (1985) *GYNESIS: Configurations of Woman and Modernity*. Ithaca, NY: Cornell University Press.

Jiang Tingsheng (1987) 'Shitan funü jiefang guannian de gengxin', *Funü Zuzhi yu Huodong* D423 (1), 13–15.

Jin Zhiyu (1986) 'Lun Nü Zuojiaqun – Xin shiqi zuojiaqun kaocha zhi san', *Dangdai Zuojia Pinglun*, 3, 25–31.

Johnson, K. A. (1983) *Women, the Family and Peasant Revolution in China*. Chicago: University of Chicago Press.

Jones, A. R. (1984) 'Julia Kristeva on Femininity: The Limits of a Semiotic Politics', *Feminist Review* (Winter), 56–73.

—— (1981) 'Writing the Body: Towards an Understanding of L'Ecriture Feminine', *Feminist Studies* 7 (2), 247–63.

Jopke, C. (1987) 'The Cultural Dimensions of Class Formation And Class Struggle: On The Social Theory of Pierre Bourdieu', *Berkeley Journal of Sociology* XXXII, 52–78.

Kakar, S. (1985) *Intimate Relations: Exploring Indian Sexuality*. Harmondsworth: Penguin.

Kang Keching (1983) 'Extract of Speech Given at the Fifth National Women's Congress', *Beijing Review* 38 (19 Sepember), 5–6.

— (1978) 'Women's Movement in China: Guiding Concepts and New Tasks', *Beijing Review* (29 September), 5–11.

Kang Zhengguo (1988) 'Nüquan zhuyi wenxue piping xuping', *Wenxue Pinglun* 1, 152–8.

Kinkley, J. C. (1990) 'The Cultural Choices of Zhang Xinxin, a Young Writer of the 1980s', in P. Cohen and M. Goldman (eds), *Ideas Across Cultures Essays on Chinese Thought in Honor of Benjamin I. Schwartz*. Cambridge, MA: Harvard University Press, 137–61.

— (1985) *After Mao: Chinese Literature and Society 1978–1981*. Harvard Contemporary China Series. Harvard University: Council of East Asian Studies Publications.

Kolodyny, A. (1980) 'Dancing through the Minefield: Some Observations on the Theory, Practice and Politics of a Feminist Literary Criticism', *Feminist Studies* 6 (1), 1–25.

— (1976a) 'Literary Criticism' *Signs* 2 (2), 404–21.

— (1976b) 'Some Notes on Defining a Feminist Literary Criticism', *Critical Inquiry* 2 (2), 821–31.

Kristeva, J. (1986) *The Kristeva Reader* ed. Toril Moi. Oxford: Blackwell.

— (1984) *Revolution in Poetic Language*. New York: Columbia University Press.

— (1974) *About Chinese Women*. Trans. A. Barrows. London: Marion Boyars.

Kubin, W. (1982) 'Sexuality and Literature in the P.R.C. Problems of Chinese Women before and after 1949, Seen in Ding Ling's Story "Diary of Miss Sophie" (1928) and Xi Rong's Story "An Unexceptional Spouse" (1962)', in W. Kubin, and G. Wagner (eds), *Essays in Modern Chinese Literature and Literary Criticism*.

Kubin, W. and Wagner, R. (eds) (1982) *Essays in Modern Chinese Literature and Literary Criticism*. Bochum: Brockmeyer.

Kuhn, A. and Wolpe, M. (1978) 'Feminism and Materialism', in A. Kuhn and A. Wolfe (eds), *Feminism and Materialism: Women and Modes of Production*. London: Routledge and Kegan Paul, pp. 1–11.

Kung Haili (1986) 'Yiban jiwei shengxing de wenyi sichao zai Meiguo – Yi nüquan zhuyi wenxue piping', *Shehui Kexue* 8, 57–9.

Kurzwell, E. (1986) 'Michel Foucault's History of Sexuality as Interpreted by Feminists and Marxists', *Social Research* 53 (4), 647–63.

Lan Chengdong (1985) 'How to Assess the Social Phenomenon of Increasing Divorce Rates' (*'Zeyang kandai lihun shuaishang sheng zhiyi shehui xianxiang'*) *Social Science (Shehui kexue)* 3 (March), 41–3.

Lang, D. (1978) *The Marxist Theory of Art: An Introductory Survey*. Hassocks: Harvester.

Lang, O. (1946) *Chinese Family and Society*. New Haven, CT: Yale University Press.

Leith, K. (1973) 'Chinese Women in the Early Communist movement', in M. Young (ed.), *Women in China*.

Lenin, I. V. (1977) 'Articles on Tolstoy', in D. Craig (ed.), *Marxists on Literature*, pp. 346–62.

Leo Ou-Fan Lee (1985) 'The Politics of Technique: Perspectives of Literary Dissidence in Contemporary China', in J. C. Kinkley (ed.), *After Mao*, pp. 159–92.

Leung Wing-Yue (1988) *Smashing the Iron Rice Pot: Workers and Unions in China's Market Socialism*. Hong Kong: Asia Monitor Resource Center.

Levy, H. S. (1966) *Chinese Footbinding: The History of a Curious Erotic Custom*. New York: Walton Rawls.

Li Jiefei and Zhang Long (1987) 'Qingqing de shuo: Nüxing Wenti Sikao', *Dangdai Zuojia Pinglun* 4, 76–9.

Li Qingxi (1985) 'Lun wenxue piping de dangdai yish', *Wenxue Pinglun* 5, 14–19.

Li Xiaojiang (1988) *Xiawa de Tansuo: Funü yanjiu congshu*. Henan: Henan Renmin Chubanshe.

Li Zhigao and Chu Yunlong (1983) 'What Young People Want in a Mate', *China Reconstructs* (June), 24–5.

Li Ziyun (1987a) 'Nüzuojia zai dangdai wenxue shi suoqi de xianfeng zuoyong', *Dangdai Zuojia Pinglun* 6, 4–10.

— (1987b) 'Jinqinian lai Zhonguo nÜzuojia chuangzuo de tedian', *Zhongguo Funü* 1, 12–14.

Lieberthal, K. G. and Lampton, D. M. (1992) *Bureaucracy, Politics and Decision-making in post-Mao China*. Berkeley: University of California Press.

Lienard, G. and Servais, E. (1979) 'Practical Sense – On Bourdieu', *Critique of Anthropology* 4 (13–14), 203–21.

Lin Shuming (1990) 'Ping Dangdai woguo de nüquan zhuyi wenxue piping', *Dangdai* 4, 36–51.

Ling Yang (1987) 'Nüzuojia shuo, shuo nüzuoji – Zhongguo dangdai wenxue guoji taolunhui ciji', *Nüzuojia* 1, 126–36.

Link, P. (1985) 'Fiction and the Reading Public in Guangzhou and Other Chinese Cities, 1979–1980', in J. C. Kinkley (ed.), *After Mao*, pp. 221–74.

Link, P. (ed.) (1983) *Stubborn Weeds: Popular and Controversial Chinese Literature after the Cultural Revolution*. Bloomington: Indiana University Press.

Liu Binyan (1988) *People or Monsters? And Other Stories and Reportage from China after Mao*, ed. P. Link. Bloomington: Indiana University Press.

Liu Jianjun (1984) 'Dangdai Wenxue yu Wenxue de Dangdai Xing', *Zhongguo Xiandai Dangdai Wenxue Yanjiu* 3, 3–12.

Liu Mei Ching (1988) *Forerunners of Chinese Feminism in Japan*. PhD thesis. University of Leiden.

Liu Min (1989) 'Tianshi yu Yaonü – Shengming de shufu yu fanban – dui Wang Anyi xiaoshuo de nüquan zhuyi piping', *Zhongguo Xiandai Dangdai Wenxue Yanjiu* 9, 137–41.

Liu Xinwu (1986) 'Yingyong shenma zhunci lai kaizhan piping', *Dangdai Wenyi Tansuo* 4, 17–18.

Lu Qingfei (1990) *Zhongguo dangdai qingnian nüzuojia pingzhuan*, Beijing: Shehui Kexue Yuan Wenxue Yanjiusuo, Zhonguo Funü Chubanshe.

Lu Wencai (1989) 'Chensi zai nüxing wenxue yanjiu de yuandili', *Zhongguo Xiandai Dangdai Wenxue Yanjiu* (Fuyin Baokan ziliao) 8, 157–62.

Lu Xun (1923) 'What Happens after Nora Leaves Home?', in *Collected Works of Lu Xun* (Lu Xun Quanji) vol. 4. Beijing: People's Publishing House, 1981, p. 86.

— (1973) 'On Women's Revolution', *Chinese Literature* 9, 30–2.

Lunacharsky, A. V. (1965) *Art and Revolution*. Moscow: Progress Publishers.

Luo Qiong (1986) *Zhongguo Funü Yundongshi* (A History of the Chinese Women's Movement). Beijing: People's Publishing House.

Macdonnel P. (1980) *Theories of Discourse*. Oxford: Blackwell.

McDougall, B. (1972) *The Introduction of Western Literary Theories into Modern China 1919–1925*. Tokyo: Centre for East Asian Cultural Studies.

MacFarquhar (1983) *The Origins of the Cultural Revolution: Vol. 2 The Great Leap Forward 1958–1960*. New York: Columbia University Press.

Ma Naru (1987) 'Dui "Liangge shijie" guanzhao zhong de xinshiqi nüxing wenxue – Lun zhongguo nüzuojia wenxue shejie de lishi bianhua', *Dangdai Wenyi Sichao* 5, 91–8.

Maloney, J. (1980) 'Women in the Chinese Communist Revolution: The Question of Political Equality', in C. Beckin and C. Lovett (eds), *Women, War and Revolution*. New York: Holmes and Meiser.

Mao Zedong (1980) *Talks on the Yenan Conference on Literature and Art: A Translation of the 1943 Text*. Trans. B. McDougall. Ann Arbor: University of Michigan, Chinese Center.

— (1982) 'Peking Forum on Mao's Literary Thinking', *SWB* (22 May), FE/7033/BII/1–3.

— (1956) *Collected Works of Mao* (4 vols). Beijing: People's Publishing House.

Marks, E. and de Courtivron, I. (eds) (1980) *New French Feminisms: An Anthology*. Amherst: The University of Massachusetts Press.

Martin, B. (1988) 'Feminism, Criticism and Foucault', in I. Diamond and L. Quinby (eds), *Feminism and Foucault*.

Martin, H. (ed.) (1986) *Cologne Workshop on Contemporary Chinese Literature*. Cologne: Deutche Welle.

Millet, K. (1971) *Sexual Politics*. London: Hart-Davis.

Mitchell, J. (1984) *Women: The Longest Revolution. Essays on Feminism and Psychoanalysis*. London: Virago.

— (1975) *Psychoanalysis and Feminism*. Harmondsworth: Penguin.

Moers, E. (1978) *Literary Women*. London: Women's Press.

Mohanty, C. (1991) 'Cartographies of Struggle: Third World Women and the Politics of Feminism', in C. Mohanty, A. Russo and L. Torres (eds), *Third World Women and the Politics of Feminism*. Bloomington: Indiana University Press.

— (1988) 'Under Western Eyes: Feminist Scholarship and Colonial Discourses' *Feminist Review* 50, 61–85.

Moi, T. (1987) *French Feminist Thought*. Oxford: Blackwell.

— (1985) *Sexual-Textual Politics*. London: Methuen.

Molyneux, M. (1981a) 'Women in Socialist Societies: Problems of Theory and Practice', in K. Young, C. Wolkowitz and R. McCullagh (eds), *Of Marriage and the Market: Women's Subordination Internationally and its Lessons*. London: Routledge and Kegan Paul, pp. 55–90.

— (1981b) *Women's Emancipation under Socialism: a Model for the Third World?* Discussion paper. Sussex University, Institute of Development Studies.

Nan Fan (1984) 'Wang Anyi xiaoshuo de guanchadian: yige renwu, yizhong chongtu', *Zhongguo Xiandai Dangdai Wenxue Yanjiu* 12, 107–13.

National Symposium on Theoretical Studies on Women (1987) 'Development of Women's Studies – The Chinese Way', *Chinese Sociology and Anthropology* 20 (1/2), 18–25.

Newton, J. and D. Rosenfelt (eds) (1985) *Feminist Criticism and Social Change; Sex, Class and Race in Literature and Culture*. New York: Methuen.

Niu Yuqiu (1985) 'Nüzuojia zai zhongpian xiaoshuo zhong de xintansuo', *Wenyibao* 7 (6), 2.

Nunn, G. R. (1966) *Publishing in Mainland China*, MIT Report no. 4. Massachusetts: MIT.

O'Hara, A. (1945) *The Position of Women in early China: According to the Lieh Nüchuan 'The Biographies of Emininent Chinese Women'*. Washington DC: Catholic University of America.

Ortner, S. and Whitehead. A. (1981) *Sexual Meanings: The Cultural Construction of Gender and Sexuality*. Stanford, CA: Stanford University Press.

Ostrow, J. M. (1981) 'Culture as a Fundamental Dimension of Experience: a Discussion of Pierre Bourdieu's Theory of Human Habitus', *Human Studies* 4, 279–97.

Owens, C. (1985) 'Feminism and Postmodernism', in H. Foster (ed.), *Postmodern Culture*. London: Pluto, pp. 57–82.

Palmer, P. (1989) *Contemporary Women's Fiction: Narrative Practice and Feminist Theory*. New York: Wheatsheaf

Pasquino, P. and Fonatana, A. (1984) '"Truth and Power", Interview with M. Foucault', in P. Rabinow (ed.), *The Foucault Reader*. Harmondsworth: Penguin, pp. 51–75.

Pearson, V. (1989) 'Behind the Steel and Glass the Oldest Profession Flourishes', *China Now* 130, 18–19.

Pei Qing (1992) Les femmes Chinoises participent activement aux affaires publiques', *Beijing Information* 10 (9 March), 20–2.

Pettit, P. (1975) *The Concept of Structuralism: A Critical Analysis*. Berkeley and Los Angeles: University of California Press.

Pickowicz, P. (1980) *Marxist Literary Thought in China: The Influence of Chu Chiu Pai*. Berkeley, CA: University of California Press.

Pieke, F. (1992) *The Structure of China's Urban Society, the Ordinary and the Extraordinary: An Anthropological Study of Chinese Reform and Political Protest*. PhD thesis. University of California at Berkeley.

Plaza, M. (1984) 'Ideology against Women', in *Feminist Issues* 4 (1) (Spring), 73–82.

Plekhanov, G. (1975) 'On the Social Basis of Style', in D. Craig (ed.), *Marxists on Literature*, pp. 76–94.

Poster, M. (1984) *Foucault, Marxism and History – Mode of Production versus Mode of Information*. London: Polity Press.

— (1982) 'The Future According to Foucault: The Archeology of Knowledge and Intellectual History', in D. LaCapra and S. L. Kaplan (eds), *Modern European Intellectual History: Reappraisals and New Perspectives*. Ithaca and London: Cornell University Press.

Price, J. (1975) 'Women and Leadership in the Chinese Communist Movement, 1921–1945', *Bulletin of Concerned Asian Scholars* 7 (1), 43–8.

Propp, V. (1966) 'Les Transformations des contes fantastiques', in Todorov, T. (ed.), *Théorie de la Littérature*. Paris: Seuil, pp. 234–62.

Prusek, J. (1980) 'Subjectivism and Individualism in Modern Chinese Literature', in Leo Ou-Fan Lee (ed.), *The Lyrical and the Epic: Studies of Modern Chinese Literature*. Bloomington: Indiana University Press

— (1974) 'Urban Centres: The Cradle of Popular Fiction', in C. Birch (ed.), *Studies in Chinese Literary Genres*. Berkeley: University of California Press

Rabinow, P. (ed.) (1984) *The Foucault Reader*. Harmondsworth: Penguin.

Rankin, M. (1975) 'The Emergence of Women at the End of the Ch'ing: The Case of Ch'iu Chin', in M. Wolf and R. Witke (eds), *Women in Chinese Society*, pp. 39–66.

Register, C. (1980) 'Literary Criticism', *Signs* 6 (2), pp. 268–82.

Reiter, R. R. (ed.) (1975) *Toward an Anthropology of Women*. New York: Monthly Review Press.

Renditions (1987) *Special Issue: Contemporary Women Writers* 27–8 (Spring).

Ren Yiwu (1988) Nüxing Wenxue de Xianddai xinghangjin', *Zhongguo Xiandai Dangdai Wenxue Yanjiu* 8, 115–20.

Renmin Ribao (1985) 'Measures to Control Knight-Errant Novels Adopted' (15 November). Translated in *JPRS-CPS* (24 January 1986), 37–9.

— (1981) 'Zuopin yu zhengji: Pianjibu zhaokai zuotanhui taolun guanyu wenyi chuangzuo ruhe biaoxian aiqing wenti de taolun', 11 November.

Rimmon-Kenan, (1983) *Narrative Fiction – Contemporary Poetics*. London: Routledge.

Risseeuw, C. (1988) *The Fish Don't Talk about the Water. Gender Transformation Power and Resistance Among Women in Sri Lanka*. Leiden: Brill.

Robinson, J. (1971) *The Cultural Revolution in China*. Harmondsworth: Penguin.

Robinson, J. C. (1985) 'Of Women and Washing Machines: Employment, Housework and the Reproduction of Motherhood in Socialist China', *China Quarterly* 101, 32–58.

Rosaldo, M., Zimbalist, T. and Lamphere, L. (1974) *Women, Culture and Society*. Stanford, CA: Stanford University Press.

Rubin, G. (1975) 'The Traffic in Women: Notes on the "Political Economy of Sex"', in R. R. Reiter, *Toward an Anthropology of Women*, pp. 157–210.

Ruthven, K. (1984) *Feminist Literary Studies*. Cambridge: Cambridge University Press.

Saich A. J. (1981) *China: Politics and Government*. London: Macmillan.

Said, E (1988) 'Identity, Negation and Violence', *New Left Review* 171 (September–October), 46–60.

— (1985) 'Opponents, Audiences, Constituencies and Community', in H. Foster (ed.), *Postmodern Culture*, London: Pluto.

Said, E. (1978) *Orientalism*. London: Penguin.

Saith, A. (ed.) (1987) *The Reemergence of the Chinese Peasantry*. London: Croom Helm.

Saussure, F. de (1974) *A Course in General Linguistics*. London: Fontana.

Sawicki, J. (1988) 'Identity Politics and Sexual Freedom: Foucault and Feminism', in I. Diamond and L. Quinby (eds), *Feminism and Foucault*.

Schipper, M. (1989) *Beyond the Boundaries: African Literature and Literary Theory*. London: Alison and Busby.

Schram, S. R. (1982) *Mao Zedong: A Preliminary Reassessment*. Hong Kong: Chinese University Press.

Schram, S. R. (ed.) (1973) *Authority, Participation and Cultural Change in China*. Cambridge: Cambridge University Press.

Schurmann, F. (1971) *Ideology and Organization in Communist China* (2nd edn). Berkeley: University of California Press.

Schwarz, V. (1986) *Intellectuals and the Legacy of the May Fourth*. Berkeley: University of California Press.

— (1975) 'Ibsen's Nora: The Promise and the Trap', *Bulletin of Concerned Asian Scholars* 7 (1), 3–5.

Selden, M. (1971) *The Yenan Way in Revolutionary China*. Cambridge: Cambridge University Press.

Sharratt, B. (1982) *Reading Relations. Structures of Literary Production: A Dialectical Text Book*. Brighton: Harvester.

Shen Rong (1981) 'Rendao Zhongnian', *Shouhou* 1, 52–91.

Shen Ying (1987) Ai de quanli, lixiang, kunhuo shilun xinshiqi nüzuojia de aiqing wenxue', *Dangdai Wenyi Tansuo* 1, 59–64.

— (1984) 'Zhencheng de Zhuiqiu – Du bufen qingnian nüzuojia xiaoshuo suixiang', *Zhongguo Xiandai Dangdai Wenxue Yanjiu* 10, 21–5.

Shen Zhi (1987) 'Development of Women's Studies – The Chinese Way', *Chinese Sociology and Anthropology* XX (1–2), 18–25.

Sheridan, M. (1976) 'Young Women Leaders in China', *Signs* 2 (1), 59–88.

Showalter, E. (1985) *The New Feminist Criticism*. London: Virago.

— (1981) *'Feminist Criticism in the Wilderness'*, *Critical Inquiry* 8, 179–205.

— (1977) *A Literature of Their Own: Women Novelists from Brontë to Lessing*. Princeton, NJ: Princeton University Press.

— (1975) 'Literary Criticism Review Essay', *Signs* 1 (2), 435–60.

Sidel, R. (1974) *Families of Fengsheng: Urban Life in China*, Harmondsworth: Penguin.

Siu, B. (1975) *Fifty Years of Struggle: The Development of the Women's Movements in China (1900–1949)*. Hong Kong: Revomen.

Snow, E. (1938) *Red Star Over China*, 1972 edn, Harmondsworth: Penguin.

Snow, H. (1967) *Women in Modern China*. The Hague: Mouton.

Sontag, S. (1977) *On Photography*. Harmondsworth: Penguin.

Spivak, G. C. (1986) *In Other Worlds: Essays in Cultural Politics*. London: Methuen.

— (1988) 'Can the Subaltern Speak', in L. Grossberg and E. Nelson (eds), *Marxism and the Interpretation of Culture*. New York: University of Illinois Press, pp. 271–316.

Stacey, J. (1983) *Patriarchy and Socialist Revolution in China*. Berkeley: University of California Press.

— (1979) 'When Patriarchy Kowtows: The Significance of the Chinese Revolution in Feminist Theory', in J. R. Eisentein (ed.), *Capitalist Patriarchy and the Case for Socialist Feminism*. New York: Monthly Review Press.

Stranahan, P. (1976) *Yenan Women Under the Communist Party*. China Research Monograph no. 27. University of California, Centre for Chinese Studies.

Su Ding (1984) 'Cong xifang wenxue piping de xintai cengci bijiao', *Jianghan Luntan* 9, 49–54.

Sun Shaoxian (1987) *Nüxing Zhuyi Wenxue*. Liaoning: Liaoning Daxue Chubanshe.

— (1986) 'Wenxue chuangzuo zhong funü diwei wenti de fansi', *Dangdai Wenyi Sichao* 4, 95–7.

Tan Li (1984) 'Reforms Improve Status of Women', *China Daily*, 25 October.

Tan Manni (1983) 'So that Women can Work without Worry', *China Reconstructs* 3 (March), 8–11.

— (1981) 'Why New Marriage Law Was Necessary', *China Reconstructs* March, pp. 17–19.

— (1980) 'Lightening the Load for Working Mothers', *China Reconstructs* 29 (3), 19–22.

Tate, M. (1985) *Black Women Writers at Work*. Harpenden: Old Castle Books.

Thakur, R. (1991) 'Western Literary Theory in China Today', *China Information* VI (2), 62–9.

Tharu, S. and Lalita, K. (eds) (1991) *Women Writing in India 600 BC – to the early Twentieth Century'*. Delhi: Oxford University Press.

Thompson, J. B. (1984) 'Symbolic Violence. Language and Power in the Writings of Pierre Bourdieu', in J. B. Thompson (ed.), *Studies in the Theory of Ideology*. Cambridge: Polity Press, pp. 42–73.

Thurston, A. F. (1988) *Enemies of the People: The Ordeal of the Intellectuals in China's Great Cultural Revolution*. Cambridge, MA: Harvard University Press.

Tianchi Martin-Liao (1985) 'Traditional Handbooks of Women's Education', in A. Gerstlacher et al. (eds), *Woman and Literature in China*, pp. 165–89.

Tianjin Women's Federation (1985) 'The Quality of Chinese Women Must Be Improved and Socialization of Household Labor Speeded Up', *Labor and Personnel* 5, 18–22.

Topley, M. (1978) 'Marriage Resistance in Rural Kwantung', in A. Wolf (ed.), *Studies in Chinese Society*, pp. 247–69.

Truong, T. (1990) *Sex, Money and Morality: The Political Economy of Prostitution in South East Asia*. London: Zed.

Tsai Mei-hsi (1975) *The Construction of Positive Types in Contemporary Chinese Fiction*. PhD thesis. University of California at Berkeley.

Tu Lin (1983) 'Shiwu zai nali – Du Zhang Xinxin tongzhi yixie xiaoshuo de chuangzuo pianxiang', *Wenhuibao* (6 December), 3.

Wang Anyi (1986) 'Nanren he Nüren, Nüren he chengren', *Dangdai Zuojia Pinglun* 5, 65–8.

— (1983) *Liushi* (short stories). Sichuan: Chubanshe, pp. 89–194.

Wang Chunyun (1986) 'Shen Rong Lun', in *Dangdai Zuojia Lun*. Beijing: Zuojia, Chubanshe, pp. 48–52.

Wang Fuxiang (1984) '"Nüxing wenxue" lunzhiyi – yu Wu Daiying tongzhi shangque jiantan jibu you zhengyi xiaoshuo de pingjia wenti', *Dangdai Wenyi Sichao* 2, 16–22.

Wang Jinhua (1984) 'Xingbie zhuanhua' de lishi yiyi – cong "Jiating shenghuo" zuopin de bijiao kan funü jiefang yundong de yiban' *Dangdai Wenyi Sichao* 5, 69–77.

Wang Meng and Wang Gang (1989) 'Shinian laide wenxue piping', *Dangdai Zuojia pinglun* 2, 4–19.

Wang Qingshu (1981) 'Rural Economic Reform and Women's Liberation', *China Reconstructs* (July), 24–6.

Wang Youjin (1985) 'Zhongguo xiandai Nüzuojia de xiaoshuo he funü wenti', *Xiandai Dangdai Wenxue Yanjiu* 13, 17–25.

Weedon, C. (1987) *Feminist Practice and Post-Structuralist Theory*. Oxford: Blackwell.

Wei Junyi (1986) 'Women a New Force in Chinese Literature', *Beijing Review* 9, 9–11.

Weinbaum, B. (1976) 'Women in transition to Socialism: Perspectives on the Chinese Case', *Review of Radical Political Economics* 8 (1), 34–59.

Wen Hua (1982) 'Red Flag (Hongqi) on Problems in Literature and Art'. Reprinted and trans., *SWB* (6 April), FE/6997/BII/6–7.

Wenyibao pinglunyuan (1986) 'Chuangzuo ziyou he wenyi gongzuozhi de shehui zirengan', *Dangdai Wenyi Sichao*, 2, 4–8.

Wertheim, W. (1974) *Evolution and Revolution: The Rising Waves of Emancipation*. Harmondsworth: Penguin.

— (1964) *East-West Parallels: Sociological Approaches in Modern Asia*. Leiden: E. J. Brill.

Whyte, M. K. (1984) 'Sexual Inequality under Socialism: The Chinese case in Perspective', in J. L. Watson (ed.), *Class and Social Stratification in post-Revolution China*. Cambridge: Cambridge University Press, pp. 198–238.

— and Parish, W. (1984) *Urban Life in Contemporary China*. Berkeley: University of California Press.

Wickham, G. (1986) 'Power and Power Analysis: Beyond Foucault', in M. Gane (ed.), *Towards a Critique of Foucault*. London: Routledge and Kegan Paul, pp. 149–79.

Widmer, E. (1989) 'The Epistolary World of Female Talent in Seventeenth-century China', *Late Imperial China* 10 (2), 1–41.

Wiegel, S. (1986) 'Double Focus: On the History of Women's Writing', in G. Ecker (ed.), *Feminist Aesthetics*. London: Women's Press, pp. 71–84.

Williams, R. (1977) *Marxism and Literature*. Oxford: Oxford University Press.

— (1965) *The Long Revolution*. Harmondsworth: Penguin.

Williams, H. (1988) *Concepts of Ideology*. New York: Wheatsheaf/St Martins Press.

Williard, F. (1985) 'The Struggle for Equality: New Legal Tools for Women's Emancipation', *China Now* 113 (Summer), 13–16.

Wittig, M. (1985) 'The Mark of Gender', *Feminist Issues* 5 (2), 3–12.

Wolf, A. (ed.) (1978) *Studies in Chinese Society*. Stanford, CA: Stanford University Press.

Wolf, M. (1985) *Revolution Postponed: Women in Contemporary China*. London: Methuen.

— and Witke, R. (eds) (1975) *Women in Chinese Society*. Stanford, CA: Stanford University Press.

Women of China (1983) 'Enhancing the Role of Women in Socialist Modernization', *Women of China* (March), 1–3.

Wu Daiying (1985) 'Cong xinshiqi nüzuojia de chuangzuo kan "nüxing wenxue" de ruogan tezheng', *Zhongguo Dangdai Xiandai Wenxue Yanjiu* 14, 12–18.

Wu Jianluo (1989) 'Shen Rong sanpian xiaoshuo bijiao tan', *Dangdai Zuojia Pinglun* 1, 45–9.

Wu Kexi and Wu Pusheng (1988) 'Mao Zedong Lun Funü Jiefang de Liang ge Wenti', *Funü Zuzhi yu Huodong* 1 (D.423), 6–9.

Xia Zhongyi (1983) 'Cong Xiang Linsao, Shafei nüshi dao Fangzhou', *Dangdai Wenyi Sichao* 5, 58–63.

Xiao Zhou (1989) 'Virginity and Premarital Sex in Contemporary China', *Feminist Studies* 15 (2), 279–91.

Xie Wangxin (1987) 'Zhongnian Nüxing Pinglun Jialun qianji moxie piping de piping', *Nüzuojia* 1, 149–64.

— (1985) 'Nüxing Xiaoshuo Jialun', *Xiandai Dangdai Wenxue Yanjiu* 18, 71–90.

Xu Ping (1988) 'Nüzuojia chuangzuo de teshu qingxu', *Xiandai Dangdai Wenxue Yanjiu* 4, 105–10.

Xu Qihua (1985) 'Wang Anyi duanpin jinzuo manping', *Xiandai Dangdai Wenxue Yanjiu* 14, 83–5.

Yan Chunde (ed.) (1985) *Xinshiqi nüzuojia bairen zuopinxuan* (2 vols). Fuzhou: Haixia Wenyi Chubanshe.

Yan Ping (1989) 'Luetan jinqishi nianlai zhongguo nüxing xiaoshuo de fazhan', *Pipingjia* 4, 16–22.

Yang, G. (1985) 'Women Writers in China', *China Quarterly* 103 (September), 510–17.

— (1980) 'A New Woman Writer: Shen Rong and her story At Middle Age', *Chinese Literature* 10, 64–78.

Yang Guixin (1984) 'Lun Zhang Jie de Chuangzuo', *Zhongguo Xiandai Dangdai Wenxue Yanjiu* 3, 22–34.

Yi Qing (1987) 'Yige chongman huoli de zhidian – ye tan "xunzhao nanren" de nüxing wenxue', *Dangdai Wenyi Sichao* 2, 16–23.

Yin Xiaomin (1987) 'Foggy Poetry: A New Wave in Chinese Literature', *China* (Spring), 54–66.

BIBLIOGRAPHY / 217

Young, M. (ed.) (1973) *Women in China: Studies in Social Change and Feminism*, Ann Arbor: University of Michigan Press.

Yu Luojin (1982) 'Chuntian de Tonghua' *Huacheng* 1, 141–221.

Yu Yan (1985) 'Nüxing wenxue de lishi yu xianzhuang – Lun shenma shi "nüxing wenxue"', *Dangdai Wenyi Sichao* 5, 32–7.

Yuan Liangsan and Jin Nan (1986) 'Women's Work, Society's Responsibility', *Beijing Review* 49 (December), 18–20.

Yue Daiyun and Wakeman, C. (1983) 'Women in Recent Chinese Fiction: A Review Article', *Journal of Asian Studies* XLII (4), 879–89.

Zeng Zhennan (1985) 'Qichuan: cong zuihou de ningpodi – du Zhang Xinxin de jinzuo suixiang', *Zhongguo Xiandai Dangdai Wenxue Yanjiu* 8, 121–4.

Zhang Fa (1984) 'Shilun Zhang Jie de chuangzuo gexing jiqi zuopin de neizai yiying', *Dangdai Wenyi Sichao* 5, 133–7.

Zhang Jie (1982) 'Fangzhou', *Shou Hou* 2, 4–59.

— (1981) 'Wode Chuan', *Wenyi Bao* (15 May).

Zhang Qing (1986) 'Nüxing wenxue de qiaoruo – Xionghua he Wuxionghua', *Dangdai Zuojia Pinglun* 5, 36–41.

Zhang Wei (1986) 'Women Writers Through Three Generations', *Beijing Review* 9 (3 March) 18–25.

Zhang Weian (1982) 'Zai wenyi xinchao zhong jueqi de zhongguo nüzuojia qun', *Dangdai Wenyi Sichao* 3, 14–22.

Zhang Xinxin (1982) *Zhang Xinxin Duanpian Xiaoshuoxuan*. Beijing: Beijing Chubanshe.

Zhang Zhong, Hong Zicheng, Zhao Zumo and Wang Yingshi (eds) (1986) 'Zhang Jie, Shen Rong, Zong Pu de xiaoshuo chuangzuo', *Dangdai Zhongguo Wenxue Gaiguan*. Beijing: Beijing University Publishing House, pp. 533–41.

Zhao Fusheng (1989) 'Xiandai Zhishi Nüxing de xinli zongji – Ding Ling he Zhang Jie de xiao shuo bijiao', *Dangdai Zuojia Pinglun* 6, 4–11.

Zhongguo Zuojia Xiehui (1986) *Dangdai Zuojia Lun*. Beijing, Zhongguo Zuojia Xiehui Chubanshe.

Zhongguo Wenhuabu (1981, 1982, 1983, 1984) *Zhongguo Chuban Nianjian*, Beijing: Zhongguo Beijing Chubanshe.

Zhongguo Shehui Kexueyuan Yanjiusuo (1987) *Xinshiqi Wenxue Liunian – 1976–1982*, Beijing: Zhongguo Kexueyuan Chubanshe.

Zhou Yang (1979) 'The Third Movement to Emancipate the Mind', *Beijing Review* 21 (25 May), 9–14.

— (1960) *The Path of Socialist Literature and Art in China*. Beijing: Foreign Language Press.

— (1954) *China's New Art and Literature*. Beijing: Foreign Language Press.

Index

9 781856 494106